톡톡튀는 생활영어

지은이_ **최창우**

경상남도 창녕에서 태어나, 경북대학교 수학과를 졸업하고 같은 대학교 대학원에서 대수학을 전공, 이학박사학위를 받았다. 영어영문학을 부전공하여 前 대구 ECA외국어학원 강사를 역임하였다. 뉴질랜드 오클랜드교육대학(현 오클랜드대학교)의 객원교수를 거쳐 현재 대구교육대학교 수학교육과 교수로 재직 중이다.

톡톡튀는 생활영어

초판 인쇄 2016년 1월 15일
초판 발행 2016년 1월 22일

지은이 최창우
펴낸이 최국주
펴낸곳 동명사
출판등록 1950년 11월 1일(제1-76호)
주소 (우 413-756) 경기도 파주시 회동길 50(문발동)
전화 031-955-7200(대표)~2, 7203(편집부), 7204(물류)
팩스 031-955-7205
전자우편 webmaster@dmsbook.com
홈페이지 www.dmsbook.com

ISBN 978-89-411-8158-3 13740
값 17,000원

東明社

머리말

우리는 지식과 정보가 넘쳐나고 있는 21세기를 살아가고 있다. 신문, 잡지, 매스컴 등을 통해서 글로벌 혹은 국제화와 같은 말은 이제 일상이 되다시피 하고 있다. 이러한 세계에 사는 우리로서는 모름지기 외국어, 특히 세계 공용 언어인 영어는 이제 필수가 아닐 수 없다.

돌이켜보면 기존의 기성세대들은 학창시절을 보내면서 그렇게 많은 영어수업을 받았음에도 정작 외국인을 만났을 때 말 한마디 하지 못했던 것이 우리의 현실이었다. 그것은 말할 나위 없이 입시 위주의 우리나라 교육제도 때문일 것이다.

그러나 요즘은 초등학교부터 영어에 많은 시간을 할애하는 우리 교육의 현실을 모두는 직시하고 있다.

대학에서 영문학을 부전공한 저자는 평소 영어에 남다른 관심이 있었고 신문이나 잡지, 인터넷, 방송 등 여러 곳에서 게재되거나 방송되고 있는 자료들을 틈틈이 스크랩하거나 기록 또는 수집하여 21세기를 살아가는 독자 여러분들에게 조금이라도 도움을 주고자 이 책을 집필하게 되었다.

이 교재에서 사용된 표현들은 생활에서 유용하게 활용할 수 있는 단어와 숙어 및 관련 표현들을 유형별로 분류하여 제시하였다.

모름지기 영어를 우리말처럼 잘하기 위해서는 독자 여러분들은 아래의 말을 꼭 명심하기 바란다.

If you wish to improve your knowledge of english conversation, please keep the followings in mind.

Don't be bashful of speaking.

Don't be afraid of making mistakes.

Practice your english at all times.

끝으로 저자로서는 최선을 다하여 조금이라도 독자의 입장에서 많은 부분을 배려하고자 하였으나 여러 가지 미비한 점은 독자 여러분들의 조언에 따라 꾸준히 수정·보완해 나갈 것임을 약속하는 바이다.

2015년을 보내며

상록동산에서 저자 씀

차례

CHAPTER 01

일상생활에서

일상생활에서 01 That's a relief — 안심이네요

A Can I have your ticket and passport, please?

B Here you go.

I don't really understand the new e-ticket system.

I wasn't sure what to bring.

A You did it correctly.

It has your confirmation number on it.

B **That's a relief.**

A 탑승권과 여권 좀 보여주실래요?

B 여기 있습니다.

새로운 전자티켓 시스템은 잘 이해가 안가더라고요.

뭘 가져오는 건지 잘 모르겠어요.

A 맞게 갖고 오셨습니다.

예약번호가 적혀있으니까요.

B 안심이네요.

일상생활에서 02 I almost forgot — 깜빡할뻔했네요

A **I almost forgot.** Here is my air miles card.

B Thank you, sir.

I'll make sure you get your mileage points.

A When can I redeem them?

I'd love to get a free flight.

B As of now, you'd only have enough points for a short domestic flight.

A 깜빡할뻔했네요. 여기 마일리지 카드요.

B 감사합니다.

마일리지 점수를 틀림없이 적립해드리겠습니다.

A 언제 그걸 쓸 수 있나요?

무료로 비행기 타고 싶어서요.

B 현재로서는 단거리 국내선은 충분히 타실 수 있는 점수를 보유하고 계십니다.

일상생활에서 03 Can you explain it in plain English? — 쉬운 말로 설명 해주실래요?

A I'm not sure if I should upgrade my computer or get a whole new machine.

B It depends on how many expansion slots you computer has.

A **Can you explain it in plain English?**

B Sure.

If there is not enough room to add more hardware, it's not worth it to just upgrade.

A 컴퓨터를 업그레이드 해야 할지 아예 새로 사야 할지 모르겠어요.

B 손님 컴퓨터의 확장슬롯이 얼마나 많은지에 따라 다릅니다.

A 쉬운 말로 설명 좀 해주실래요?

B 그러죠.

하드웨어를 추가할 공간이 충분하지 않으면 업그레이드 할 가치도 없습니다.

일상생활에서 04 Bear with me, please. 기다려주세요 / 참아주세요

A May I speak to Kenny?

B Speaking.

A Hi, Kenny. This is Regina calling about the park I ordered last week.

B What was the part number, Regina?

A Daewon-092735.

B OK. **Just bear with me.**

B 나야.

A 안녕, 케니. 나 레지나인데 지난주에 주문한 부품 때문에 전화해.

B 부품 번호가 뭐였지?

A 대원-092735.

B 알았어, 잠깐만 기다려.

일상생활에서 05 I always chicken out! 무서워서 무슨 일을 못하겠어!

A I think I'm falling in love.

B With whom?

A A girl in my office. I want to tell her how I feel, but **I always chicken out** when I talk to her.

B What's she like?

A She's smart, Beautiful, and nice.

B You really should ask her out. What are you afraid of?

A My boss. She's his daughter.

A 나 사랑에 빠졌나봐.

B 누구랑?

A 사무실에 있는 사람이야. 내 감정을 얘기하고싶은데, 무서워서 못하겠어.

B 어떤 사람이길래?

A 그녀는 아주 똑똑하고 예쁘고 착해.

B 그럼, 그녀에게 고백해야겠다. 근데, 뭐가 그렇게 두려운거야?

A 우리 사장님. 그녀가 사장님 딸이거든.

일상생활에서 06 Is he housebroken? 개가 용변을 잘 가려요?

A Do you have a pet?

B Yes. I have a little puppy. He's like one of the family.

A I see. **Is he housebroken?**

B Yes, he is and he's really well-trained.

A 애완 동물 키우세요?

B 네. 작은 강아지를 키워요. 가족이나 다름없죠.

A 그렇군요. 개가 용변 잘 가려요?

B 네, 그럼요. 그리고 아주 말을 잘 들어요.

일상생활에서 07 No doubt about it. 의심할 여지도 없어

A Good! Seems like your date went really well.
I thought you guys might get doing well together.
B I saw him in the office this morning,
and we had a little chat about your date.
A I get the feeling that he likes you very much.
No doubt about it.
I'm sure he will call you to ask you out again.
I hope everything goes well.

A 잘됐다! 데이트 정말 좋았나 보네.
둘이 잘 맞을 거라 생각했었지.
B 오늘 아침에 사무실에서 그 사람 만나서, 소개팅에 대해서 좀 얘기했었어.
A 그 사람 네가 아주 마음에 드는 눈치야.
틀림없어, 얘.
확실히 그 사람이 곧 애프터 신청할 거야.
모든 것이 잘 되길 바래.

일상생활에서 08 You look familiar to me. 낯이 익네요

A Hi! **You look familiar to me.**
B You, too.
Maybe we've bumped into each other somewhere.
A Oh, wait a moment....
We met at Kelly's birthday party.
B Yes, that's right. I remember now.

A 안녕하세요. 낯이 익네요.
B 저도 그러네요.
어디선가 우연히 봤겠죠.
A 아, 잠깐만요….
캘리 생일 파티 때 만났네요.
B 네, 맞아요. 이제 기억이 나네요.

일상생활에서 09 Don't get your hopes up too high. 너무 기대 많이 하지 마

A Have you made your Christmas list?
B As a mater of fact, I haven't gotten around to it yet.
A Well, I look forward to getting something wonderful from you again this year.
B OK, but **don't get your hopes up too high.**

A 너 크리스마스 선물 리스트 만들었어?
B 사실, 아직 손도 못 댔어.
A 음, 나 올해에도 너한테 어떤 근사한 것을 받을지 기대되는데.
B 알았다구, 그래도 너무 큰 기대는 하지 마.

일상생활에서 10 Loosen up! | 맘 편안히 가져!

A Hey, Sophie, you look nervous. Are you all right?

B Just the person I wanted to see.

You know I'm not comfortable being with a bunch of strangers.

A Oh, don't tell me you are too shy to talk to anyone.

Just **loosen up** and be yourself! You will be fine.

B Thanks. I'll try, schmoozing around.

A 소피, 왜 그렇게 긴장하고 있어? 괜찮아?

B 너 마침 잘 왔다.

너 나 모르는 사람들 많은 데 있으면 불편해 하는 것 알잖아.

A 야, 네가 부끄러워서 사람들한테 말 못하는 건 아니지?

그냥 맘 편안하게 갖고 너답게 행동해. 괜찮을 거야.

B 고마워. 어울려 볼게.

일상생활에서 11 Today is not my day. | 오늘 일진이 별로 안 좋아

Today is not my day. I left home earlier than usual, so I decided to take my car instead of the subway.

On the way to work I made a wrong turn and I got stuck in traffic for more than an hour.

That really stressed me out and put me in a rotten mood.

When I finally arrived at work, my boss, of course, got angry and didn't want to listen to my excuses.

Great way to start the day, huh?

오늘 일진이 사나워. 평소보다 좀 일찍 집을 나와서 지하철을 안 타고 차를 가지고 갔거든.

출근하는데 방향을 잘못 바꾸는 바람에 한 시간 넘게 교통체증 때문에 오도가도 못했어.

그거 때문에 스트레스 많이 받고 기분이 나쁘더라구.

겨우 출근했는데 당연히 상사가 화가 나서 내 변명은 들으려고 하지도 않는 거야.

정말 상쾌하게 하루를 출발했다.

일상생활에서 12 Christmas is just around the corner. | 크리스마스가 바로 코앞에 다가왔어

A Do you have any plans for this weekend?

B I need to go shopping for christmas presents.

A Right. **Christmas is just around the corner.**

Can I tag along with you?

B Be my guest.

Let's hit all the big department stores and malls.

A 너 이번 주말에 무슨 계획 있어?

B 크리스마스 선물 사러 가야해.

A 맞다. 크리스마스가 코앞에 다가왔지?

나 따라가도 돼?

B 같이 가자.

우리 큰 백화점이나 대형 매장은 전부 들르자.

일상생활에서 13 Would you get a grip? 좀 진정하지 그래?

A I don't know why I let you convince me to come here. I hate parties.

B **Would you get a grip** on yourself?
This is going to be a blast!

A Well, I don't know. I'm just not that into parties.

B Come on, don't be a party poorer.
Just enjoy it as if you belong here.

A 도대체 왜 네 꼬임에 넘어가서 여길 왔는지 모르겠다.
나 진짜 파티 싫은데.

B 좀 진정하지 그래?
이 파티 진짜 재밌을 거야!

A 글쎄, 잘 모르겠다. 난 파티에 별로 관심이 없어.

B 제발 파티 좀 망치지마.
그냥 네 집이다 생각하고 즐겨.

일상생활에서 14 It really takes the cake. 진짜 대단하다

A What a great party! **It really takes the cake.**
Thanks for inviting me here, Susan.

B Likewise. Having you is such a great pleasure for me. Thanks for coming.

A Well, now that I've seen you. I have to hit the road.
I have to get an early start tomorrow.

B Already? I wish you could stay longer.
We have tons of things to catch up on.

A 진짜 멋진 파티인데! 진짜 대단하다.
초대해 줘서 고마워, 수잔.

B 나도 마찬가지야. 너랑 같이 있으면 너무 즐거워. 와줘서 고마워.

A 그나저나 너 봤으니까 이제 집에 가야겠다.
내일 일찍 일어나야 하거든.

B 벌써? 조금만 더 있다가 가.
우리 아직도 할 얘기 많이 있잖아.

일상생활에서 15 Time certainly flies. 시간 정말 빨리 간다

A It's almost the end of the year already.

B Wow, **Time certainly flies.**
I don't feel like I've accomplished anything this year.

A Looking back, I can't say it was a real productive year for me either.

B Let's talk it over at the year-end bash.
Tomorrow night, all right?

A 벌써 올해가 다 지나가네.

B 우와, 시간 정말 빨리 간다.
올해 아무것도 해놓은 게 없는 것 같아.

A 돌아보니, 나에게도 그다지 생산성 있는 해는 아니었던 것 같다.

B 우리 송년파티하면서 얘기해보자.
내일 밤 괜찮아?

일상생활에서 16 Can I have a rain check? 다음 기회로 미루면 안 될까?

A Hey, Jess. Will you be free this Saturday.

B **Can I have a rain check?**

I have a blind date this Saturday.

A Wow, awesome. Who fixed you up with the guy?

B My friend, Michael.

I hope he has picked Mr. right for me this time.

A 제스, 이번 주 토요일에 시간돼? 나 콘서트 티켓 있는데.

B 우리 다음번으로 미루면 안 될까?

나 이번 주 토요일에 소개팅이 있거든.

A 진짜? 좋겠다. 누가 주선한 거야?

B 내 친구 마이클.

이번에는 제대로 된 남편감을 소개해 줬으면 좋겠어.

일상생활에서 17 Stop putting me on. 농담 그만 해

A Hi, you must be Jess. I'm Joshua.

So, finally we get to see each other.

B It's great to meet you at last. How are you?

A I am thrilled. Actually I'm a little flusterd. I didn't expect such a beautiful girl like you to show up.

B **Stop putting me on.**

But thanks, It's very good of you to say so.

A 안녕하세요, 제스 맞죠? 저 조슈아예요.

마침내 만나게 되네요.

B 드디어 만나서 너무 반가워요. 안녕하세요?

A 저 기분 너무 좋아요. 솔직히 말하면 약간 떨리네요. 이렇게 아름다운 분이 나오실 줄 몰랐거든요.

B 농담 그만하세요.

그래도 그렇게 말씀해 주시니 고마워요.

일상생활에서 18 Live a little. 걱정하지 말고 즐겨!

A You want a refill, Jesse?

B No thanks, I've had enough already. I'm a bit tipsy.

A Come on.

This is supposed to be a New Year's party!

Live a little, huh?

B Well I'm not really a big drinker,

but I guess just one more for the road won't kill me.

A 한 잔 더 마실래, 제시?

B 아니 괜찮아. 이미 많이 마셨어. 약간 취기가 있네.

A 이봐,

지금 송년회잖아!

걱정 말고 한잔 더해.

B 글쎄, 나 술은 잘 못 마시지만

딱 한 잔 더 한다고 죽기야 하겠어.

일상생활에서 19 Wake up and smell the coffee! 정신 좀 차려!

A I think I'm going to ask Paul out tomorrow.

B What do you mean? Paul has a girlfriend already.

A Yeah, but who knows when they might break up?

B Girl, **Wake up and smell the coffee!** They are crazy about each other and Paul will never leave her.

A 나 내일 폴한테 데이트 신청할까봐.

B 무슨 소리야. 폴 여자 친구 있잖아.

A 알아. 그래도 걔네들 언제 헤어질지 누가 알아?

B 야, 정신 좀 차려! 걔네들 서로한테 얼마나 빠져있는데. 그리고 폴은 절대 그 여자 안 떠나.

일상생활에서 20 I'll try make time. 시간을 한 번 내볼게

A Can you find time to meet tonight?
We have some things to go over.

B I'm pretty tied up today,
but if it's an emergency **I'll try make time.**

A It's about the Anderson firm we've been working on.
We were planning on meeting at 7.

B Oh, I think I'll be able to make it. See you then.

A 오늘 밤에 만날 시간 좀 있어요?
검토해야할 일들이 있는데.

B 오늘 좀 바쁜데,
그래도 긴급한 일이면 시간을 낼게요.

A 우리가 처리중인 앤더슨 회사에 관한 일이에요.
7시에 미팅하기로 했거든요.

B 어, 갈 수 있을 것 같아요. 그럼 그때 봅시다.

일상생활에서 21 Let's start moving stuff in. 어서 짐을 들입시다

A That was a good lunch. I needed a break.

B **Let's start moving stuff in.**

A Okay!

A 점심 맛있었어요. 좀 쉬고 싶었거든요.

B 어서 짐을 들입시다.

A 알았어요!

일상생활에서 22 Don't pick on your brother. 동생 괴롭히지 마

A Mom, Brian's hitting me!

B Brian, **don't pick on your brother.**

A 엄마, 브라이언이 절 때려요!

B 브라이언, 동생 괴롭히지 마.

일상생활에서 23 I'll heat up some left-overs. 남은 음식 있는데 데워줄게요

A I'm pretty hungry.

Have you made anything for dinner?

B No, not yet. **I'll heat up some left-overs.**

A 나 배고파 죽겠어.

저녁 준비했어?

B 아직요. 남은 음식이 있는데 데워 줄게요.

일상생활에서 24 Would Saturday work better? 그럼 토요일은 어때?

A I'm busy Friday.

B **Would Saturday work better?**

A I'll be out of town this weekend.

A 난 금요일에 바빠

B 그럼 토요일은 어때?

A 이번 주말엔 시내에 없어.

일상생활에서 25 Get off my back! 그만 좀 해!

A You need to finish your work soon.

B **Get off my back!** I'm working as hard as I can.

A You don't have to get angry at me.

A 너 일 얼른 끝내야 해.

B 그만 좀 해! 최대한 열심히 하고 있단 말야.

A 나한테 화낼 필요는 없잖아.

일상생활에서 26 School was OK today. 오늘 학교에서 그냥 그랬어요

A **School was OK today.**

The teacher told me that I was making good progress.

B That's excellent! I'm proud of you.

A 오늘 학교에서 그냥 그랬어요.

선생님이 나보고 많이 좋아졌대요.

B 잘했어! 네가 자랑스럽구나.

일상생활에서 27 It looks cozy. 참 안락해 보인다

A What do you think of our place?

B **It looks cozy.**

A We thinks so, too.

A 우리 집 어때?

B 참 안락해 보인다.

A 우리 생각도 그래.

일상생활에서 28 The toilet won't flush. | 변기가 물이 안 내려가네

A Oh,no! **The toilet won't flush.**

B We'll have to take the lid off the tank to see inside.

Maybe we can solve this problem.

A 아, 이런! 변기 물이 안 내려가네.

B 그럼 수조 뚜껑을 열고 안을 들여다보자. 우리가 고칠 수 있을지도 모르니까.

일상생활에서 29 Let's put some tunes on. | 음악을 틀자

A I want people to dance! **Let's put some tunes on.**

B I've got a great CD full of dance music.

Let's put that one on.

A 사람들이 춤을 추었으면 좋겠어! 음악을 틀자.

B 댄스 음악이 가득한 굉장한 CD가 있어. 그걸 틀자.

일상생활에서 30 We'll go cold turkey on January 1st. | 1월 1일부터 (담배를) 딱 끊을 거야

A I'm finally going to quit smoking.

B I'm going to cut down on smoking and try to drink less, too.

A Perfect. We can help motivate and support each other.

B Right, but let's not start until after the New Year's Eve party. **We'll go cold turkey on January 1st.**

B 나도 담배를 줄이고 술도 덜 마시려고.

A 좋아. 우리 서로 동기를 부여하고 용기를 주면서 도와주자.

B 그래. 하지만 새해전야 파티까지는 하지 말자. 1월 1일부터 딱 끊자고.

일상생활에서 31 It is nice to get away from it all. | 일상생활을 벗어나니 좋다

A It feels great to get out into nature and breathe some fresh air.

B **It** sure **is nice to** be out of the office and **get away from it all.**

A I can't wait to get out and lose myself in nature.

B Me, too. But, first let's find a place to park the car.

It looks like this lot is full.

A 자연으로 나와서 신선한 공기를 마시니까 기분이 아주 좋아.

B 사무실을 벗어나 일상생활을 털어버리니 정말 좋구나.

A 밖에 나와 자연에 묻히는 걸 얼마나 기다렸는데.

B 나도 그래. 그런데 주차할 곳부터 찾아보자.

여기는 주차장이 꽉 찬 거 같아.

일상생활에서 32 Cost me an arm and a leg — 돈 좀 들였어요

A Ta-dah! It's the max Murdoch action figure.

B Where did you get that?

All the stores have been out of stock for weeks.

A I bought it on the Internet.

Cost me an arm and a leg.

B Well, Billy will be thrilled come Christmas morning.

A 짜잔! 맥스 머도크 전투 인형이요.

B 어디서 샀어요?

가게마다 품절된 지 몇 주 됐는데.

A 인터넷으로 샀죠.

돈 좀 들였어요.

B 그렇군요. 크리스마스날 아침에 빌리가 감격하겠어요.

일상생활에서 33 I just clip coupons from the newspaper — 신문에서 쿠폰을 잘랐어요

A Do you have one of our preferred costumer coupon cards?

B No. **I just clip coupons from the newspaper.**

What are the benefits of having a card?

A You get all the discounts automatically.

All I do is swipe the card at the register

and your total is automatically adjusted.

A 우리 점포의 우대고객 쿠폰카드를 가지고 계신가요?

B 아니요. 신문에서 자른 쿠폰이 있어요.

카드가 있으면 어떤 혜택이 있나요?

A 자동으로 할인 받을 수 있습니다.

카드를 금전등록기에 긁기만 하면 손님이 쓰신 총액이 자동적으로 할인 적용됩니다.

일상생활에서 34 Have a seat — 앉으세요

A I have an appointment with Tony for three.

It's for highlights.

B I see. He's running a bit behind today

Michael is available.

A No thanks. I'll wait.

I dont' trust anyone else with my hair.

B I understand. **Have a seat**

and Tony will be with you as soon as he can.

A 3시에 토니 미용사에게 예약했습니다.

하이라이트를 하려고요.

B 네. 토니가 오늘 일이 좀 밀려 있는데 마이클은 시간이 괜찮습니다.

A 아니에요. 기다릴게요.

제 머리를 아무나 믿고 맡길 수 없잖아요.

B 알겠습니다. 앉으세요.

토니는 가능한 한 빨리 올 거예요.

일상생활에서 35 I've socked away about $30 thousand. 3만 달러를 모았어요

A You seem to have a good steady job, so it's not like you're going to be suddenly unemployed anytime soon.

B And I have some savings, too. Over the last few years **I've socked away about $30 thousand.**

A Excellent. That could be a nice size down payment.

A 안정적인 좋은 직장을 갖고 계시니 당분간 갑작스런 실업의 우려는 없겠군요.

B 그리고 저축해놓은 돈도 있어요. 지난 몇 년 동안 3만 달러를 모았죠.

A 아주 좋습니다. 계약금도 어느 정도 내실 수 있겠네요.

일상생활에서 36 Just don't go overboard 적당히 해둬

A Do you think I'd look good with highlights?
The stylist at the salon said I should get them.

B Highlights? What are those?

A It's where you just dye some of your hair a lighter color.

B OK. **Just don't go overboard.**
You don't want them to be too obvious.

A 하이라이트를 하면 괜찮아 보일까? 미용사가 하라고 해서.

B 하이라이트? 그게 뭐야?

A 머리 일부를 더 밝은 색으로 염색하는 거야.

B 좋은데. 적당히 해.
너무 튀는 건 안 좋아.

일상생활에서 37 I never actually keep any of them. 그것들을 실제로 한 번도 지킨 적이 없어

A Have you made any resolutions for the coming year?

B I've made three New Year's resolutions every year, but **I never actually keep any of them.**

A So, your resolution is to not make any more resolutions?

B No. This year I'm making a fourth:
To keep the other three resolutions.

A 내년 결심을 정했니?

B 해마다 세 가지씩 새해결심을 정했는데 실제로 한 번도 지킨 적이 없어.

A 그럼, 너의 새해결심은 더 이상 다른 결심을 하지 않겠다는 거야?

B 아니야. 올해 네 번째 결심을 덧붙이기로 했어.
다른 세 가지를 지킨다는 결심이지.

일상생활에서 38 This one is pressing | 이건 매우 급합니다

A How soon would you like to have them done?

B well, **this one is pressing**, but the other one can wait.

A When is this one due?

B At the latest, by February, 28

A 언제까지 그것들을 완료시키면 되겠습니까?

B 음, 이건 아주 급합니다만 다른 것들은 여유가 있어요.

A 언제가 마감일입니까?

B 늦어도 2월28일까지입니다.

일상생활에서 39 It's a been a full day | 꼬박 하루 걸렸어요

A So, we cleaned the bathroom, vacuumed the carpets, swept and mopped the floors, and washed the dishes.

Did I miss anything?

B We also did the laundry. Separated, washed, dried and folded it.

A **It's been a full day.**

Let's take a quick break and then have dinner.

A 자, 화장실 청소를 했고, 진공청소기로 카펫도 밀었고, 바닥을 쓸고 닦았고, 설거지도 했어요.

빠진 거 있어요?

B 빨래도 했잖소. 색깔 별로 분류해서 세탁하고 건조한 후 갰어요.

A 꼬박 하루 걸렸네요.

좀 쉬었다가 저녁 먹어요.

일상생활에서 40 It totally slipped my mind | 완전히 잊고 있었네

A Are you all set for the potluck party tomorrow night?

B **It totally slipped my mind.**

I could just bring a slad, or a jelly mold.

A That'll be sort of embarrassing.

Can't you whip up something nice?

B Right. I'm sure I can find something quick and easy in one of these cookbooks.

A 내일 밤에 있을 음식지참 파티에 갈 준비는 다 했니?

B 완전히 잊고 있었네.

그냥 샐러드나 젤리를 가져가면 어떨까.

A 그건 좀 창피할거야.

잽싸게 맛있는 거 만들면 안 될까?

B 그래. 이 요리책에서 빠르고 쉽게 하는 요리를 찾아봐야겠다.

일상생활에서 41 My family is as poor as church mice. 우리 가족은 찢어지게 가난해

A One day I'll bo telling you "My ship's come in."
I'm going to be rich.

B Do you have a rich old uncle?
Are you planning on inheriting the family fortune?

A No, everyone in **my family is as poor as church mice.**

B In that case, you better make plans to win the lottery.

A 언젠간 너한테 "나 부자 됐어"라고 말할 거야.
난 부자가 될 거니까.

B 나이 드신 부자 삼촌이라도 있어?
가족 유산 물려받을 계획이라도 있니?

A 아니, 우리 가족은 다 찢어지게 가난해.

B 그렇다면 복권에 당첨될 계획을 세우는 게 낫겠네.

일상생활에서 42 My husband and I are empty nesters. 아이들 없이 남편과 저만 있어요

A What kind of home were you thinking about?

B Well, **my husband and I are empty nesters.**

A So, you're looking for something smaller and easier to manage.

B And it should be a bungalow, not a two-story.
We've both got bad knees.

A 어떤 집을 생각하고 있었나요?

B 글쎄요, 저희 내외만 살 거라서요.

A 그렇다면, 크기가 작고 관리하기 쉬운 집을 찾고 있으시군요.

B 그리고 이층집 말고 베란다가 있는 단층집으로요.
우리 둘 다 무릎이 불편하거든요

일상생활에서 43 I can't say offhand. 당장은 말씀드릴 수가 없군요

A How soon do you think you can make the shipment?

B I'd say somewhere around the first of next month.

A Do you know if it'll be a direct shipment?

B Well. **I can't say offhand.**
I'll have to check.

A 선적을 얼마나 빨리 해 주실 수 있겠습니까?

B 다음달 1일쯤 될 것입니다.

A 직항으로 선적을 하나요?

B 글쎄요. 당장은 말씀드릴 수가 없군요.
확인해 봐야겠습니다.

일상생활에서 44 That's typical. 그럴 줄 알았다

A **That's typical** of human resources.

B Well, I am also from ICM.

I represent the programming division.

A Anyway, nice to meet you. I remember now being told that I would have company.

B I believe I have previously worked with you on a project.

A Really?

A 인사관리부에서 그럴 줄 알았어요.

B 실은 저도 ICM 소속입니다.
전 프로그래밍 사업부 소속이죠.

A 어쨌든 반가워요. 일행이 있을 거라던 말이 이제야 기억나네요.

B 전에 우리 어느 프로젝트에서 같이 일한 적이 있는 것 같아요.

A 그래요?

일상생활에서 45 How arrogant! 저런 건방진!

A The principal said that foreign teachers and instructors are not educators.

B **How arrogant** the principal is!

A He thinks they're only "teaching machines or work horses." What the hell is the difference between an educator and a teaching machine?

B I guess an educator deserves retirement pay and a pension, but the teaching machine can be fired anytime.

A 교장이 외국인 선생과 강사들은 교육자가 아니라고 했네.

B 저런 건방진 사람이 있나!

A 외국인과 강사들은 단지 '가르치는 기계나 일꾼'이라고 생각하나 봐. 교육자와 가르치는 기계의 차이가 도대체 뭐야?

B 교육자는 퇴직금과 연금을 받을 자격이 있고 가르치는 기계는 언제든지 해고될 수 있는 것 아니겠어.

일상생활에서 46 It's kind of a bittersweet thing. — 시원섭섭합니다

A I'm leaving this school next month.

B Are you? How long have you been working here?

A Thirty years.

B That long? What are your feelings about leaving a workplace after such a long time?

A **It's kind of a bittersweet thing.**

A 다음 달에 이 학교를 떠납니다.

B 그래요? 근무한 지 얼마나 되셨는데요.

A 30년이오.

B 그렇게나 오래요? 그렇게나 오랜 세월이 지난 후 직장을 떠나는 심정이 어떠세요?

A 시원섭섭하죠.

일상생활에서 47 That's a cheap shot — 치사한 행동입니다

A Did you see the TV debate between the two men running for congress in our district?

B No. I missed it. How did it go?

A They didn't debate polices. They just exchanged **cheap shots** about each other's personal life.

B They did?

A Yes. They spent the whole hour hitting each other below the belt.

A 우리 선거구에서 국회에 출마한 두 사람이 TV 토론하는 것 봤니?

B 아니, 못 봤는데. 어땠는데?

A 정책 토론은 하지 않더군. 단지 서로의 사생활을 가지고 치사한 공방만 하더군.

B 그랬어?

A 그래. 치사한 말을 주고받는데 온 시간을 할애하더라고.

일상생활에서 48 Shake a leg! — 서둘러!

A Hey, kido! It's almost 8:00.
You've gotta really hurry up.

B Okay, mom. I'm doing it as fast as I can.

A What keeps you so long?
I told you to prepare everything for class last night.

B Mom, bare with me. I didn't sleep well last night.

A **Shake a leg,** or you're gonna miss the bus.

B Yes yes. I'm coming down.

A 꼬맹아! 벌써 여덟 시야.
어서 서둘러라.

B 네, 엄마. 빨리 하고 있어요.

A 왜 이렇게 오래 걸리니?
수업 준비는 어젯밤에 다 해놓으라고 그랬잖아.

B 좀 봐주세요, 엄마. 어젯밤에 잠을 설쳤단 말이에요.

A 빨리 해라. 이러다간 버스를 놓치겠다.

B 네. 지금 내려가요.

일상생활에서 49 It's OK to brag a little bit here 여기서는 자랑을 좀 해도 돼

A OK. Next, it's asking here about my past work experience. What should I include?

B Write your past jobs, starting with the most recent.

A I guess I should put my job titles, too. Anything else?

B Any special responsibilities or projects you completed. And **it's OK to brag a little bit here.**

A 자, 다음은 과거 경력을 묻고 있네. 어떤 걸 써야 하지?

B 가장 최근 것부터 시작해서 과거의 직업을 쓰면 돼.

A 그럼 직책도 써야겠구나. 또 포함시킬 게 있니?

B 네가 완수했던 특별과업이나 프로젝트도 써. 경력란에는 자랑 좀 해도 돼.

일상생활에서 50 Just make sure you don't get caught 들키지 않도록 조심해

A See? I've hidden the microphone under my hat.

B What? Are you sure that's legal? Aren't you breaking copyright, or something?

A Don't worry. Lots of people do it. It's called a "bootleg."

B Well, **just make sure you don't get caught.**

A 보여? 모자 아래 마이크를 숨겨왔어.

B 뭐? 그거 법적으로 문제없는 거니? 저작권 같은 것을 어기는 거 아니야?

A 걱정 마. 많이들 이렇게 해. 이런 복제품을 '해적판'이라고 하는 거야.

B 음, 들키지 않도록 조심해

일상생활에서 51 Do you mind if I tag along? 나도 따라가도 될까?

A I'm going to run down to the store to pick up a few items. Is there anything you need?

B You're going shopping? **Do you mind if I tag along?** I need to look for shoes.

A Oh, in that case, we can go and do some serious shopping.

B Sure. We'll make an afternoon of it.

A 물건 좀 사려고 백화점에 갈 건데 너 필요한 거 뭐 있니?

B 쇼핑하러 가는 거야? 나도 따라가도 될까?
신발을 좀 봐야 해서.

A 아, 그럼 가서 본격적으로 쇼핑을 하면 되겠다.

B 좋아. 쇼핑하면서 오후를 보내자.

일상생활에서 52 Give me a hug! 날 안아주렴!

A Aunt Sandra! Hi!

B **Give me a hug!**

A Hi, uncle Herbie!

A 샌드라 숙모! 안녕하세요!

B 날 안아주렴!

A 안녕하세요, 허비 삼촌!

일상생활에서 53 You are a sight for sore eyes. 만나서 정말 반갑다

A Brian! How are you? **You are a sight for sore eyes!**

B It has been a while hasn't it? How have you been?

A I've been okay, but it's great to see a friendly face.

A 브라이언! 잘 지냈어? 만나서 정말 반갑다!

B 정말 오랜만이네. 그동안 어떻게 지냈어?

A 난 잘 지냈지. 오랜만에 반가운 얼굴을 보니 정말 좋다.

일상생활에서 54 She gave me a hard time about it. 나를 힘들게 하더라고

A I need to get home before my wife gets upset again.

B She doesn't like it when you come home late?

A I was late one time last month, and **she gave me a hard time about it** for weeks!

A 집사람이 또 화내기 전에 집에 가는 편이 좋겠어.

B 집에 늦게 오면 싫어해?

A 지난달에 한 번 늦게 귀가했더니 몇 주 동안이나 나를 힘들게 하더라고!

일상생활에서 55 That's sort of hard to say. 뭐라 말하기 어렵네요

A What do you consider to be your greatest weakness as an employee?

B **That's sort of hard to say.**
I guess I tend to work too hard.

A That can be a problem.
It puts a lot of pressure on your co-workers.

B That's why I started reading books about how to relax.

A 사원으로서 귀하의 가장 큰 단점이라고 생각되는 것은 무엇인가요?

B 뭐라 말하기 어렵네요.
너무 열심히 일하는 거라고 할까요?

A 그것도 문제가 될 수 있겠군요.
동료들에게 많은 압박을 주니까요.

B 여유롭게 사는 방법이 실린 책을 읽기 시작한 것도 그 때문이에요.

일상생활에서 56 Time is really dragging on for me today / 오늘은 시간이 지독히도 안 가는군요

A May I spreak to Il-Hyung Kim?

B Speaking.

A Hi, Il-Hyung. This is Kenny. How is it going today?

B **Time is really dragging on for me today.**

A You must be tired or something.

B No. This job I'm doing is really boring.

A 김일형씨 부탁합니다.

B 접니다.

A 일형아, 나 케니인데, 오늘 어떻게 지내고 있냐?

B 오늘 진짜 시간 안 가네.

A 피곤한 모양이구나.

B 아니. 내가 하고 있는 일이 지겨워서 그래.

일상생활에서 57 I was just in the neighborhood. / 잠깐 근처에 들렀어요

A What's new with you?

B **I was just in the neighborhood.**

I couldn't resist sneaking a preview of the opening.

A Did Nancy come along with you?

B No, she couldn't make it,

because she is swamped with work.

A What a pity!

By the way, what time does the opening start?

B 1 p.m. on the dot.

A 어쩐 일이야?

B 잠깐 근처에 들렀어.

개업식을 미리 보고 싶어서 참을 수가 없었거든.

A 낸시도 같이 왔니?

B 아니, 그녀는 오지 못했어.

그녀는 너무 일이 많거든.

A 유감이군!

그런데 개업식은 몇 시에 시작이야?

B 오후 1시 정각이야.

일상생활에서 58 Not your usual slapdash work. / 늘 하듯 대충하지 마세요

A Kenny, could you mow the lawn today?

B Don't worry, Dad.

A And **not your usual slapdash work.** Lately you've been getting sloppy in a lot of things.

B I've got a lot of things to do. I don't have enough time for all your work.

A 케니야, 오늘 잔디 좀 깎아줄래?

B 걱정 마세요, 아빠.

A 네가 늘 하듯 대충하지 말거라. 요즘 들어 많은 일을 대강 아무렇게나 해 왔잖니.

B 저도 할 일이 많이 있어요. 아빠가 시키시는 일을 다 할 시간이 충분치 못해요.

일상생활에서 59 Let's face it. 현실을 직시하세요

A I want my daughter to go to Princeton no matter what.

B **Let's face it.** Mr. Huh.
Your daughter's high school GPA and SAT score are not good enough for her to be admitted to Princeton.

A My daughter's extra curricular activities and writing skills are perfect.

B Whatever you say,
the most important thing is school GPA.

A 내 딸을 무슨 일이 있어도 프린스턴대학에 보내고 싶어요.

B 허 선생님. 현실을 직시하시죠.
따님의 학교성적과 수능성적은 프린스턴대학에 입학하기에 충분치 못해요.

A 내 딸의 과외 활동과 글 솜씨가 완벽하잖아요.

B 뭐라 하시건,
가장 중요한 것은 내신성적입니다.

일상생활에서 60 I'm about ready to wrap it up. 거의 끝나가요

A Kenny, please finish building the dog house.

B Morn! Don't worry. **I'm about ready to wrap it up.**

A Your nephew, Sebastian, wants you to go to a movie with him.

B Really? I scolded him just before.
He didn't keep the important promise.

A Forgive him and be generous to him.
He is still young.

A 케니야, 개집 짓는 것 빨리 끝내렴.

B 엄마 걱정 마세요. 거의 끝나가요.

A 네 조카 세바스천이 너랑 영화 구경을 가길 원하고 있다.

B 정말요? 내가 조금 전에 꾸짖었는데요.
중요한 약속을 지키지 않아서요.

A 용서해 주고 너그럽게 대해줘라.
아직 어리잖아.

일상생활에서 61 It's just my gut feeling. 그저 내 직감이 그래요

A Something tells me that the Stevens will break up soon.

B You mean they may divorce?

A Yes.

B Why do you think so?

A **It's just my gut feeling.**

A 스티븐 부부가 곧 헤어질 예감이 드는데.

B 이혼할 수도 있다는 말이니?

A 그래.

B 왜 그렇게 생각하니?

A 그저 내 직감이 그래.

일상생활에서 62 It will come in handy. 상당히 도움이 될 것입니다

A Do you have any special plans for this summer?

B Yes, I'm going to New York to visit Stuybesant High School and Baruch College.

A Really? I went there a couple of years ago.

B Could you give me some advice?

A Take this book with you when you go to New York. **It'll come in handy.**

B Oh, thank you.

A 이번 여름에 무슨 특별한 계획이라도 있어요?

B 네, 스타이브슨 고교와 버룩대학교를 방문하러 뉴욕에 갈 거에요.

A 정말요? 이삼년 전에 저도 갔었어요.

B 조언 좀 해주세요.

A 뉴욕에 갈 때 이 책을 갖고 가세요. 상당히 도움이 될 거에요.

B 감사합니다.

일상생활에서 63 I haven't cracked it yet. 아직 못 알아냈어

A Hey, buddy, How's it going?

B Oh, good to see you. I', in grave peril. I need your help.

A Okay, what is the problem?

B I spent a whole night trying to find the code but **I haven't cracked it yet.**

A You haven't? Then I can't.
You're second to none cracking codes.

A 이봐, 친구. 일은 잘 돼가?

B 야, 마침 잘 만났네. 심각한 문제가 생겼어. 네 도움이 필요해.

A 알았어. 뭐가 문젠데?

B 밤새 암호를 풀어보려고 애썼는데 아직도 못했어.

A 네가 못했다면 나도 못해.
넌 암호 해독엔 최고잖아.

일상생활에서 64 Beats (the hell out of) me. 난 전혀 모르겠다

A What's that one about?

B **Beats the hell out of me.**

A Well, it's got Brad Pitt and Johnny Depp in it.

B Did you say Jonny Depp? Then it's got to be a flop.

A Come on, John. You can't brand him as a bad actor just because of one movie.

B I know you're a big fan of his, so don't even try.

A 저건 어떤 내용이지?

B 전혀 모르겠는데.

A 글쎄, 브래드 피트와 자니 뎁이 나오는데.

B 자니 뎁이라고 했니? 그럼 분명 실패작이겠네.

A 그러지 마, 존. 영화 하나 때문에 그를 나쁜 연기자로 낙인찍을 순 없잖아.

B 자니 뎁의 열렬한 팬인 거 아니까 시도도 하지 마.

일상생활에서 65 I hear you loud and clear. 무슨 말인지 잘 알겠어

A Mona, would you join me and Cathy for a movie tonight?

B I'd love to. But isn't it weird, me and Cathy?
We had a big fight a month ago.

A I know. But it happened a month ago.

B Well.... I'd like to hang around with you but....

A Come on! Don't you wanna make up with her?

B **I hear you loud and clear.**

A 모나, 오늘 나랑 캐시랑 영화 보러 갈래?

B 가고는 싶지만 캐시랑 같이 가면 불편하지 않을까?
한 달 전에 크게 싸웠는데.

A 나도 알아. 하지만 한 달 전 일이잖아.

B 글쎄…. 너랑은 가고 싶지만 그래도 좀….

A 같이 가자! 너도 화해하고 싶지 않아?

B 무슨 말인지는 잘 알겠어.

일상생활에서 66 I'll go for broke. 모든 것을 걸고 최선을 다하겠다

A I've decided to invest all my savings in this business venture.

B If it fails, you will go broke. Think twice.

A I'm so certain of succeeding in this business that **I'll go for broke.**

B Well, I'll keep my fingers crossed.

A 나는 그동안 저축한 돈 전부를 이 사업에 투자하기로 마음먹었습니다.

B 실패하면 망하는 것이니 재고해 보세요.

A 이 사업의 성공에 자신이 있기에 모든 것을 걸겠어요.

B 그렇다면 행운을 빌겠습니다.

일상생활에서 67 Don't get any hopes up. 어떤 희망도 기대하지 마세요

A Could you do me a favor?.

B Sure, what can I do for you?

A You filmed a lot on my wedding day, right?
I wondered if I could look at your videotape because mine has come out all blue.

B OK, but I'm pretty sure I wiped it,
so **don't get any hopes up.**

A 저 부탁 하나 할까요?

B 그래요, 뭐죠?

A 제 결혼식 때 식장에서 촬영 많이 하셨죠?
제가 가진 녹화 테이프의 상태가 엉망이라 그러는데요. 당신이 찍은 비디오테이프 좀 볼 수 없을까요?

B 저런. 제 테이프는 이미 확실히 지워버린 것 같은데요.
(미안하지만) 제게는 기대하지 않는 게 좋을 것 같군요.

일상생활에서 68 I'm afraid I was taken for a ride. 내가 속은 것 같아요

A Could you give me a ride home, please?

B Yes, but what happened to your car?

A It broke down again. I think I got a lemon from the used car dealer.

B Maybe. It's not easy to buy a used car without **being taken for a ride**, you know.

A 우리 집까지 차 좀 태워주시겠어요?

B 그래요. 그런데 당신 차에 무슨 문제가 있나요?

A 또 고장 났어요. 결함 있는 중고차 딜러에게서 엉터리 차를 구입한 것 같아요.

B 그럴지도 모르죠. 속지 않고 중고차를 사는 게 쉬운 일이 아니지요.

일상생활에서 69 It's all been taken care of. 다 처리됐어

A Did you see the telephone bill?
I think the due day was a few days ago.

B Yes, it was due last Friday. But don't worry.

A What do you mean?

B **It's all been taken care of.**
I already paid it online last week.

A Whew, I am relieved now.

A 전화요금 고지서 봤니?
납부 기한이 며칠이나 지난 것 같던데….

B 응, 지난 금요일이 납부 마감일이었지.
그러나 걱정하지 마.

A 무슨 소리니?

B 납부됐어.
지난주에 온라인으로 지급했거든.

A 후유, 다행이야.

일상생활에서 70 You're barking up the wrong tree. 넌 잘못 짚었어

A What're you going to do this afternoon?

B Nothing. What about you?

A Nothing either. I thought you might go out with Brent.

B What's that supposed to mean?
Why would I go out with Brent?

A Isn't something going on with you two?

B Me and Brent? No way.
You're barking up the wrong tree.

A 오늘 오후에 뭐해?

B 아무것도 안 해. 너는?

A 나도 별일 없어. 넌 브렌트를 만나러 외출할 줄 알았는 데.

B 그게 무슨 소리야?
내가 왜 브렌트를 만나?

A 너희 둘 사이에 뭔가 있지 않아?

B 나랑 브렌트랑? 아니.
너 완전히 잘못 짚었어.

일상생활에서 71 Don't use four-letter words. 나쁜 말을 쓰지 마라

A Kenny, what do you think of our new vice president?

B He strikes me as a mean SOB.

He **uses** a lot of **four-letter words**, doesn't he?

A Yes, he does.

B Did you attend the board meeting yesterday?

A Yes I did.

A 케니, 새로운 부사장은 어때?

B 인상이 아주 안 좋아.

말끝마다 욕을 하잖아. 안 그래?

A 맞아.

B 너 어제 이사회에 참석했었니?

A 응. 했어.

일상생활에서 72 Think nothing of it. 별말씀을요

A Here is the paper you asked to get done by today.

B It was nice of you to do that for me.

Without your help, I wouldn't be able to submit it to my boss on time. How can I thank you?

A It's no big deal. **Think nothing of it.**

B I really appreciate your help.

A 당신이 오늘까지 해달라고 부탁했던 서류에요.

B 부탁한 일을 해주셔서 감사해요.

당신이 아니었더라면 제시간에 상사에게 제출하지 못할 뻔했어요.

A 별것 아닙니다. 별말씀을요.

B 당신의 도움에 정말 감사드립니다.

일상생활에서 73 Could you be a little more specific? 좀 더 구체적으로 말씀해 주시겠어요?

A Mr. Kim, your letter is a bit vague.

Could you be a little more specific?

B Well, in what ways, for example?

A Well, it states that you are interested in importing electronic parts, but it doesn't specify which items.

B Oh, I see. Okay, I'll complete the details and send them off to you when I get back to the States.

A 김선생, 편지 내용이 좀 모호하군요.

좀 더 구체적으로 말씀해 주시겠어요?

B 예를 들어 어떤 점들을 말씀하시는 거죠?

A 편지에는 귀사가 전자 부품의 수입에 대해 관심이 있다고 되어있는데, 어떤 품목인지에 대해서는 구체적으로 명시되어 있지 않아서요.

B 아, 알겠습니다. 미국으로 돌아가 세부사항을 완성해서 보내지요.

일상생활에서 74 The suspense is killing me. 궁금해서 미치겠어

A You have to tell me what's going to happen next.

B No way. Just watch the movie and see for yourself.

A **The suspense is killing me.** I have to know now.

B Sorry.

I don't want to ruin the ending for you.

A 이다음에 어떻게 되는지 말 좀 해봐.

B 절대로 안 돼. 그냥 영화 보고 알면 되잖아.

A 궁금해서 죽겠어. 난 지금 알아야겠단 말이야.

B 미안해.

괜히 결말을 말해 줘서 네 영화감상을 망치고 싶지 않아.

일상생활에서 75 I haven't seen you for ages! 진짜 오랜만이다!

A Look who's here! Jane Johnson!

B Mark! Gosh, **I haven't seen you for ages!**

How are getting along?

A Can't complain. How are you keeping?

B Well, the same old thing.

Anyways, it's great to see you again.

A 이게 누구야! 제인 존슨 아냐?

B 마크! 어머 진짜 오랜만이다.

그 동안 어떻게 지냈어?

A 잘 지내지. 너는 잘 지내?

B 글쎄, 똑같지 뭐.

그나저나 다시 만나서 정말 반갑다.

일상생활에서 76 Don't bother 그럴 필요 없어

A Hey, Ian. Where're you headed?

B I'm going to the downstairs to make a copy.

A **Don't bother.**

The copy machine is not working right now.

B What? Are you sure? I'm in a rush to do this.

A Sure. I was just there. Why don't you use a copy machine on the 9th floor?

A 안녕, 이안. 어디가?

B 아래층에 복사하러 가는 길이야.

A 가봤자 헛수고야.

지금은 복사기가 작동이 안 돼.

B 뭐야? 확실해? 내가 좀 급해서.

A 확실해. 방금 거기서 오는 길이야. 9층에 있는 복사기를 사용하지 그래?

일상생활에서 77 Crime doesn't pay. 죄를 지으면 벌을 받기 마련이지

A I heard that the CEO of ABC Company was sent to jail for insider trading!

B I saw that in the newspaper.
He was sentenced to fifteen years in prison.

A Wow! I guess **crime doesn't pay!**

A ABC사의 사장이 내부자 거래로 구속되었대!

B 나도 신문에서 봤어.
15년형을 선고 받았더라.

A 와! 죄를 지으면 벌을 받기 마련이지!

일상생활에서 78 Holy cow! 야, 세상에!

A Oh, my gosh! Look over there!

B **Holy cow!** I can't believe my eyes!

A What is it?

B I don't know, but it looks like a UFO.

A 어머나! 저기 좀 봐!

B 세상에! 도저히 내 눈을 믿을 수가 없어!

A 저게 뭐야?

B 모르겠어. 하지만 UFO같이 보이는데.

일상생활에서 79 Where's the beef? 이게 다야?

A Here is my report. I'm all finished!

B **Where's the beef?**

A What do you mean? I wrote four pages.

B But it's supposed to be a twenty-page paper.

A 여기 제 보고서요. 다 끝났습니다!

B 이게 다야?

A 무슨 말씀이세요? 4페이지나 썼는데.

B 20페이지짜리여야 하잖아.

일상생활에서 80 Have we met before? 우리 전에 만나지 않았니?

A **Have we met before?**

B No, but I think I've seen you around campus.
My name's Kim.

A I'm Mark.

A 우리 전에 만나지 않았나?

B 아니, 근데 학교에서 본 적이 있는 것 같아.
내 이름은 킴이야.

A 난 마크야.

일상생활에서 81 Period — 확실해!

A Did you make up your mind about going to Hong Kong?

B Yes. I told Mr. Paulman that I'd accept his proposition.

A **Period?**

B **Period!** I slept on it almost a week.

That's more than enough, I believe.

A Good for you.

I'm sure this will be a once-in-a-lifetime opportunity.

B I hope so.

A 홍콩에 갈지 말지 결정했어?

B 응. 폴먼씨에게 제안을 받아들이겠다고 했어.

A 확실해?

B 확실해! 일주일이나 고민했는걸.

그 정도면 충분히 생각하고도 남은 것 같아.

A 잘됐다.

내게 일생일대의 기회가 될 거야.

B 나도 그랬으면 좋겠어.

일상생활에서 82 You could have gone to an ATM and got a cash advance. — 현금자동지급기에서 현금서비스를 받을 수도 있어

A I was at a small store that only took cash.

B **You could have gone to an ATM and got a cash advance.**

A If it had been an emergency. But those advances can be expensive, and the interest rates are really high.

A 작은 가게에 갔더니 현금만 받는대.

B 현금자동지급기에서 현금서비스를 받을 수도 있었잖아.

A 급한 일이었으면 그랬겠지. 하지만 현금 서비스는 비싼데 다가 이자율이 아주 높아.

일상생활에서 83 The faucet keeps dripping. — 수도꼭지에서 물이 계속 떨어져요

A **The faucet keeps dripping.**

We're wasting a lot of water.

B I'll get my tools and try to fix the problem.

A 수도꼭지에서 물이 계속 떨어져요.

이건 물 낭비에요.

B 제가 공구를 가지고 와서 고쳐볼게요.

일상생활에서 84 The table is set for dinner. 저녁상 다 차렸어

A **The table is set for dinner.**

B Is the ketchup on the table?

A Yes.

A 저녁상 다 차렸어?

B 상 위에 케첩 있니?

A 응.

일상생활에서 85 After today they expire 유효기간이 오늘까지야

A I've got a lot of coupons I have to use, because **after today they expire.**

B One is for peanuts and another for hot sauce.
What can you make with all of these things?

A Well, they don't really go together, but I can save them for later.

B Right. And think of all the money you'll save.

A 써야 할 쿠폰이 많이 있어.
유효기간이 오늘까지거든.

B 하나는 땅콩, 또 하나는 핫 소스 쿠폰이네.
이걸 갖고 뭐 해 먹을 수 있지?

A 글쎄, 어울리는 재료는 아니지만 나중을 위해서 아껴두면 되잖아.

B 맞아. 그리고 절약되는 돈을 생각해봐.

일상생활에서 86 They jack up the prices. 그들은 가격을 올려 팔아요

A Before we head off, let's make sure we have everything we'll need for the day.

B Don't they have shops there?
I'm sure we can pick up anything we forget.

A But **they jack up the prices** at the stores in the park.

B I guess you're right.
Hand me that extra bottle of water.

A 가기 전에 오늘 하루 필요한 걸 다 챙겼는지 확인 해봐요.

B 거기에 가게 없어요?
잊고 안 챙긴 물건은 사면 돼요.

A 하지만 공원에 있는 가게들은 가격을 올려서 팔아요.

B 당신 말이 맞아요.
물을 더 가져가게 내게 줘요.

일상생활에서 87 It sure is dismal out today. 오늘은 정말 바깥 날씨가 음산하네

A How do you like this weather?

B **It sure is dismal out today.**

A 오늘 날씨 어때?

B 오늘은 정말 바깥 날씨가 음산하네.

일상생활에서 88 There is a slight discount on dented cans 찌그러진 통조림은 약간 할인이 됩니다

A This can appears to have a dent in it.

B I'm sorry, sir, but that's all we have in stock. I'm sure the contents are fine.

A Well, I guess I could try. I'll be able to return it and get my money back if there's a problem?

B Of course. And **there is a slight discount on dented cans**, too.

A 이 통조림은 찌그러졌어요.

B 손님, 죄송하지만 이것밖에 없습니다. 내용물은 괜찮을 거예요.

A 그럼 사겠어요. 만일 내용물에 이상이 있으면 반납하고 돈을 되돌려 받을 수 있는 거죠?

B 물론입니다. 그리고 찌그러진 통조림은 약간 할인이 됩니다.

일상생활에서 89 How did they track me down all the way across the country? 전국 방방곡곡을 뒤져서 어떻게 나를 찾아냈지?

A Did you get your letter from the class reunion committee?

B Mine came last week. **How did they track me down all the way across the country?**

A I don't know how they found me either.

B Well, I guess we'll have to go to our class reunion. There's no way around it.

A 동창회에서 온 편지 받았니?

B 지난주에 왔더라. 전국 방방곡곡을 뒤져서 어떻게 나를 찾아냈을까?

A 그 사람들이 나도 어떻게 찾았는지 모르겠네.

B 음, 동창회에 가야 할 거 같아. 어쩔 수 없지.

일상생활에서 90 The toilet is blocked up. 화장실이 막혔어요

A Hey, **your toilet is blocked up.**

B What did you do to it?

A Nothing, it was already like that when I went in.

A 저기요, 화장실이 막혔는데요.

B 어떻게 해서 막혔나요?

A 아무 짓도 안 했어요. 제가 들어갔을 때 이미 막혀 있던데요.

일상생활에서 91 Is our account overdrawn? 한도를 넘었나요?

A Your transaction was denied.

B **Is our account overdrawn?**

A I don't know.

A 카드가 안 되는데요.

B 한도를 넘었나요?

A 저도 모르겠습니다.

일상생활에서 92 Are you going to vegetate in front of the TV all day? 하루 종일 텔레비전만 보고 있을 거니?

A **Are you going to vegetate in front of the TV all day?**

B Why not? I've finished my final exam,

so I have nothing to do but watch TV.

I want to catch up on Ally Mcbeal.

A That program has recently gone down hill.

B You mean the show is boring now?

A 하루 종일 텔레비전만 보고 있을 거니?

B 왜 안돼? 기말고사 끝나고 텔레비전 보는 것 밖에 할 것이 없어.

Ally Mcbeal 볼 거야.

A 요즘에는 내용이 점점 형편없어지는 것 같아.

B 지루하다는 거니?

일상생활에서 93 I'm tickled to death. 너무 좋아 죽겠다

A **I'm tickled to death** that you are getting married at last.

B Thank you.

A I hear your bride is coming from Russia. Is that true?

B Yes, I'm dying to see her.

A I'll bet.

A 드디어 당신이 결혼한다니 더할 나위 없이 기쁩니다.

B 감사합니다.

A 듣기론 러시아에서 신부가 온다던데 사실입니까?

B 네. 그녀가 보고 싶어 죽을 지경입니다.

A 그러시겠죠.

일상생활에서 94 It was a really long day. 정말 힘든 하루였어

A **It was a really long day.**

B I'm sorry to hear that. Here at home, you can relax.

A 정말 힘든 하루였어.

B 안됐군요. 이제 집에 돌아왔으니 쉬세요.

일상생활에서 95 She was mugged in an alleyway — 그녀는 골목길에서 강도를 당했대

A Did you hear about Kate? **She was mugged in an alleyway** last week.

B That's horrible! Was she hurt?

A No, but the man had a knife and demanded her purse. She wasn't going to argue!

A 너 지난주에 케이트가 골목에서 강도를 당한 일을 들었어?

B 저런! 다치지 않았대?

A 응, 칼을 든 강도가 핸드백을 달라고 해서 주저 없이 줬대!

일상생활에서 96 I got this second-hand. — 이거 헌옷 가게에서 샀어

A You look stunning in that coat. Where did you buy?

B Does it look good? **I got this second-hand.**

A No way! It doesn't look old at all.

B I had it altered a bit and I think that helped.

A 너 그 코트 입으니까 정말 멋지다. 어디서 샀어?

B 괜찮아 보여? 이거 헌 옷 가게에서 산 거야.

A 말도 안 돼! 전혀 오래된 것 같지 않은데?

B 조금 수선했지. 아마 그래서일 거야.

일상생활에서 97 I can't wait for it to snow. — 눈이 안 오면 견딜 수가 없어

A **I can't wait for it to snow.**

B Really?

A Yes. Where I grew up there was lots of snow in the winter.

A 눈이 안오면 견딜 수가 없어.

B 정말?

A 응, 내가 자란 곳은 겨울이면 눈이 엄청 많이 내렸거든.

일상생활에서 98 They startled me — 너무 놀랐으니까

A Why did you jump back when they all started yelling and screaming?

B Because **they startled me.**

A 사람들이 모두 소리치기 시작했을 때 왜 뒤로 물러났어?

B 너무 놀랐으니까.

일상생활에서 99 They're all out of style. (옷들이) 전부 유행이 지났어

A I need to go shopping. I don't have a thing to wear.

B Oh, not again. Check your closet. You've got tons of clothes.

A **They're all out of style.** I need to update my wardrobe to the latest fashion.

B Well, enjoy your shopping spree but take care not to wear yourself out.

A 나 쇼핑하러 가야 해. 입을 옷이 하나도 없어.

B 어휴, 또 그런다. 네 옷장 좀 봐. 얼마나 입을 옷이 많은데.

A 그 옷들 모두 유행지난 거야. 최신 유행에 맞춰 입고 싶단 말이야.

B 그렇다면 마음껏 쇼핑해. 그래도 지치지는 않게 조심하고.

일상생활에서 100 I hope it doesn't get too bumpy. 지나치게 난기류가 아니었으면 좋겠네요

A Could you fasten your seat beat?

B Sorry?

A We have the 'Fasten Seat Belt' sign. We may have some turbulence.

B I get it. **I hope it doesn't get too bumpy.**

A Don't be concerned about it. We will be fine.

A 안전벨트 착용해 주시겠어요?

B 네? 뭐라고요?

A 안전벨트착용 표시등이 동작 중입니다. 기체가 아마 좀 흔들릴 것 같습니다.

B 네 알았어요. 지나치게 난기류가 아니었으면 좋겠네요.

A 너무 걱정하지 마세요. 괜찮을 겁니다.

일상생활에서 101 Have you thought about being a candy striper? 간호보조원 해보는 게 어떠니?

A I have to choose which volunteer work to do.

B **Have you thought about being a candy striper?**

A No way! I don't want to be stuck around a bunch of sick people.

B Oh, well. I guess I'll give up my dream of you becoming a doctor, then.

A 어떤 봉사활동을 할지 선택해야 돼요.

B 간호보조원 해보는 게 어떠니?

A 싫어요! 아픈 사람들 속에 갇혀 있고 싶지는 않아요.

B 그래. 네게 의사를 기대했던 내 꿈은 포기해야 할 거 같구나.

일상생활에서 102 You get paid when you volunteer | 봉사활동을 하면 얻는 게 있단다

A Mom! The school say I have to complete twenty-five volunteer hours before the end of twelfth grade.

B You're just starting ten now. That's plenty of time.

A But all those hours of unpaid work!

B **You get paid when you volunteer**; you get paid in practical experience.

A 엄마! 학교에서 12학년이 끝날 때까지 25시간 봉사활동을 끝마쳐야 한대요.

B 이제 10학년을 시작했으니 시간은 많이 있구나.

A 그런데 그 시간을 다 무급으로 일해야 돼요!

B 봉사활동을 해도 얻는 게 있단다. 세상 경험이라는 거지.

일상생활에서 103 There are rolls of unexposed film in the bag. | 쓰지 않은 필름 몇 통이 가방에 있어요

A I'm worried about the camera in my bag. Will this machine damage it?

B Is your camera digital or film?

A It's an old film camera, and **there are rolls of unexposed film in the bag, too.**

B If you like, we can hand check the film for you, to make sure it's not harmed by the machine.

A 가방 안에 있는 카메라가 걱정되네요. 이 기계 때문에 망가질까요?

B 디지털 카메라인가요, 필름 카메라인가요?

A 구식 필름 카메라인데 쓰지 않은 필름 몇 통이 가방에 있어요.

B 원하시면 필름을 손으로 확인해볼게요. 기계에 손상되지 않도록요.

일상생활에서 104 It's a bit pricey. | 가격이 좀 비싸다

A Are you looking for anything in particular?

B How much is the necklace?

A It's 300 bucks.

B **It's a bit pricey.** Will you give a discount?

A Oh, It's already marked down.

B OK, I will take it.

A Would you like it gift-wrapped?

B Sure.

A 뭐 특별하게 찾으시는 것이 있으세요?

B 저 목걸이 얼마에요?

A 300달러입니다.

B 어머, 좀 비싸네요. 할인 안 되나요?

A 죄송합니다. 이미 인하된 가격입니다.

B 할 수 없군요. 주세요.

A 선물용으로 포장해 드릴까요?

B 네.

일상생활에서 105 I'm little short on dough. 내가 돈이 좀 부족해서 말이야

A **I'm a little short on dough.**

B I'll pay it this time, but next time you bring a check book.

A Thanks.

A 내가 돈이 좀 부족해서 말이야.

B 이번엔 내가 낼 테니까 다음 번엔 네가 수표책을 가져와[네가 내라].

A 고마워.

■ dough는 원래 '반죽'을 가리키는 단어지만 구어에서는 '돈'(money)이라는 뜻으로도 사용됩니다.

일상생활에서 106 I'll write a check for it. 내가 개인 수표를 쓸게

A Do you have any cash with you?

B No. Sorry.

A **I'll write a check for it.**

A 현찰 좀 있니?

B 없는데. 미안해.

A (그럼) 내가 개인 수표를 쓸게.

■ 미국 사람들은 대부분 신용 카드만큼 개인 수표(personal check)를 씁니다. write a check은 '개인 수표를 발행하다'라는 의미입니다.

일상생활에서 107 The clock is running out. 시간이 다 되어가고 있거든

A We're down by five points. Can we pull this out?

B I don't know. **The clock is running out.**

A 우리 5점 뒤지고 있어. 역전시킬 수 있을까?

B 모르겠어. 시간이 다 되어가고 있거든.

■ 'Can we pull this out?'은 'come from behind to win'의 의미로 역전승을 말합니다.

일상생활에서 108 They link to that other page. 그것들은 다른 페이지로 링크되어 있어

A Why do these words look different?

B **They link to that other page.** If you click your mouse over them, the other page will be displayed.

A 이 단어들은 왜 달라 보이지?

B 그것들은 다른 페이지로 링크되어 있어. 그 위에 대고 마우스를 클릭하면 다른 페이지가 나올거야.

일상생활에서 109 Would you like to wear these out? 신고 가시겠어요?

A These shoes are great.

B I'm glad you like them.

Would you like to wear these out?

A Yes, and you can throw away my old shoes.

A 이 신발 너무 맘에 드네요.

B 맘에 드신다니 다행입니다.
신고 가시겠어요?

A 예, 제가 신고 온 신발은 버려주세요.

일상생활에서 110 I did it on the spur of the moment. 충동적으로 했어

A Did you think twice before you quit your job at Acme Company?

B No, **I did it on the spur of the moment.**

A Wow - that's a very brave of you.
I could never do that.

A 직장 그만둘 때 신중히 생각한 거야?

B 아니, 충동적으로 했어.

A 와, 용기 한번 대단한데.
난 절대 그렇게 못 할 거야.

일상생활에서 111 Enough is enough. 그만하면 충분해

A Jess, do you have any idea for how many hours you stick to the computer?

B It's driving me crazy! I'm almost there.

A That's exactly the same thing as what you said an hour ago.

B It's just a little short of something and I can't find it.

A Hey, **enough is enough.**
Just give a call to the service department, okay?

B Yeah, you're right. **Enough is enough.**

A 제스, 너 지금 그 컴퓨터에 몇 시간째 매달려 있는 거니?

B 정말 돌겠어! 거의 다 고쳤는데.

A 한 시간 전에도 그렇게 말했었잖아.

B 뭔가가 약간 모자라는데 그걸 못 찾겠단 말이야.

A 이봐, 그만하면 충분해.
그냥 서비스센터에 전화해, 응?

B 그래, 네 말이 맞다. 난 할 만큼 했어.

일상생활에서 112 Times have changed | 세상이 많이 변했습니다

A According to recent statistics, every fourth newly wed couple in Korea will eventually divorce.

B Well, **times have changed.**

When I was young, divorces were very rare.

A So, Kenny, please don't push your son-in-law.

B How dare! None of your business.

A Calm down. I am saying as a friend.

Don't get me wrong.

A 최근 통계에 따르면 한국은 신혼부부 네 쌍 중 한 쌍은 결국 이혼한다는군.

B 그래, 세상 많이 변했군.

내가 젊었을 때는 참 드문 일이었는데.

A 그러니, 케니, 자네 사위를 몰아세우지 말게.

B 감히 어디다. 자네 상관할 바 아니야.

A 진정하게. 친구로서 하는 말일세.

곡해하지 말게.

일상생활에서 113 My condolences! | 삼가 조의를 표합니다

A **My condolences!**

B Please accept my condolences.

C Please accept my deepest sympathy.

D I am so sorry to hear that your grandmother had passed away.

E I am so saddened to hear of your beloved grandmother passing away.

A 삼가 조의를 표합니다.

B 조의를 받아주세요.

C 슬픔을 같이 나누고 싶습니다.(애도합니다.)

D 할머니께서 돌아가셨다니 유감입니다.

E 사랑하는 할머니께서 별세하셨다는 소식을 들으니 매우 애통하군요.

- C에서 sympathy는 동정이 아니라 '슬픔을 같이 나눔'을 뜻한다.

일상생활에서 114 I'm afraid I have a cramp in my foot. | 발에 쥐가 난 것 같아

A **I'm afraid I have a cramp in my foot.**

B It feels like I'm walking on pins and needles.

A My leg is asleep, too.

B I'm not surprised. You have sat cross-legged over five hours playing cards.

A 발에 쥐가 난 것 같아요.

B 나는 다리가 저려요.

A 내 다리도 저려요.

B 그럴 수밖에 없지요. 다섯 시간 이상 다리를 꼬고 앉아 포커를 치니 그렇지요.

일상생활에서 115 A penny for your thoughts. 네 생각을 말해 봐

A Hey. You look so serious. What are you thinking?

B Nothing.

A It can't be nothing.
You didn't say a word for half an hour. What is it?

B Well.... Just a couple of things about you and me.
Nothing big.

A About us? Now, I've gotta know. What's brewing in your mind? **A penny for your thoughts.**

B If you insist. Do you really think we can work out well?

A 되게 심각하네. 무슨 생각해?

B 아무 생각 안 해.

A 그럴 리가.
30분 동안 한마디도 안 했잖아. 뭔데?

B 그냥…. 너랑 나에 대해서 좀….
별거 아니야.

A 우리에 대해서? 이제, 진짜 알아야겠어.
무슨 생각인데?
말 좀 해봐.

B 네가 정 알고 싶다면. 우리가 정말 잘 어울린다고 생각해?

일상생활에서 116 No dice! 절대로 안 돼!

A What's going on with you and your father?

B What? Something weird?

A Yeah. You guys didn't say anything to each other at dinner.

B Actually, I asked him for a raise in my allowance.
And you know what he said? **"No dice!"**

A Is that why? How old are you?
Don't be such a baby!

B Come on! Do you have any idea how hard it is to live it up with 20 bucks a week?

A 너 아버지랑 무슨 일 있어?

B 왜? 이상해 보여?

A 당연하지. 저녁 식사 동안 서로 한마디도 안했잖아.

B 사실은 아빠한테 용돈을 좀 올려달라고 말씀드렸는데 뭐라 그러신 줄 알아?
"절대로 안 돼!"

A 그게 이유야? 너 몇 살이야?
철 좀 들지!

B 뭐야? 일주일에 20달러로 사는 게 얼마나 힘든지 너 알아?

일상생활에서 117 It's a bed of roses. 이건 천국이지

A Hello, Justin. Long time no see.

B Hi, Neo. What's up? I've lost track of you.

A Oh, I got a new job on Madison Avenue.

B You did? Wow.... So, how's your new job?

A Pretty good. Compared to my old one, **it's a bed of roses.**

B That's awesome!

A 안녕, 저스틴. 정말 오랜만이다.

B 그래, 네오. 잘 있었어? 어떻게 지내나 궁금했는데.

A 아, 나 광고 쪽에 새로 취직했어.

B 그래? 와…. 새 일은 어때?

A 꽤 좋아. 예전 직업에 비하면 이건 천국이야.

B 정말 잘됐다!

일상생활에서 118 the fruit will get crushed at the bottom of the cart 과일을 카트 바닥에 놓으면 뭉개질 거야

A I guess we should start over on the other side of the supermarket.

B Why walk all the way there and then back again? We can start here, in the fruit section.

A But then **the fruit will get crushed at the bottom of the cart**

B I see. Let's go to the canned goods first, then.

A 슈퍼마켓 저쪽 끝에서부터 쇼핑을 시작하는 게 어때.

B 왜 저기까지 걸어갔다가 다시 돌아와야 하는데? 여기 과일 코너부터 보자.

A 하지만 과일을 먼저 사서 카트 바닥에 놓으면 뭉개질거야.

B 그렇구나. 그럼 통조림류 코너부터 가자.

일상생활에서 119 It's a once-in-a- lifetime chance! 평생에 한 번 올까 말까 한 기회야

A You should invest heavily in Acme Company. I've heard some hot tips about it!

B I don't know. It seems like a risky company to invest in.

A But you could make millions. **It's a once-in-a- lifetime chance!**

A Acme 회사에 집중 투자해. 좋은 정보를 들었거든.

B 글쎄. 투자하기엔 좀 불안한 회사 같은데.

A 하지만 떼돈을 벌 수 있을걸. 평생에 한 번 올까 말까한 기회야!

일상생활에서 120 Can I ring of these up for you? | 이것으로 계산해 드릴까요?

A **Can I ring of these up for you?**

B I still haven't made up my mind, thanks.

A 이것으로 하나 계산해 드릴까요?

B 아직 결정을 못 내렸어요. 감사합니다.

일상생활에서 121 Can I see something a little more compact? | 좀 소형으로 볼 수 있나요?

A **Can I see something a little more compact?**

B Sure. our ultra-compact video cameras are here.

A 좀 소형으로 볼 수 있나요?

B 물론이죠. 초소형 비디오카메라가 이쪽에 있습니다.

일상생활에서 122 Paper or plastic? | 종이 백 드릴까요, 비닐 백 드릴까요?

A **Paper or plastic?**

B Are those my only choices? I'm worried the paper bags might rip, but I hate to use too much plastic.

A We also sell re-usable cotton bags.

B Perfect. I'll take two, please.

A 종이 백 드릴까요, 비닐 백 드릴까요?

B 그 두 가지 뿐인가요? 종이 백은 찢어질까 봐 걱정되고, 비닐 백을 너무 많이 쓰는 건 싫은데

A 재사용할 수 있는 면 가방도 팔고 있습니다.

B 좋군요. 두 개 주세요.

일상생활에서 123 You can count on me | 제게 맡기세요

A My wife says, "No boys allowed."

B Don't worry.

I have a bunch of homework to do anyway.

A Then, if the phone rings, just let the machine get it.

And don't answer the door.

B **You can count on me.** if there are any problems, your number is on the fridge, right?

A 아내가 남자는 절대로 데려오지 말라고 하네요.

B 걱정 마세요.

해야 할 숙제도 많아요.

A 그리고 전화가 오면 자동응답기가 받도록 두세요.

누가 와도 문을 열어 주지 말고요.

B 제게 맡기세요. 문제가 생기면

냉장고에 써 있는 번호로 연락드리면 되죠?

일상생활에서 124 I'm green with envy

매우 부러워하는

A You'll never guess what happened to me last Saturday.

B You found tha man of your dreams?

A Oh, very funny, but you're not so far off. I got Stephen Laure's autograph.

B You mean that really gorgeous looking actor in the detective series on TV?

A Well they were filming some scenes on location just round the corner from my apartment and I managed to catch him during a break.

B Oh, **I'm green with envy.** What did he say to you.

A 너는 지난 토요일에 내게 무슨 일이 일어났는지 짐작도 못할거야.

B 너 이상형이라도 만났니?

A 오 아주 웃겨. 하지만 아예 틀리진 않아. 내가 Stephen Laurie의 사인을 받았어.

B TV탐정시리즈에 나오는 외모가 멋진배우 말이지?

A 우리 아파트 근처에서 몇 장면을 찍고 있어서 휴식시간에 가까스로 그를 만날 수 있었어.

B 오, 정말 부럽군. 그가 너에게 무슨 말이라도 했니?

일상생활에서 125 Bob's your uncle!

걱정할 필요 없어 그렇게 하면 되는 겁니다

A What are you wailing about?
Has your computer crashed?

B No, I am trying to make this photo bigger on the screen.

A Oh, it's not difficult.

B I've been trying to do it for half an hour without success.

A I'll show you. Look, you open this menu. click here, click on the percentage you want, say 200% and **Bob's your uncle.** There it is, twice as large.

A it's easy when you know how. Thanks a lot

A 너 왜 울부짖고 있니?
너의 컴퓨터가 부서졌니?

B 아니, 이 사진을 화면에 확대하려고 하고 있어.

A 오, 그건 어렵지 않지.

B 30분 동안 해매고 있었어.

A 내가 보여주지. 봐. 이 메뉴를 연 후, 여기를 클릭한 후에 네가 원하는 퍼센트로 클릭해봐 200%로,
그렇게 하면 되는 거야. 2배로 말이야.

B 방법을 알고 나니 쉽군, 고마워.

일상생활에서 126 He's a handful — 귀찮은 것

A Good afternoon. Jessica. How's the baby?

B **He's a handful.** but very healthy.

A You know, you're looking great. I'm amazed you were able to get back into such good shape so soon after having a baby.

B Oh, thanks, Sue.

A What's your secret?

B I don't know.

I have been trying to exercise a lot, I guess.

A Well, whatever you're doing. it's working.

B If you keep this up, I'm going to start blushing.

A 안녕, Jessica. 애기는 좀 어때?

B 애보기가 너무 힘들지만 애기는 건강해.

A 너 정말 멋져 보여. 애기를 낳은 후로 그렇게 빨리 몸매가 돌아올수 있다니 놀라워.

B 고마워, Sue.

A 비법이 뭐야?

B 모르겠어.

꾸준히 운동한 덕분이 아닐까?

A 넌 무엇을 하든 효과가 있구나.

B 네가 계속 칭찬하면 내 얼굴이 붉어진다니까!

일상생활에서 127 Every cloud has a silver lining. — 고생 끝에 낙이 온다

A I heard you went to Jan's wedding. It must be strange seeing your high school sweetheart marry another guy.

B I was not looking forward to going, but it worked out fine. I met a nice girl at the reception, and now we're dating.

A Well, I guess it's true what people say.

Every cloud has a silver lining.

A 조앤 결혼식에 갔다고 들었어요. 고등학교 때 애인이 다른 남자랑 결혼하는 걸 보는 기분이 좀 묘했을 거예요.

B 가고 싶지 않았는데 가길 잘했어요.

피로연에서 괜찮은 여자를 만나서 지금 사귀고 있어요.

A 흠, 옛말이 맞는 것 같아요.

고생 끝에 낙이 온다잖아요.

일상생활에서 128 The thorn just poked me

가시에 찔렸어

A Well, Betty, what do you think?

Are you having a good time so far?

B What a perfect day! I loved the chocolates.

They're sweet, just like you are.

A And what about the card and the poem?

B Right. And the flowers are so....

Ouch! **The thorn just poked me!**

A 베티, 어때? 오늘 즐거웠어?

B 정말 멋진 하루였어! 초콜릿도 마음에 들어.

당신처럼 달콤한 것 같아.

A 그럼 카드와 시는 어때? 그것도 나처럼 로맨틱하지?

B 맞아. 그리고 꽃은 아주….

아야! 가시에 찔렸어!

일상생활에서 129 Their work ethic might rub off on you.

그 아이들 학습태도를 네가 배울 수 있어

A I found the perfect way to stick to my resolution to improve my grades.

B Good for you.

A I'm going to get together with all the other students who are having problems.

B Why not hang out with successful students instead?

Their work ethic might rub off on you.

A 성적 향상 결심을 지키기 위한 좋은 방법을 알았어.

B 잘됐구나.

A 성적 때문에 골치 썩이는 다른 애들과 어울릴 생각이야.

B 그러지 말고 공부 잘하는 애들과 어울리지 그러니?

걔네 학습태도를 네가 배울 수 있어.

일상생활에서 130 New cameras are idiot-proof

새로 나온 카메라는 전자동이야

A My father has an old film camera he still uses.

B A lot of people are like that. They're called purists.

They think using a digital camera is cheating.

A Because the camera does everything for you?

B Right. **New cameras are idiot-proof**, and purists think that's no fun at all.

A 우리 아버지는 필름 카메라를 갖고 계신데 아직도 사용하셔.

B 많이들 그래. 그런 사람들은 '순수주의자'라고 하지. 그들은 디지털 카메라로 사진을 찍는 건 진짜 사진이 아니라고 생각해.

A 카메라가 다 알아서 해주니까 그런 거야?

B 맞아. 새로 나오는 카메라는 전자동이라서 그들한테는 전혀 흥미롭지 않지.

일상생활에서 131 The years have sure been unkind to her. 그녀는 힘든 세월을 보낸 거 같아

A Look over there, It's Jill Henson.
Boy, **the years have sure been unkind to her.**

B You can say that again. Although, to be fair, I heard she's had two kids.

A Wow. I never expected her to settle down and start a family.

B Oh, she never settled down.
She has two kids by two different men.

A 저기 좀 봐. 질 헨더슨이야.
저런, 힘든 세월을 보낸 거 같네.

B 정말 그렇네. 거짓말 안 보내고, 쟤한테 아이가 두 명 있대.

A 와. 쟤가 결혼해서 가정을 꾸릴 거라곤 상상도 못했는데.

B 아, 결혼은 한 번도 안했어.
아빠가 다른 아이가 둘이래.

일상생활에서 132 It's sort of cliche, isn't it? 그건 좀 뻔하지 않니?

A What do you think about giving my girlfriend a box of chocolates for Valentine's Day?

B That's it? **It's sort of cliche, isn't it?**

A I guess you're right. I don't want to get her the same thing everyone else is.

B But at the same time, it is aort of a tradition.

A 발랜타인데이에 여자 친구에게 초콜릿 한 상자를 주는 건 어떨까?

B 그게 다야? 초콜릿을 주는 건 좀 뻔하지 않니?

A 네 말이 맞는 것 같아. 다른 사람들이랑 똑같은 걸 주고 싶지는 않은데.

B 그런데 또 그게 관례이긴 해.

일상생활에서 133 He struck it rich in computers soon after graduation. 그는 졸업하고 얼마 후 컴퓨터로 벼락부자가 됐어

A Is that Ted Johnson over there? That suit looks like it's worth more than my house.

B I bet it is.
He struck it rich in computers soon after graduation.

A That figures. He was a huge math nerd in school.

B Look at him now. All the single women here are fawning over him.

A 저기 저 사람 테드 존슨이니? 쟤가 입은 정장이 우리 집값보다 더 비싸 보여.

B 틀림없이 그럴 거야. 졸업하고 얼마 후에 컴퓨터로 벼락부자가 됐대.

A 생각한 대로네.
학교 다닐 때도 수학밖에 모르는 따분한 애였잖아.

B 쟤 좀 봐. 결혼 안 한 여자애들이 다 쟤한테 비위를 맞추고 있어.

일상생활에서 134 Did you turn him down? 너 그 사람 말 거절했어?

A Tom invited us out for drinks this evening.

B What did you tell him? **Did you turn him down?**

A Of course. My resolution was not to drink during the week.

B Good for you. Now, I think I'll call Tom and accept his invitation. My resolution was to get out of the house more often.

A 톰이 오늘 저녁에 술 한 잔 하자고 우리를 초대했어.

B 그래서 톰에게 뭐라고 했어? 거절했어?

A 물론이지. 내 새해결심은 평일에 술을 마시지 말자는 거였잖아.

B 잘했네. 난 톰한테 전화해서 간다고 해야지. 내 결심은 외출을 더 자주 하자는 거였어.

일상생활에서 135 I have terrible handwriting 내 글씨는 엉망이야

A Look at this job application!
It's going to take forever to fill out.

B The company really wants to know a lot about the applicants.

A Well, I guess that's to be expected.
It's not just some fast food, part-time job.

B Let me get a pen. Actually, can you write in the answers? **I have terrible handwriting.**

A 이 입사지원서 좀 봐!
다 쓰려면 끝도 없겠네.

B 회사에서 지원자에 대해 속속들이 알고 싶은 거야.

A 예상했던 일이긴 해. 패스트푸드점 아르바이트를 뽑는 것도 아니니까.

B 내가 펜을 가지고 올 테니 지원서 좀 써 줄 수 있어? 난 글씨가 엉망이라서.

일상생활에서 136 Proper posture is essential. 올바른 자세가 가장 중요해요

A Now that I can read music a little bit, I'm all ready to learn to play.

B The first thing you have to do is sit up straight.
Don't bend your back at all.

A Like this? It feels a bit awkward.

B **Proper posture is essential.**
Otherwise, you'll hurt your back.

A 악보를 조금 읽을 수 있으니까
연주할 준비가 된 거네요.

B 가장 먼저 해야 될 일은 똑바로 앉는 거예요.
허리를 구부리지 마시고요.

A 이렇게요? 어색한데요.

B 올바른 자세가 가장 중요해요.
그렇지 않으면 허리가 아플 거예요.

일상생활에서 137 Looks don't matter. 겉모양은 중요하지 않아

A What do you think of these hiking shoes? They look great, don't they?

B **Looks don't matter.** How do they fit? Are they tight anywhere?

A A little bit around the toes, but I still think they look good. They match my pants.

B They'll give you blisters if they're not the right size. Try on another pair.

A 이 하이킹 신발 어때? 괜찮아 보이는데, 안 그래?

B 겉모양은 중요하지 않아. 잘 맞아? 꽉 끼는 데 있니?

A 발가락 주위가 좀 끼는데 그래도 모양이 괜찮잖아. 바지와 잘 어울리고.

B 사이즈가 안 맞으면 물집이 생길 거야. 다른 걸로 신어봐.

일상생활에서 138 What else will I need besides the monitor? 모니터 말고 뭐가 더 필요할까요?

A **What else will I need besides the tower and the monitor?**

B Will you just install the OS from your old computer onto the new one?

A Can't I buy something that already has an OS?

B Sure. We'll put everything together and load the OS right here in the store.

A 탑이랑 모니터 말고 뭐가 더 필요할까요?

B 예전 컴퓨터의 OS를 새 컴퓨터에 설치하시겠어요?

A OS가 이미 깔려 있는 것을 살 수는 없나요?

B 사실 수 있죠. 여기 가게에서 저희가 다 편집하고 OS를 깔아 드립니다.

일상생활에서 139 It says an honorarium is available. 사례금이 있다고 나와 있구나

A The center for the blind actually pays money!

B Well, **It says an honorarium is available.**

A But they give you money, right?

B The center is far away, so the money is to help volunteers pay for the subway rides there and back.

A 시각장애인 센터에서는 보수를 지급한대요!

B 사례금이 있다고 나와 있구나.

A 그럼 거기서 돈을 준다는 거 맞죠?

B 센터가 멀어서 왕복 지하철 요금을 보태주는 거란다.

일상생활에서 140 I'm not a picky eater. 나는 아무거나 잘 먹어

A Do you like Italian cuisine?

I find a website full of recipes.

B I love pizza. Can you make us one for dinner?

A Actually, these are authentic Italian dishes.

Real Italian pizza is different from what you'd expect.

B Well, I'll give it a try anyway. **I'm not a picky eater.**

A 이탈리아 요리 좋아하니?

요리법으로 가득한 웹사이트를 찾았어.

B 피자 정말 좋아해. 저녁에 피자 만들어 주는 게 어때?

A 그런데 이건 정통 이탈리아 요리야.

네가 생각하는 것과 다른 진짜 이탈리아 피자지.

B 그럼 일단 먹어보지 뭐. 나는 아무거나 잘 먹어.

일상생활에서 141 It's a point-and-shoot camera. 이건 보고 누르기만 하면 되는 전자동 카메라야

A I don't know what half of these buttons do.

B Set the camera to full auto.

Then, **it's** like **a point-and-shoot camera.**

A But I spent all this money to get one with all the bells and whistles.

B You can learn how to use it one feature at a time.

Eventually, you'll be shooting in full manual.

A 이 버튼들 중에서 절반은 뭔지 모르겠어.

B 카메라를 전부 자동으로 설정해봐.

그럼 완전 자동카메라 같이 돼.

A 그렇지만 카메라 부속품 사는데 들인 돈이 얼마인데.

B 한 번에 기능 하나씩 배우면, 나중엔 전부 수동 기능으로 사진을 찍을 수 있을 거야.

일상생활에서 142 We just try to get the most out of each volunteer. 자원봉사자들을 최대한 활용하려는 거예요

A Excuse me.

I'm here to sign up for the volunteer project.

B Great. Fill in this form and I'll get you a T-shirt.

A Hey, way are there questions about my work experience on this form?

B Don't worry, it's not an interview. **We just try to get the most out of each volunteer.**

A 실례합니다만 자원봉사 프로젝트에 등록하러 왔어요.

B 좋아요. 서류를 작성해주시면 티셔츠를 갖다 드릴게요.

A 저기요, 이 서식에 왜 경력을 묻는 질문이 들어있죠?

B 인터뷰가 아니니 걱정 마세요. 자원봉사자들의 경험을 최대한 활용하려는 거예요.

일상생활에서 143 He's half the size he used to be. 그는 몸이 반쪽이 됐어

A Did you see Mark Hill?

He's half the size he used to be.

B A few years back he dropped all the weight and opened a chain of gyms.

A I heard he married Jane Henderson. She was the most popular girl at school.

B Good for him. In the end, he got the girl.

A 너 마크 힐 봤어?
몸이 반쪽이 됐어.

B 걔 몇 년 전에 살을 전부 빼고 체육관 체인점을 열었어.

A 제인 헨더슨과 결혼했다고 하던데, 그 애가 학교에서 제일 예뻤잖아.

B 잘됐네. 결국 헨더슨과 결혼했구나.

일상생활에서 144 It's not easy to find someone on such short notice. 급하게 부탁할 수 있는 사람 찾기가 쉽지 않네요

A **It's not easy to find someone on such short notice.**

B Let me call my sister.

A You mean, she'll come over and look after the kids for a few hours?

B No, but she should be able to recommend someone.
I know she has a few babysitters she usually uses.

A 급하게 부탁할 수 있는 사람 찾기가 쉽지 않네요.

B 여동생한테 전화해볼게요.

A 처제가 와서 몇 시간 동안 아이를 본다는 말이에요?

B 아니요, 그 애가 아이 봐줄 사람을 추천해줄 거예요.
자주 부르는 사람이 몇 명 있거든요.

일상생활에서 145 You can leave any valuables at the front desk 귀중품은 카운터에 맡길 수 있습니다

A Do I have to bring my own lock for the lockers?

B No. All the lockers have built-in locks and we'll give you a key every time you come.

A Are the locks any good?
I don't want my stuff to get stolen.

B **You can leave any valuables at the front desk** if you're worried.

A 사물함을 잠글 자물쇠를 제가 갖고 와야 하나요?

B 아니요, 모든 사물함에 자물쇠가 붙어 있어서
오실 때 마다 열쇠를 드려요.

A 자물쇠는 잘 잠기나요?
소지품을 도난당하면 안 되잖아요.

B 걱정되시면 귀중품은 카운터에 맡길 수 있습니다.

일상생활에서 146 That depends on how old she is

그녀의 나이에 따라 달라요

A What's a good CD for my daughter?

B **That depends on how old she is** and what sort of music she likes.

A She's twelve and to be honest I have no idea what kind of music she listens to.

B The new Cindy is a safe bet.
She is really popular with young girls.

A 딸에게 줄 CD로 뭐가 좋을까요?

B 몇 살인지, 또 어떤 음악을 좋아하는 지에 따라 달라요.

A 12살인데, 솔직히 어떤 음악을 듣는지 잘 모르겠어요.

B 새로 나온 Cindy음악이라면 틀림없이 좋아할 거예요.
여자아이들에게 인기가 아주 많아요.

일상생활에서 147 What would you describe as your worst quality?

본인의 단점을 말해 볼래요?

A **What would you describe as your worst quality?**

B In the past, I used to work too hard.
What I mean is, I would push myself too much.

A And is this something you still do?

B A little bit, but I also try not to be so hard on myself.

A 본인의 단점을 말해 볼래요?

B 예전에는 일을 너무 열심히 했습니다.
제 스스로를 지나치게 다그쳤다는 뜻이죠.

A 그럼 지금도 그런 가요?

B 조금 그렇긴 하지만, 제 자신에게 너무 심하게 하지는 않으려고 노력합니다.

일상생활에서 148 The machine is beeping

기계에서 삑 소리가 나요

A I'd like to pay for everything with my credit card.
Here it is.

B Thank you. I'll just swipe the card and then ask you to sign the receipt.

A **The machine is beeping.**
It looks like there's something wrong with the card.

B Actually, it says your card has been declined.
You might have to try another one.

A 신용카드로 다 계산할게요.
여기 있습니다.

B 감사합니다. 제가 카드를 긁고 나면 영수증에 서명을 부탁드릴게요.

A 기계에서 삑 소리가 나는데요.
카드에 무슨 문제가 있는 거 같아요.

B 손님, 카드가 승인되지 않았다고 나오네요.
다른 카드로 해봐야겠네요.

일상생활에서 149 It's a great chance to see a living legend 유명인을 볼 수 있는 굉장한 기회야

A How much longer are we going to have to stand in line?

B Be patient. This is a once in a lifetime chance to meet the author.

A I know. **It's a great chance to see a living legend.**

B Well, I just want him to sign this book.
Then I can double my money selling it on e-bay.

A 줄을 얼마나 더 서야 할까?

B 조금만 참아. 작가를 만날 기회는 평생 한 번 뿐이야.

A 알아. 유명인을 볼 수 있는 굉장한 기회라는 거.

B 난 이 책에 사인을 받을 거야.
그러면 이-베이에서 이걸 두 배 가격으로 팔 수 있어.

일상생활에서 150 You don't need a lot of detergent. 세제는 많이 필요 없어요

A **You don't need a lot of detergent.**

B Right. Look at this shirt. Everything looks OK, but the collar is really dirty.

A "Ring around the collar." You'll need to add some stain remover directly to the fabric.

B OK. Let me take care of that for you.

A 세제는 많이 필요 없어요.

B 맞아요. 이 셔츠 좀 봐요. 깃의 때만 아니면 다 멀쩡해 보여요.

A "깃 주위에 때 탄 거네요." 옷깃에 직접 얼룩 제거제를 뿌려요.

B 알겠어요. 당신 거니까 신경 쓸게요.

일상생활에서 151 Did you make your payment last month? 지난달 카드 대금 냈어?

A It says my card was declined. What should I do?

B **Did you make your payment last month?**
The bank might have cancelled your card.

A That can't be it. Could it be something else?

B Well, if the purchase is really large, it might exceed your daily limit.

A 카드 사용이 정지됐다고 나오네. 어떻게 해야 하니?

B 지난달 카드 대금 냈어?
은행에서 네 카드를 취소했을지도 몰라.

A 그건 아닐 거야. 다른 이유 때문 아닐까?

B 음, 구매 금액이 아주 클 경우 하루 사용 한도액을 초과할 수도 있어.

일상생활에서 152 I guess they're afraid of credit card fraud. 신용카드 사기를 염려하는 거 같아

A The guy in the store spent a long time looking at my card.

B He was just making sure your signature matched the one on the card.

A **I guess they're afraid of credit card fraud.**

B Sure. If you lose your card, you should call and cancel is as soon as possible.

A 가게 점원이 내 카드를 오랫동안 살펴보고 있었어.

B 저 사람은 네 서명이 카드에 있는 것과 같은지 확인하고 있던거야.

A 신용카드 사기를 염려하는 거구나.

B 그럼, 만일 카드를 잃어버리면 최대한 빨리 전화해서 카드사용을 금지시켜야 해.

일상생활에서 153 I guess a fixer-upper is out of the question. 리모델링용 주택은 안 되겠군요

A Tell me about your husband. Is he handy with tools?

B My husband has to hire someone to change light bulbs.

A **I guess a fixer-upper is out of the question**, then.

A 남편에 대해 얘기를 좀 해주세요. 연장을 잘 다루시나요?

B 제 남편은 전구 바꿀 때도 사람을 불러야 해요.

A 그럼 리모델링용 주택은 어렵겠군요.

일상생활에서 154 The lyrics are all about violence. 가사가 전부 폭력에 관한 거예요

A What does this label on the front of the CD mean?

B That's the parental advisory sticker.

A I guess **the lyrics are all about violence.**

B Right. It's store policy to not sell any CD with that sticker on it to kids under the age of fifteen.

A CD앞에 붙은 이 라벨은 뭔가요?

B 부모의 동의가 있어야 판다는 스티커입니다.

A 가사들이 전부 폭력에 관한 거군요.

B 네. 이런 스티커가 붙은 CD는 15세 이하의 아이들에게 팔지 않는 게 가게 방침입니다.

일상생활에서 155 What if the market crashes? 집값이 떨어지면 어떡해요?

A This house has a lot of potential.
You're looking at a really nice ROI.

B ROI? What's that?

A It's "return on investment" You buy the house, do some quick cosmetic improvements and then sell it at a profit.

B But **what if the market crashes?**

A 이 집은 개발 가능성이 많아요.
ROI가 정말 괜찮네요.

B ROI? 그게 뭐예요?

A '투자 수익률'요. 집을 사서 빨리 외관을 바꾸어 팔면 이익이 남죠.

B 그런데 집값이 떨어지면 어떡해요?

일상생활에서 156 That's the last straw 더 이상 못 참아!

A **That's the last straw** Sam.
You don't respect me at all.

B I do. You have done great work as the vice-president of this company.

A Then why do you constantly refer to me as "honey"?

B I just thought that you looked sexy in that red dress.

A That's borderline sexual harassment.
Do you want me to sue you?

B You know that's the last thing I want, honey.

A That's it. i'm finished here. I quit.
I'm cleaning out my office this afternoon.

A 더 이상 못 참겠어요.
당신은 나를 전혀 생각하지 않는군요.

B 그래요. 당신은 이 회사의 부회장으로 많은 일을 했어요.

A 근데 당신은 왜 나를 계속해서 애인으로 취급하나요?

B 당신이 빨간 드레스를 입으면 섹시해보일거라 생각했지요.

A 그건 성희롱에 가까운데요.
내가 고소하길 바라세요?

B 아니 그러고 싶지 않아요.

A 그럼 여기까지 하죠. 오늘 오후에 회사를 정리하겠어요.

일상생활에서 157 Don't get me started. | 말도 꺼내지 마세요

A Have you seen Tom's latest numbers? It looks like the department is having some real problems.

B **Don't get me started.** The whole department needs to be fired. they're driving me nuts.

A Well, it's something that needs to be deal with. let's schedule a meeting for this afternoon, at the latest.

A 톰의 최근 실적 봤어요? 그 부서는 심각한 문제가 있는 것 같아요.

B 말도 꺼내지 마요. 부서 직원을 전부 다 해고시켜야 해요. 그 부서 때문에 정말 미치겠어요.

A 음, 이건 꼭 짚고 넘어가야 할 문제예요. 늦어도 오늘 오후에는 회의 일정을 잡으세요.

일상생활에서 158 That's a wrap. | 끝났어요

A And **that's a wrap!** Thanks everyone for all your hard work. I really appreciate it.

B That's it? But I thought we would spend more time hammering out the details.

A Nope. I just needed your help with the general ideas.
I can take it from here and finish it on my own.

A 오늘은 여기까지요! 모두들 정말 수고 많았어요. 정말 고마워요.

B 끝이라고요? 세부적인 내용들을 좀 더 논의할 줄 알았는데요.

A 아니요. 전반적인 계획에 대해서만 여러 분들의 도움이 필요했어요. 오늘 의견을 바탕으로 내가 혼자서 끝내도록 할게요.

일상생활에서 159 I'd rather not ask someone in the family | 가족에게 부탁하고 싶진 않아요

A We're running out of options.
Thereis only a few more names on our list.

B If worse comes to worst, we can call your nephew and ask him.

A **I'd rather not ask someone in the family.**
It's better to hire a stranger.

B I agree. It feels strange to pay someone in your own family.

A 선택할 수 있는 사람이 얼마 없어요.
생각나는 사람이 거의 없거든요.

B 정 안되면 당신 조카한테 전화해서 물어봐요.

A 가족에게 부탁하고 싶진 않아요.
아예 모르는 사람이 낫죠.

B 그러게요. 가족에게 돈을 주기가 좀 껄끄럽긴 해요.

일상생활에서 160 What a trip down memory lane! | 그리운 추억이여!

A **What a trip down memory lane!**

B I agree.

It was interesting to see how everyone turned out.

A For some people, high school was the only happy part of their lives.

B And it's been all down hill for them. But for a lot of people, they moved on to bigger and better things.

A 그리운 추억이여!

B 맞아.

다들 어떻게 변했는지 보니까 정말 즐겁다.

A 몇몇 친구들에겐 고등학교 때가 인생에서 유일하게 행복한 시절이었어.

B 그들에게는 그 후로 쭉 내리막길이었나 봐. 하지만 많은 사람들이 더 성공하고 발전했어.

일상생활에서 161 It's my treat. | 내가 한턱낼게

A Put your wallet away. These coffees are on me.

It's my treat.

B But I thought you didn't have any cash on you.

How are you going to pay?

A I'll charge it. I've got my credit card with me.

B In that case, thanks.

A 지갑은 넣어둬. 이 커피는 내가 살게.

내가 한턱 낼 거야.

B 그런데 너 돈 없는 거 같던데 어떻게 계산하려고?

A 카드로 계산할 거야. 신용카드를 가져왔거든.

B 그렇다면 고마워.

일상생활에서 162 He's had his eye on you. | 그가 너를 눈여겨 봐왔어

A Do you remember George from my office?

He's had his eye on you since last Christmas.

B Really? He is kind of cute. Can you set us up?

A No sweat. I'll invite the two of you over for dinner on the same night.

B Good, That way it won's feel like a blind date at all.

A 우리 회사 다니는 조지 기억나?

그가 지난 크리스마스부터 너를 눈여겨 봐왔어.

B 정말? 그 사람 멋있잖아. 우리 주선 좀 해줄래?

A 물론이지. 너희 둘을 같은 날 밤 저녁식사에 초대할게.

B 좋아 그런 경우 소개팅 같은 분위기도 없을 거야.

일상생활에서 163 Get your priorities in order. 우선순위를 정해

A I have so many things to do but I don't know where to begin.

B You've taken on too many projects again. You always spread yourself too thin.

A I know. I keep digging myself into a deeper hole by continuing to do it.

B Just **get your priorities in order** and know your limits.

A 할 일이 너무 많은데 어디서부터 시작해야 할지 모르겠어.

B 너 또 일 너무 많이 맡았구나. 넌 항상 네가 할 수 있는 것보다 너무 많은 일을 한꺼번에 맡는 것 같아.

A 나도 알아. 계속 그러면서 내 상황을 악화시키는 것 말이야.

B 일단 일의 우선순위를 정하고 네 한계를 인정해.

CHAPTER 02

스포츠와 건강

스포츠와 건강 01 None of them are in good shape. 몸매 좋은 사람은 아무도 없어요

A Matt is a great trainer. And look at him! He's got huge muscles.

B But look at his clients. **None of them are in good shape.**

A I see what you mean. It's possible that Matt is not very good at explaining how to exercise.

B Right. A good personal trainer has to be a good teacher, too.

A 매트는 아주 좋은 코치에요. 보세요! 근육도 대단하잖아요.

B 그런데 그가 지도하는 회원들 좀 봐요. 몸매 좋은 사람은 아무도 없네요.

A 무슨 말인지 알겠어요. 매트는 운동방법을 설명하는 데는 서툴지 모르겠군요.

B 맞아요. 좋은 코치가 되려면 가르치는 것도 잘해야 되니까요.

스포츠와 건강 02 I'm highly motivated. 의욕이 넘쳐요

A You will have to come into the gym about four times a week. Can you promise to come?

B **I'm highly motivated**, so I'll come here every day, except Sundays.

A That is not a good idea, actually. Getting enough rest is just as important as getting enough exercise.

A 일주일에 네 번 정도는 체육관에 오셔야 합니다. 꼭 오실 수 있죠?

B 운동이 하도 하고 싶어서 일요일 빼고는 매일 여기에 올 거예요.

A 사실 매일 오는 게 좋은 생각은 아니에요. 충분한 휴식을 갖는 것도 충분한 운동만큼 중요하거든요.

스포츠와 건강 03 They were knocked out of the tournament. 그들은 대회에서 탈락했습니다

A Jennifer's team didn't do very well in the tournament.

B They didn't win the championship?

A They weren't even close. **They were knocked out of the tournament** in the first round.

A 제니퍼네 팀이 대화에서 잘 못했어.

B 우승을 못했어?

A 근처도 못 갔어.
대회 1회전에서 탈락했어.

스포츠와 건강 04 It's possible to get into shape. | 몸매 관리가 가능해요

A I think that Janet should be my personal trainer. She seems perfect for me.

B Did you know that before she was a trainer, she was really overweight?

A I know. So, now she really understands what it takes to lose weight.

B Right. She's living proof that **it's possible to get into shape.**

A 자넷이 제 개인코치를 맡아야할 것 같아요. 저한테 딱 맞는 것 같거든요.

B 자넷이 코치가 되기 전에 아주 뚱뚱했던 거 아세요?

A 알아요. 그럼 체중감량이 얼마나 힘든 일인지 정말 잘 아시겠네요.

B 맞아요. 몸매관리가 가능하다는 걸 보여주는 좋은 본보기죠.

스포츠와 건강 05 You have a potbelly. | 배가 많이 나왔군요

A Hey, man, what brings you in here?

B I decided to work out.

A You should. You look like you are getting fatter. Wow, **you have a potbelly!**

B Are you pulling my leg?

A 야, 너 여기에 웬일이야?

B 운동하기로 결심했어.

A 갈수록 더 뚱뚱해지니까 당연히 그래야겠지. 어머, 배 나온 것 좀 봐!

B 너 지금 나 놀리는 거야?

스포츠와 건강 06 I think you're really athletic. | 만능 스포츠맨이신 것 같네요

A **I think you're really athletic.**

B Yes. I'm a fitness buff. I love all kinds of sports. What about you?

A Well. I don't like sports that are too strenuous. I sometimes use a hula-hoop. I used to go bowling, but I'm a bit rusty now.

B Okay. Why don't we go bowling sometime?

A 정말 운동 좋아하시는 것 같네요.

B 네. 전 헬스 광이에요. 모든 종류의 스포츠를 다 좋아하죠. 그 쪽은 어떠세요?

A 저는 너무 과격한 운동은 좋아하지 않아요. 가끔 훌라후프 정도 하고요. 예전엔 볼링도 좀 쳤는데, 예전 같지 않아요.

B 그렇군요. 언제 한 번 볼링장에 같이 가는 거 어때요?

스포츠와 건강 07 I want to watch my weight. 체중 조절을 하고 싶어

A I'm planning on losing some weight this year. What about you?

B **I want to watch my weight**, too.

I'm planning on joining a gym.

A I'm sure you can stick to it.

B Out with the old and in with the new. So long, old me. Say hello to the new me!

A 올해는 살을 좀 빼야겠어.
넌 어떠니?

B 나도 체중 조절을 하려고.
체육관에 등록할 계획이야.

A 넌 반드시 해낼 수 있을 거야.

B 오래된 건 버리고 새 것을 맞이하려고.
예전의 나는 안녕. 새로운 내가 돼야지!

스포츠와 건강 08 I never realized how physically draining it was 체력 소모가 그렇게 많은지 몰랐어

A Now that we're out here, I have to admit it's harder than it looks.

B What's the hardest part of snowboarding?

A **I never realized how physically draining it was.** And my hands hout, too.

B Sure, because you spend a lot of time trying to break your falls with your hands.

A 막상 여기 나와 보니까 보기보다 어렵다는 걸 알겠구나.

B 스노보드 타면서 어떤 게 가장 어려우세요?

A 체력 소모가 그렇게 많은지 몰랐어.
손도 다쳤단다.

B 그렇죠, 넘어지지 않으려고 손을 사용하실 때가 많으니까요.

스포츠와 건강 09 I've finally got the hang of kicking. 발차기 요령을 드디어 터득했어

A I think **I've finally got the hang of kicking.**

B Good. Now move your arms, one at a time, like windmils.

A This sure takes a lot of energy, and I can't really move that fast at all.

B It's the same for everyone when they're just learning.

A 발차기 요령을 드디어 터득한 거 같아.

B 좋아. 이제 풍차가 도는 것처럼 한 번에 한 팔씩 움직여.

A 확실히 힘이 너무 들어서 그렇게 빨리는 못 나가겠어.

B 누구나 배울 때는 똑같아.

스포츠와 건강 10 You'll get soaking wet.

흠뻑 젖을 거예요

A You can't wear that jacket to snowboard in. **You'll get soaking wet.**

B Why? This is the jacket I use for skiing. It's nice and warm.

A But you need a jacket that's long enough for you to sit on.

B Right! Snowboarders spend a lot of time sitting in the snow adjusting their bindings.

A 스노보드 탈 때 저 재킷을 입으면 안돼요. 다 젖을 거예요.

B 왜?
스키 탈 때 입었던 건데 따뜻하고 괜찮단다.

A 그렇지만 눈에 앉아있어도 괜찮은 긴 재킷이 필요해요.

B 그렇지! 스노보드 타는 사람들은 바인딩을 조절하느라 눈 위에 앉아 있는 시간이 많구나.

스포츠와 건강 11 You have to avoid slamming into other people

다른 사람과 부딪치지 않도록 해야 해

A So, I point my skis downhill and just let myself slide along?

B No. **You have to** be able to slow down and **avoid slamming into other people.**

A OK. So, to stop I stick my poles in the ground really quickly?

B No! Point the tips of your skis together and dig the edges into the snow.

A 그럼, 스키를 아래쪽으로 향하게 하고 그냥 미끄러져 내려가면 돼?

B 아니. 속도를 줄일 수 있어야 다른 사람과 부딪치지 않아.

A 알겠어. 그럼 멈추려면 스키 폴을 땅에다 잽싸게 꽂으면 되니?

B 안 돼! 스키앞 쪽 끝을 함께 모으고 날 부분을 눈 속으로 넣어야지.

스포츠와 건강 12 Bank it off the wall.

쿠션을 이용해서 쳐봐

A **Bank it off the wall.**

B I'm no good at banking my shots.

A 쿠션을 이용해서 쳐봐.

B 나는 쿠션엔 약한데.

스포츠와 건강 13 There's going to be a pinch hitter. 대타가 나올 거야

A **There's going to be a pinch hitter.**

B What's that?

A A substitute batter.

A 대타가 나올 거야?

B 그게 뭔데?

A 교체 타자라는 말이지.

스포츠와 건강 14 I think I'm starting to get the hang of this. 이제 요령이 생기는 거 같아

A **I think I'm starting to get the hang of this.**

B You're a fast learner. You'll be.... Hey! That guy almost crashed into me!

A Well, there are five of us, two adults and three kids. And we need ticktets that cover the entrance fees and unlimited redes.

B Let me double-check.

A 이제 요령이 생기는 거 같아. 연습만 좀 하면 돼.

B 아주 빨리 배우는구나. 너는…. 야! 저 사람 나랑 부딪힐 뻔했어!

A 저 사람은 자기가 먼저 갈 권리가 있다고 생각했나봐.

B 저 사람이 잘못했어. 항상 아래쪽에 더 가까이 있는 사람한테 우선 통행권이 있어.

스포츠와 건강 15 This slope has a ski lift. 이 슬로프에는 스키 리프트가 있습니다

A **This slope has a ski lift.** It'll be easy to get to the top.

B That's good, because I don't want to climb this slope. I'm exhausted.

A 이 슬로프에는 스키 리프트가 있습니다. 꼭대기까지 올라가기가 아주 쉽죠.

B 잘 됐네요. 꼭대기까지 기어 올라가고 싶진 않으니까요. 전 완전히 지쳤어요.

스포츠와 건강 16 The bases are loaded. 만루야

A **The bases are loaded.**

B If this batter hits a home run, it'll be a grand slam.

A 만루야.

B 이 타자가 홈런을 치면 만루 홈런이네.

스포츠와 건강 17 I think I'm under the weather. 몸이 좋지 않은 것 같아

A You don't look very well, Kenny.

B **I think I'm under the weather.**

A Really? I hope it's not the flu.

B I don't know, but I have a mild fever.

A Do you?

In that case, why don't you all in sick today?

B I think I will.

A 케니, 안색이 안 좋아 보이는데.

B 몸이 안 좋은 것 같아.

A 그래? 독감은 아니겠지.

B 모르겠어. 그런데 열이 좀 있네.

A 그래?

그럼, 아파서 출근 못 한다고 전화하는 게 어때?

B 그래야겠네.

스포츠와 건강 18 Who are you rooting for? 어느 편을 응원하고 있습니까?

A **Who are you rooting for?**

You seem to be egging both teams on.

B That's exactly what I'm doing.

A Why?

B Because neither is my hometown team.

A Oh, I see. What is your hometown team?

B New York Yankees.

A 너 누구 응원하니?

둘 다 응원하는 것 같은데.

B 맞아. 둘 다 응원하고 있어.

A 왜 그러니?

B 둘 다 우리 고향팀이 아니라서 말이지.

A 이해가 가네. 고향팀은 어디니?

B 뉴욕 양키스야.

스포츠와 건강 19 He must think he's going to be the next Tiger Woods! 제 2의 타이거 우즈가 될 거라 생각하나 보네!

A I haven't seen David around lately.

Where is he these days?

B He goes to the golf course for lessons every single night. He's really dedicated.

A **He must think he's going to be the next Tiger Woods!**

A 데이비드 본 지 오래됐네.

요즘 뭐해?

B 매일 밤 골프레슨 받으러 다녀.

진짜 열심이야.

A 제 2의 타이거 우즈가 될 거라 생각하나 보네!

스포츠와 건강 20 The game ended in a draw. 경기가 무승부로 끝났거든

A What was the final score of the game?Did your team win?

B No, but the other team didn't win either. **The game ended in a draw.**

A Well, that's better than losing, I suppose!

A 경기 결과가 어땠어? 네 팀이 이겼어?

B 아니, 하지만 상대편도 못 이겼어. 경기가 무승부로 끝났거든.

A 지는 것보단 낫지 뭐!

스포츠와 건강 21 The game went into extra innings. 게임이 연장전에 들어갔거든

A You were late getting home from the baseball game last night.

B **The game went into extra innings** because the score was tied at the end of the ninth.

A So, who won?

A 어제 야구 경기에서 늦게 돌아왔더라.

B 9회 말에 동점이 돼서 게임이 연장전에 들어갔거든.

A 그래서 누가 이겼어?

스포츠와 건강 22 I need to take some blood. 채혈을 해야 돼요

A Hold still, please. **I need to take some blood.**

B I hate needles. Is there any way you could do this without sticking that thing in me?

A Don't worry. It just feels like a pinch. See? We're already done.

B Wow. I hardly felt that at all. You have a really soft touch, nurse.

A 가만 계세요. 채혈을 해야 돼요.

B 바늘이 너무 끔찍한데 그걸 찌르지 않고 채혈할 수 있는 방법은 없나요?

A 걱정 마세요. 그냥 따끔할 뿐이에요. 보이죠? 벌써 다했어요.

B 우와. 전혀 느낌이 없었어요. 선생님, 안 아프게 잘 해주시네요.

스포츠와 건강 23 All that just will rot their teeth. 그런 정크푸드 때문에 이가 썩어요

A Let's bring a nice healthy bag lunch for the kids.

B But the kids will want hot dogs and drinks.

A Cotton candy and candy apples and popcorn.... **All that junk will rot their teeth.**

B I'll pack lunch, but we should allow the kids one treat each.

A 아이들에게 영양가 있는 도시락을 가져다 줍시다.

B 하지만 아이들은 핫도그와 음료수를 먹고 싶어할 거에요.

A 솜사탕, 사과엿, 팝콘…. 그런 정크푸드 때문에 이가 썩는 거에요.

B 점심을 쌀게요. 그렇지만 아이들이 좋아하는 것 한 가지씩은 사먹게 하죠.

스포츠와 건강 24 I don't have an athletic bone in my body 난 운동신경이 없어

A Did you see Tim run the 100 meters? He was so fast!

B Wow. But I guess ti's easy for him, because he has such long legs.

A You should give credit where credit's due. You know that he also trains a lot.

B I know. I guess I'm just a bit jealous. **I don't have an athletic bone in my body.**

A 팀이 100미터 달리기하는 거 봤니? 정말 빠르더라!

B 와, 하지만 그 애한테는 쉬웠을 거야. 다리가 정말 길잖아.

A 칭찬할 일은 칭찬해야지. 팀은 훈련도 많이 했어.

B 알아, 샘나서 그런 거야. 난 운동 신경이 없거든.

스포츠와 건강 25 The symptoms won't go away. 증상이 나아지지 않는다

A How is your blood pressure?

B I am getting much better. The diet I'm on is doing wonders for it.

A If you stick to the diet, you can stop taking the medication in another few weeks.

B That's good to hear. I will keep in mind whatever you tell me to do.

A But if **the symptoms don't go away** after three weeks, come back.

A 요즘은 혈압이 어때요?

B 점점 좋아지고 있어요. 식이요법 중인데 놀랄 만큼 효과가 있네요.

A 음식 조절을 꾸준히 잘 하면 몇 주 후에는 약을 안 먹어도 됩니다.

B 듣던 중 반가운 소식이군요. 선생님 말씀 명심하겠습니다.

A 3주 후에도 증상이 나아지지 않으면 다시 오십시오.

스포츠와 건강 26 I think it's just a minor sprain. 그냥 살짝 접지른 것 같아요

A So your file says you slipped on the stairs and twisted your ankle?

B That's correct. **I think it's just a minor sprain.**

A Even so, you need an X-ray. Your ankle might be broken.

A 차트에는 계단에서 미끄러져서 발목을 접질렸다고 쓰여있는데 맞나요?

B 네 맞아요. 그냥 살짝 접지른 것 같아요.

A 그래도 X선 촬영을 해봐야 합니다. 발목이 부러졌을 수도 있으니까요.

스포츠와 건강 27 That was slop. 우연의 일치였어

A That was a nice shot.

B No, **That was slop.**

A 샷 죽이는데.

B 아니야. 우연이었어.

- pool(포켓볼)을 칠 때 slop이란 말은 '우연(an accident)'이란 의미입니다.

스포츠와 건강 28 I can bench-press 105 pounds. 난 벤치 프레스 105파운드는 할 수 있어

A **I can bench-press 105 pounds.** I could probably beat you up.

B You're a weakling! I can bench-press twice that weight.

A 난 벤치 프레스 105파운드는 할 수 있어. 넌 상대가 안 되지.

B 약골께서 무슨 말씀! 난 너보다 두 배 더 무거운 걸 들 수 있어.

- bench-press는 '의자에 누워서 역기를 들어올리는 운동'을 말하는 것으로 아래 예문에서는 동사로 쓰였습니다.

스포츠와 건강 29 I'm working on my biceps. 이두박근 운동 중이야

A What are you doing now?

B **I'm working on my biceps.** Soon, I'll have huge, muscular arms.

A 지금 뭐 해?

B 이두박근 운동 중이야. 조만간 엄청난 근육질 팔이 될 거야.

- work on~은 '~ 운동 중이다'의 의미. 그리고 biceps는 '이두박근'을 가리킨다.

스포츠와 건강 30 Bull's-eye! 명중이다!

A I'm not very good at darts.

B **Bull's-eye!**

A That's my first bull's-eye!

A 나는 다트를 잘 못해.

B 명중이다!

A 태어나서 처음이야!

■ Bull's-eye는 표적의 한가운데 부분, 즉 점수가 가장 높은 부분에 명중되었음을 말합니다.

스포츠와 건강 31 I got the double. 나 더블이야

A **I got the double!**

B That's the second time in this game! Keep it up!

A 나 더블이야!

B 벌써 두 번째네! 계속 살려봐!

■ 다트 표적(dartboard)에는 double이 있고 triple이 있는데 표적 바깥 부분에 얇게 그어진 선을 맞히면 double이 됩니다. 점수는 두 배.

스포츠와 건강 32 Nice scratch! 자~알 했다!

A **Nice scratch!**

B Well, I gave it my best try.

A Don't hit it so hard next time.

A 자~알 했다!

B 글쎄, 난 최선을 다해 친 건데.

A 다음번에는 그렇게 세게 치지 마.

■ Nice scratch!는 상대편이 잘못하여 내 공을 포켓에 넣는 실수를 했을 때 던지는 비꼬는 식의 멘트(a sarcastic comment).

스포츠와 건강 33 They get a corner kick. 코너킥을 얻었어

A What's happening?

B **They get a corner kick.**

A 어떻게 됐어?

B 코너킥을 얻었어.

■ 코너에서 차는 볼을 corner kick이라고 한다.

스포츠와 건강 34 Hold your horses. — 좀 천천히 가

A It's so lovely to have a stroll in the park.

B Is it so? Then who is the person I asked a hundred times to go out and walk?

A Come on! I'm not a fitness-freak as you are.

B You really need to work out, though.

A By the way, **hold your horses.** Why are you walking so fast?

B Let's speed up a little bit. It's fun.

A 공원을 산책하는 건 정말 상쾌해.

B 그래? 나가서 좀 걷자고 해도 꼼짝하지 않던 게 누구더라?

A 이봐! 난 너처럼 운동광이 아니야.

B 넌 정말 운동이 꼭 필요해.

A 그런데, 좀 천천히 가.
너 왜 그렇게 빨리 걷는 거야?

B 조금만 빨리 걷자. 재밌잖아.

스포츠와 건강 35 I want everyone to see how I've stayed in shape. — 내가 몸매 유지를 얼마나 잘했는지 모두에게 보여주고 싶어

A I'm thinking of wearing my graduation tuxedo to the reunion.

B It's twenty years old! Why in the world would you do that?

A It still fits, sort of. **I want everyone to see how I've stayed in shape.**

B I can see what you're saying, but I still think it's one of your top ten worst ideas of all time.

A 졸업식 때 입었던 턱시도를 입고 동창회에 갈까 생각 중이야.

B 20년 전 옷이야!
도대체 왜 그걸 입으려는 거야?

A 아직도 대충 맞아. 내가 몸매 유지를 얼마나 잘했는지 보여주고 싶어.

B 무슨 말인지 알겠는데, 그건 아주 안 좋은 생각 같아.

스포츠와 건강 36 Take it on an empty stomach. — 공복에 드세요

A Here's your prescription. You should take two tablets, three times a day.

B Before meals or after meals?

A **Take it on an empty stomach.**

A 여기 처방전입니다.
두 알씩 하루 세 번 드세요.

B 식전에요, 식후에요?

A 공복에 드세요.

스포츠와 건강 37 We had to learn CPR. 심폐소생술을 알아야 돼

A What experience did they require you to have to be a lifeguard?

B **We had to learn CPR.**

A 인명구조원이 되려면 어떤 경력이 있어야 돼?

B 심폐소생술을 알아야 돼.

스포츠와 건강 38 I have an upset stomach. 배탈 났어

A Are you feeling okay?

B Not really. **I have an upset stomach.**

A You should avoid spicy foods for a while.

A 몸 좀 괜찮아?

B 아니. 배탈 났어.

A 매운 음식은 한동안 피해야겠다.

스포츠와 건강 39 I've been recuperating well. 몸조리를 잘 하고 있었어

A Hey! I haven't seen you in ages. How is it going?

B Not bad. I was quite sick last month.

A I'm sorry to hear that. How do you feel now?

B Much better. **I've been recuperating well.**

A 정말 오랜만이네. 어떻게 지내?

B 그럭저럭. 지난달에 많이 아팠거든.

A 그랬구나. 지금은 좀 어때?

B 훨씬 좋아졌어. 몸조리를 잘 하고 있었어.

스포츠와 건강 40 What are your symptoms? 증상이 어떤데?

A I think I'm sick. I feel errible.

B **What are your symptoms?**

A I have a stuffed-up nose and a sore throat.

B You may want to try a decongestant.

A 아무래도 아픈 것 같아. 몸이 너무 안 좋아.

B 증상이 어떤데?

A 코도 막혔고 목도 아파.

B 소염제를 먹어야겠네.

CHAPTER 03

직장에서

직장에서 01 I'll keep my eyes open for you. 앞으로 눈여겨 지켜보겠다

A My secretary got married and quit. She was a very efficient secretary.

B Really? You must miss her very much.

A I sure do. Can you recommend anyone?

B Not at the moment
but **I'll keep my eyes open for you.**

A 내 비서가 결혼을 하고는 사직했어요. 아주 유능한 비서 였는데.

B 정말요? 당신, 그녀를 몹시 그리워하겠는데요.

A 그럼요, 누구 추천할 사람 없어요?

B 당장은 없지만,
앞으로 눈여겨보도록 할게요.

직장에서 02 He may not be pulling his weight. 그는 제 몫을 하는 것 같지 않아

A Hiring Tom for our department doesn't seem to be working out.

B Well, **he may not be pulling his weight** just yet, but he's still new. Give him a little more time.

A Well, he'd better get his act together soon.

B Have a little more patience. I'm sure he will be alright.

A 톰을 우리 부서에 뽑은 건 잘 못한 일 같아.

B 뭐, 아직 제 몫을 하는 것 같지 않지만, 신입이잖아. 조금만 시간을 더 줘.

A 글쎄, 빨리 자리를 잡는 것이 좋을 텐데.

B 좀 기다려봐. 좋아질 거야.

직장에서 03 Your input shed a light on our work. 당신의 생각이 우리 일을 이해하는 데 도움이 됐어요

I'm e-mailing you to let you know that I appreciate how helpful you've been to us on this project. **Your input shed a great deal of light on our work** and thanks to you we've finally worked out a good deal with our client and everything is falling into place. I'm going to throw a party next week and we would love for you to drop by and join our celebrations. Thank you again for everything.

당신이 이번 일에 얼마나 큰 도움이 되었는지 감사드리기 위해서 이메일을 보냅니다. 당신의 아이디어는 우리 일을 이해하는 데 정말 많은 도움이 되었고 덕분에 거래처와 좋은 계약을 성사시킬 수 있었습니다. 모든 일이 다 잘 되고 있어요. 제가 다음 주에 파티를 열 계획인데, 오셔서 함께 축하해 주시면 좋겠습니다. 다시 한 번 여러 가지로 감사드립니다.

직장에서 04 I will get caught up with everything. 모든 일을 마무리 지을 수 있을 거야

How have you been? I'm terribly sorry for the late reply. I have been under tremendous pressure with the workload, not to mention the fact that I was already behind schedule. But don't worry. Eventually **I will get caught up with everything.** I can't find time to meet you at the moment but as soon as things get better let's hook up and have a good time. Take care.

잘 지냈어? 답장 늦게 보내서 정말 미안해. 나 요즘 너무 일이 많아서 스트레스를 너무 받고 있어. 그런데다 이미 일도 많이 밀려 있고, 그래도 걱정하지 마. 결국은 다 잘 처리할 수 있을 거야. 지금은 널 만날 시간이 없지만 상황이 나아지는 대로 우리 만나서 좋은 시간 갖자. 잘 있어.

직장에서 05 I've got to tie up a few loose ends. 나 남은 일 좀 마무리할게

M Working overtime again?
Do you realize it's already 11:00?

W Already? Gosh, I feel like I have no social life outside of work these days.

M Wrap it up and let's have a cold one.
Mike and Angela are at the bar already.

W Why don't you go ahead? **I've got to tie up a few loose ends** and then I'll catch up with you guys a little later.

M 또 야근하고 있어?
지금 벌써 11시인 것 알아?

W 벌써? 이런, 요즘 일 외에 다른 사회생활은 전혀 없는 것 같아.

M 일 그만 마무리 짓고 시원한 맥주나 마시러 가자.
마이크하고 앤젤라는 벌써 바에 가 있어.

W 먼저 가 있을래? 난 남은 일만 좀 마무리하고 조금 이따 거기로 갈게.

직장에서 06 We're not in the red yet. 아직 적자는 아니야

W How's our revenue for this month?

M Well, **we're not in the red yet** but I don't see much reason to be optimistic.

W We should be doing much better than this.

M Perhaps, but we're not through yet.
We'll come up with something to turn things around.

W 우리 이번 달 수익이 어떻게 돼?

M 아직 적자는 아닌데 낙관적이지는 않아.

W 지금보단 훨씬 더 잘해야만 하는데.

M 하지만 아직 끝나지 않았잖아.
뭔가 개선방안을 생각해 낼 거야.

직장에서 07 Things are all under control | 일이 계획대로 잘 진행되고 있어요

A Is there anything I can help you with?
I habe a little time on my hands.
B Perfect! I was just going to ask you to take this equipment down to the meeting.
A Got it. Looks like **things are all under control**, doesn't it?
B Yep, I just hope everything goes smoothly.

A 내가 도울 일 좀 없어?
나 시간 좀 있어.
B 잘 됐다. 안 그래도 지금 너한테 이 장비 좀 아래 회의 장소에 갖다 놔 달라고 하려고 했어.
A 알았어. 일이 계획대로 잘 진행되는 것 같지, 안 그래?
B 응, 모든 일이 순조롭게 진행되길 바랄 뿐이야.

직장에서 08 Our department might be downsized soon. | 우리 부서는 곧 축소될지도 모릅니다

As I reported, **our department might be downsized soon.** Our business is going south and we are barely managing to get by. I'm guessing more than 30% of our employees might get the axe. I hope you can find a way to bail us out of this mess. I am definitely not looking forward to being the bad guy who has to let good people go.

보고 드렸듯이, 우리 부서는 곧 축소될지도 모르겠습니다. 사업이 하향세라 간신히 버티고 있습니다. 아마도 30% 이상의 직원들을 해고해야 할 것 같습니다. 이 위기에서 벗어날 방법을 찾아주셨으면 합니다. 전 죄 없는 사람들을 내보내야 하는 악역이 되고 싶지 않습니다.

직장에서 09 I'm in over my head on this one. | 이 일이 내 능력 밖인 것 같아

A There's no way I can meet the deadline.
I'm in over my head on this one.
B Our clients will hit the ceiling if you don't get it done on time.
A I will see what I can do.
But to be honest I'm not very optimistic.
B I understand you've had your hands full with too much work, but let's try to work it out together.

A 절대 마감시간 못 지킬 것 같아. 이 일 내 능력 밖이야.
B 너 이 일 제시간에 안 끝내면 우리 고객이 난리가 날 거야.
A 내가 어떻게든 해 볼게.
그래도 솔직히 낙관적이진 않아.
B 네가 지금 일이 너무 많은 것 알고 있지만 그래도 우리 함께 일을 풀어나가도록 노력해 보자.

직장에서 10 We're going to have to face the music. 우리가 대가를 치러야 할 거야

A Why the long face? Something wrong?

B I've just got stuck with the Anderson account. No one seems to know how to figure out what to do with it.

A Well, perhaps everyone feels that you can take care of these kinds of things the best.

B Maybe, but sooner or later **we're going to have to face the music.**

A 얼굴 표정이 왜 그래? 뭐가 잘못 됐어?

B 앤더슨 회사와 문제가 생겼어. 아무도 이것을 어떻게 처리해야 할지 모르는 것 같아.

A 아마도 모두들 네가 이 일을 처리하는 데 최고라고 생각하나 보지.

B 그럴지도 모르지. 그렇지만 조만간에 우리가 대가를 치러야 할 거야.

직장에서 11 I was trapped at work. 꼼짝 못하고 일만 했어

A How come you didn't show up at my party last night?

B Sorry, **I was trapped at work** all last weekend.

A Well, you missed out on a great party although we all ended up getting plastered.

B Maybe it's best that I didn't go then.
I'm a bit behind in my work.

A 너 왜 어젯밤 파티에 안왔어?

B 미안해. 나 지난 주말 내내 꼼짝 못하고 일만 했어.

A 너 진짜 재밌는 파티 놓친거야. 결국엔 우리 다 취해서 뻗어버리긴 했지만.

B 그럼 안간게 잘한 걸지도 모르겠다. 일이 좀 밀려서 말이야.

직장에서 12 Things are really going downhill. 일이 정말 안 좋게 돌아간다

A How's it going with your new boss?

B **Things are really going downhill.**
All he does these days is complain and yell at us.

A Maybe he thinks that's the way to manage employees.

B Maybe, but he'd better lighten up soon.
We've all had enough.

A 너 새로운 상사와 좀 어때?

B 일이 정말 안 좋게 돌아가. 그 사람 요즘 하는 일이라곤 우리한테 불평하고 소리치는 게 다야.

A 아마도 그게 사람들 관리하는 방법이라고 생각하나 보지.

B 그럴지도 모르지. 그렇지만 그 사람 이제 좀 덜 그러는 게 좋을 거야. 우리 모두 많이 참았거든.

직장에서 13 Our boss is falling asleep at the wheel. 우리 상사는 일을 게을리 하고 있어

A **Our boss is falling asleep at the wheel.**

B What's wrong with him? He should show a little more responsibility for his work.

A We really need someone in charge who stays on top of things better.

B Well, we can't really advise him to be more careful. After all be is our boss.

A 우리 상사 또 일을 게을리 하고 있어.

B 그 사람 왜 그래? 자기일에 좀 더 책임감을 보여야 하잖아.

A 우리에겐 정말 제대로 일 처리 잘하는 상사가 필요해.

B 글쎄, 그렇다고 우리가 좀 더 조심하라고 충고할 순 없잖아.
그래도 우리 상관인데.

직장에서 14 Let me briefly go over 간단하게 요약해 드리겠습니다

A How was the meeting with our American buyer?

B It went well. **Let me briefly go over** what was covered in the last meeting.

A Why don't we do it over lunch?

B That sounds fine. It'll give me some time to get organized.

A I'll see you around 12:00

A 미국 바이어들과 회의가 잘 됐나요?

B 잘됐어요. 지난 회의에서 다룬 내용을 간단하게 요약해 드리겠습니다.

A 점심 먹으면서 하는 것이 어떨까요?

B 좋아요. 그럼 그때까지 정리할 시간이 좀 있겠네요.

A 그럼 12시쯤에 보도록 하죠.

직장에서 15 Time to go back to the salt mines. 다시 돌아가 일할 시간이다

A What time is it?

B Oh, it's already ten to one.

A Yeah? Lunch is over.
Time to go back to the salt mines.

B Are you prepared for the marketing meeting this afternoon?

A Almost there. Just a couple of numbers to check out.

A 지금 몇 시야?

B 아, 벌써 1시 10분 전이네

A 그래? 점심시간이 끝났군.
다시 돌아가 일할 시간이야.

B 오늘 오후에 있을 마케팅 회의 준비는 끝났어?

A 거의. 숫자 몇 개만 확인하면 돼.

직장에서 16 I'm open to that — 그것에 대해선 상의할 용의가 있습니다

A I have an importer in New York who's hot for your new model. He says he'll start with 500 sets a month.

B Oh, that's good. What are we looking at price-wise?

A He says you need to come down a ways from your original asking price.

B Well, **I'm open to that**, but the question is how far.

A 귀사의 새 모델에 관심이 많은 뉴욕의 수입업자를 알고 있어요. 우선 한 달에 500 세트로 거래를 시작하고 싶다고 하더군요.

B 좋네요. 가격은 어떻게 하고요?

A 귀사가 요구하는 가격에서 좀 할인해 줬으면 합니다.

B 음 그 점은 상의해 볼 용의가 있습니다만, 얼마냐가 문제죠.

직장에서 17 We are short-handed. — 일손이 모자란다

A Are you finished with the market analysis report, Gilbert?

B I am working on it now. It'll take a couple of more hours.

A What? Oh, no. You need to speed things up.

B Stop pushing me, please. **We are just short-handed.** I am doing what I can.

A 길버트, 시장 분석 보고서 끝냈어?

B 지금 하는 중이야. 한두 시간 더 걸릴 거야.

A 뭐? 안 돼. 그럴 시간이 없어.

B 그만 좀 재촉해. 우리 일손이 부족하잖아. 난 지금 최선을 다하고 있단 말이야.

직장에서 18 As soon as we get the green light from upstairs. — 상부로부터 정식허가가 나오는 대로요

A When do you think we can sew up the deal?

B **As soon as we get the green light from upstairs.**

A Well, when do you figure that will be?

B The way things look now, it may be a little while yet.

A 언제쯤 이 거래를 확정지을 수 있을 것 같습니까?

B 상부로부터 정식허가가 나오는 대로요.

A 그래요. 그게 언제쯤 될 것 같아요?

B 현재의 상황으로는 시간이 조금 걸리겠는데요.

직장에서 19 We must go into it fully before deciding. 결정 전에 충분히 검토해야 합니다

A Do you think you can give me a definite answer on our offer later today?

B I'm afraid I can't. I need a chance to take it up with the board of directors.

A Can't you make a decision on your own?

B No, not without the board's approval.

We must go into it fully before deciding.

A 저희 오퍼에 대한 분명한 답변을 오늘 오후에 해 주실 수 있습니까?

B 힘들겠는데요. 이사진과 그 문제를 이야기해 볼 필요가 있어서요.

A 혼자서는 결정을 못 내리시나요?

B 예, 이사진의 승인 없이는 안 돼요.

결정전에 충분히 검토해야 해요.

직장에서 20 Don't pass the buck to me. 내게 책임을 미루지 마라

A Who drove and wrecked my car?

B I did, Kenny. But the accident wouldn't have happened if Regina hadn't rushed me while I was giving her a ride to her friend's home.

C **Don't pass the back to me**, Michael.

I didn't tell you to speed.

A Ok. It's my fault. Forget it! Get out of my sight!

A 누가 내 차를 몰고 나가서 망가뜨렸지?

B 내가 그랬어, 케니야. 그렇지만 레지나를 자기 친구 집에 데려다 줄 때 재촉하지만 않았어도 사고가 나진 않았을거야.

C 마이클! 내게 덮어씌우지 마.

난 과속으로 달리란 말은 안 했어.

A 알았어. 내 잘못이야. 신경 끄고 내 눈 앞에서 사라져!

직장에서 21 Our company is cutting jobs. 우리 회사는 감원하고 있어요

A Please take a seat.

B Sure.

A As you know due to the economic downturn **our company is cutting jobs.** I am sorry to say this, but we have to lay you off.

B I got it. How about my severance pay?

A We will definitely pay you; so don't be concerned about it.

A 앉으세요.

B 네.

A 당신도 알다시피 경기침체로 인해 회사에서는 정리해고를 하고 있어요. 이런 말씀을 드려서 죄송하지만 당신을 일시 해고해야만 합니다.

B 알겠습니다. 그러면 저의 퇴직금은 어떻게 되나요?

A 확실하게 지급할 겁니다. 그러니 그 문제에 대해 걱정하지 마세요.

직장에서 22 She's in the driver's seat. 그녀가 책임자이다

A Did you hear that Mr. Sanders got in an accident?

B What? When did that happen? Is he hurt?

A This morning on the way to this office.

He seems to be in serious condition.

B Who's gonna be in charge of this company now?

A Now that Mr. Sanders is not available, **Mrs. Bender must be in the driver's seat.**

A 미스터 샌더스에게 교통사고가 났다는 소식 들었어?

B 뭐? 언제? 많이 다쳤대?

A 오늘 아침 출근길에.

상태가 심각한가 봐.

B 그럼 이제 누가 우리 회사의 책임자가 되는거지?

A 샌더스씨가 없으니 벤더가 책임자겠지.

직장에서 23 Guilty as charged 제가 맡고 있어요

A Are you the volunteer coordinator?

I'm here to volunteer, but I don't know where to go.

B **Guilty as charged.** My name is Gail.

A Glad to meet you. So, you're a volunteer, too.

B Actually, the title means I coordinate the volunteers.

But, it's a paid position.

A 자원봉사 책임자이신가요?

봉사활동 하러 왔는데 어디로 가야 할지 몰라서요.

B 제가 맡고 있어요. 제 이름은 게일입니다.

A 만나서 반갑습니다. 그럼 선생님도 자원봉사자이시군요.

B 사실 자원봉사자들을 책임지고 있는 일이긴 한데요, 유급직입니다.

직장에서 24 Opinion is divide 의견이 분분하다

A Did you see the minutes of the last board meeting?

Has the board made a decision?

B Almost. They've all agreed to merge the company's subsidiaries in the US. But **opinion is divided** on which offer to take.

A How much longer do you think it'll take?

A 지난번 이사회 회의록 봤어?

이사회에서 결론은 났어?

B 거의. 미국 내의 자회사를 합병하자는 데 모두 합의했어.

하지만 어느쪽 제안을 받아들일지에 대해서는 의견이 분분해.

A 결론이 날 때까지 앞으로 얼마나 걸릴 거라고 생각해?

직장에서 25 I'll take care of this right away — 즉시 처리할게요

A I would like to change my presentation topic for the conference this weekend. I hope it is not too late to change.

B Well, I'll have to find out about it, but I am positive it is still possible.

A Thank you. And I hope so, too.

B Yes it is possible and **I'll take care of this right away.**

A Thank you very much.

A 이번 주말 학회에서 발표할 발표 제목을 수정하고 싶습니다. 너무 늦지 않았겠지요?

B 글쎄요. 알아봐야겠지만 아마도 가능하리라 생각합니다.

A 감사합니다. 그랬으면 좋겠네요.

B 네, 가능하고요.
즉시 알아봐서 처리할게요.

A 감사합니다.

직장에서 26 How should I phrase it so it sounds good? — 어떻게 써야 그럴듯해 보일까?

A It's sort of hard to explain all of the things I did at my old jobs.

B The trick is to use really active verbs. Never say, "I did this and that." It sounds weak.

A **How should I phrase it so it sounds good?**

B Use word like "completed," supervised," and "organized."

A 예전에 했던 일들을 전부 설명하기가 좀 까다롭네.

B 능동적인 동사를 사용하는 게 요령이야. "이거 했다, 저거 했다"같은 말은 약해 보이니 쓰지 마.

A 그럼 어떻게 써야 그럴듯해 보일까?

B "완수했다", "지도했다", "조직했다"와 같은 단어를 써 봐.

직장에서 27 Let's put it in writing and sign it. — 그것을 문서화해서 서명합시다

A Now I think we've been able to come to an agreement.

B Yes, all the problems have been ironed out, as far as we can see.

A Right. So **let's put it in writing and sign it.**

A 이젠 계약을 해도 될 것 같습니다.

B 그렇군요. 저희가 보기에도 모든 문제점들이 조정된 것 같습니다.

A 맞습니다. 그렇다면 문서화해서 서명을 합시다.

직장에서 28 She's living on borrowed time. 지금까지만 해도 오래 버틴 거야

A Mary has made so many mistakes.

B She can't last much longer.

She's living on borrowed time.

A If it weren't for her personality,

She'd have been canned a long time ago

A 메리는 실수가 많은데 아직도 회사에 남아있는 것이 신기해!

B 아마 오래가지 못할걸.

지금까지만 해도 오래 버틴 거야.

A 성격마저 좋지 않았다면 오래 전에 해고 되었을 거야.

직장에서 29 We just can't assume full responsibility for it. 우리가 전적으로 책임을 다 질 수는 없다

A We've just got to settle this claim somehow.

B I understand your position, Mr. Smith. But, I'm sorry, **we just can't assume full responsibility for it.**

A Then that'd leave me no choice but to take legal action.

A 어떻게든 이 클레임을 해결해 줘야겠습니다.

B 스미스씨의 입장은 이해합니다만, 우리가 그에 대한 책임을 전부 질 수는 없습니다.

A 그렇다면 법적 조치를 취할 수밖에 없겠네요.

직장에서 30 James should be dismissed for his poor record-keeping. 기록 보관을 제대로 못해서 제임스를 해고시켜야겠어

A **James should be dismissed for his poor record-keeping.** He's made a mess of things!

B That's too bad. I really like him!

A I do too, but he's been warned repeatedly.

A 기록 보관을 제대로 못해서 제임스를 해고시켜야겠어.

일을 아주 엉망으로 만들었어!

B 안됐다. 난 그 사람 진짜 좋은데.

A 나도 좋아하지만 여러 번 경고했다고.

직장에서 31 How long is your commute? 출퇴근 시간이 얼마나 걸려?

A I wish I lived closer to work. I spend too much time driving to and from the office.

B **How long is you commute?**

A It's ninety minutes each way.

That's a three hours lost every day!

A 회사에서 조금 더 가까운 데 살았으면 좋겠어. 출퇴근하는 데 시간이 너무 많이 걸려.

B 출퇴근 시간이 얼마나 걸리는데?

A 편도 1시간 반 걸려.

매일 3시간씩이 날아간다고!

직장에서 32 We have a performance -based pay system. 우리는 성과급체제야

A At my company, our pay is determined by seniority.

B Our company is different; **we have a performance-based pay system.**

A I like that idea better. I work really hard, but I'm not compensated enough!

A 우리 회사는 근속 연수에 따라 급여가 지급돼.

B 우리 회사는 달라.

우리는 성과급체제야.

A 그게 더 낫다. 난 진짜 열심히 일하는데 충분한 보상을 못 받아.

직장에서 33 Here goes nothing. (잘 안 되겠지만) 한 번 해보는 거야

A Are you ready for the presentation?

I hear the VP will be sitting in.

B I'm so nervous. But there's no looking back now.

A Right. Just think to yourself, **"Here goes nothing!"**

A 발표 준비 다 됐어요?

부사장님께서 참석하신대요.

B 너무 떨려요. 하지만 이제 돌이킬 수 없어요.

A 맞아요. 그냥 "별 거 아니야!"라고 생각해요.

직장에서 34 Are you willing to relocate? 파견 나가실 의향이 있습니까?

A Our headquarters are herein New York, but this position is based in Hong Kong. **Are you willing to relocate?**

B I'm interested in hearing about your relocation package.

A 저희 본사는 이곳 뉴욕에 있지만 이 업무는 홍콩 지사에서 하시게 됩니다. 파견 나가실 의향이 있습니까?

B 파견 근무 시 제공되는 혜택에 대해 듣고 싶습니다.

직장에서 35 What can you bring to the company? 회사에 어떤 기여를 할 수 있죠?

A **What can you bring to the company?**

B From my previous jobs, I gained experience in working in a variety of environments. I feel confident that I can handle any situation that might arise in the workplace.

A 회사에 어떤 기여를 할 수 있죠?

B 저는 여러 직장에서 다양한 상황별 업무 경험을 쌓았습니다. 직장에서 발생하는 어떤 상황에도 대처할 자신이 있습니다.

직장에서 36 What is your educational background? 학력이 어떻게 됩니까?

A **What is your educational background?**

B I majored in electrical engineering. Also, I worked for two years as a research assistant in the Math department.

A 학력이 어떻게 됩니까?

B 전기공학을 전공했습니다. 또한 수학과에서 2년간 연구조교로도 일했습니다.

직장에서 37 He needs to be given a written warning. 서면경고를 줘야겠어

A Did you see the complaint that James made about Charlie?

B I did. That kind of behavior at work can't be tolerated. What should we do?

A **He needs to be given a written warning.** This is a serious situation!

A 제임스가 찰리에 대해 제기한 문제들을 봤어?

B 응. 그런 행동은 직장에서 허용될 수 없어.
어떻게 해야할까?

A 서면경고를 줘야겠어.
이건 심각한 상황이라고!

직장에서 38 I'm the low man on the totem pole. 저는 말단 직원입니다

A I hate **being the low man on the totem pole.** I always get the worst tasks in the office!

B We were all in your position once. I'm sure you'll be promoted soon.

A I hope so. I', tired of doing all the thankless jobs!

A 저는 말단인 게 정말 싫어요. 사무실에서 제일 하찮은 일만 맡긴다고요!

B 우리도 다 너 같았던 때가 있었어.
금방 승진될 거야.

A 그러면 좋겠어요. 하찮은 일 하는 데 지쳤어요.

CHAPTER 04

영화관에서

영화관에서 01 It's being called the sleeper hit of the year 이게 올해 예상외의 흥행작이래

A Hey, let's check out this one.
It's being called the sleeper hit of the year.

B I've never heard of it.

A You only pay attention to movies with multimillion-dollar advertising campaigns.

B But that's park of the fun. There are the teasers and then the trailers and then the movie!

A 야, 이것 좀 봐.
올해 예상외로 흥행하고 있는 영화래.

B 처음 듣는데.

A 넌 수백 만 달러를 들여 광고하는 영화에만 관심이 있더라.

B 그것도 영화의 재미야. 광고 보고, 예고편 보고, 그 다음 영화 보는 거!

영화관에서 02 That movie was for the birds. 그 영화는 정말 형편없었다

A Did you have a nice weekend?

B Almost, except the terrible movie I saw Saturday night.

A Uh-uh. How terrible was it?

B In a nut shell, **it was strictly for the birds.**

A That bad, huh? What did your boyfriend say?

B He was barely awake through the whole movie.

A 좋은 주말 보냈어?

B 대충, 토요일 밤에 봤던 끔찍한 영화만 빼면.

A 이런. 얼마나 끔찍했는데?

B 한 마디로 말하자면, 정말 형편없었어.

A 그렇게 나빴어? 네 남자친구는 뭐래?

B 영화 내내 거의 졸던데.

영화관에서 03 That was a surprising plot twist. 반전이 정말 놀랍더라

A When the main character found out that his brother was really a spy, **that was a surprising plot twist.**

B I agree. I was surprised that that happened.

A 주인공이 자기 형이 스파이인 걸 알았을 때 반전이 정말 놀랍더라.

B 맞아. 나도 그 장면에서 놀랐어.

영화관에서 04 This flash movie is hilarious. 이 플래시 무비 정말 재미있다

A **This flash movie is hilarious.**

B Are those hard to make?

A The Flash program makes it easy.

A 이 플래시 무비 정말 재미있다.

B 그런 거 만들기 힘드니?

A 플래시 프로그램만 있으면 만들기 쉬워.

What a tearjerker! 정말 슬픈 영화야!

A **What a tearjerker!**

That film told an emotionally moving story.

B Yeah. It was a very sad movie.

A 너무 슬픈 영화야!

영화 정말 감동적이다.

B 그래. 아주 슬픈 영화였어.

CHAPTER 05

음주

음주 01 I drank so much I blanked out. | 술을 너무 많이 마셔서 필름이 끊겼어요

A I think you had too much to drink.

B Yeah. Last night was a little crazy.

A Do you remember what you did?

B No. **I drank so much I blanked out.**

A 너 너무 많이 마신 것 같던데.

B 응. 어젯밤에 장난 아니었어.

A 네가 무슨 짓을 했는지는 기억나니?

B 아니. 너무 많이 마셔서 필름이 끊겼거든.

음주 02 Why don't we go for another round? | 우리 2차 갈까요?

A It's getting boring here. **Why don't we go for another round?**

B Good idea. I saw a fancy singing room nearby.

A Shouldn't we call to book a table first?
The place might be full on a night like this.

B Good thinking! I'll call right now.

A 여기 지루해진다.
우리 2차 갈까?

B 좋은 생각이야. 나 이 근처서 근사한 노래방 봤었는데.

A 전화해서 미리 예약해야 하는 거 아니야? 오늘 밤 같은 날은 자리가 다 찼을지 몰라.

B 그래! 내가 지금 전화할게.

음주 03 Leave out the rum and just give me the coke. | 럼주 빼고 콜라만 주세요

A Would you like a complimentary beverage as we wait, sir?

B Sure. I'd love a rum and coke, please. Not too much ice.

A Only non-alcoholic beverages are free of charge.
There is a fee for alcoholic drinks.

B In that case, **leave out the rum and just give me the coke.**

A 손님, 기다리시는 동안 서비스 음료 좀 드릴까요?

B 좋습니다. 콜라 넣은 럼주 한 잔 주세요. 얼음은 많이 주지 마시고요.

A 무알코올 음료만 무료이고, 알코올 음료는 돈을 내셔야 합니다.

B 그렇다면 럼주는 빼고 콜라만 주세요.

음주 04 Let's have just one more round, Okay?

한 잔만 더 하시죠?

A Oh it's getting very late, I should go now.

B **Let's have just one more round, okay?**

A I would, but I don't have enough money to cover it.

B Don't worry, it'll be my treat.

A 야, 이거 시간이 너무 늦어 지금 가야겠는데요.

B 한잔만 더 하시죠?

A 그러고 싶지만 감당할 돈이 충분히 없는데요.

B 걱정하지 마세요. 제가 냅니다.

음주 05 Do you stock alcohol?

술 있어요?

A **Do you stock alcohol?**

B Sure, but we don't sell hard alcohol.

A So, you have beer and wine? Is that it?

B And wine coolers, too. Those are like wine flavored soft drinks. But they have some alcohol in them.

A 술 있어요?

B 물론이죠. 하지만 도수 높은 술은 팔지 않습니다.

A 그럼 맥주와 와인이 있겠네요? 그렇죠?

B 와인쿨러도 있습니다. 와인 맛이 나는 음료수인데 알코올도 좀 들어 있어요.

음주 06 a bartender sometimes offers drinks to people on the house.

바텐더가 가끔은 사람들에게 술을 무료로 줍니다

A I don't see why we are out in this noisy place with all this smoke. We could be home relaxing together!

B I heard that this bar is fabulous. You know **a cool bartender sometimes offers drinks to people on the house.**

A Really? But I guess we'd better not have any more drinks. I feel a bit tipsy.

A 왜 우리가 이렇게 담배 연기가 가득하고 시끄러운 곳에 왔는지 모르겠어. 집에서 함께 쉴 수 있었는데도 말이야.

B 이 술집이 굉장하다고 들었어. 바텐더가 사람들에게 가끔 공짜로 술을 준대.

A 정말? 하지만 더 이상 술을 안 마시는 것이 좋겠어. 나 좀 취했거든.

음주 07 We really tied one on. 우리 정말 과음했어

A I'm still hung over from the New Year's Eve party. How about you?

B I'm about 80% recovered. **We really tied one on.**

A Tell me about it. I have never been that sick before in my life.

B Me neither. Oh well. It was worth it, though. It was the perfect way to bring in the new year.

A 새해전야파티 때의 숙취가 아직도 있어. 넌 어때?

B 난 거의 깼어. 우리 정말 과음했어.

A 그러게 말이야. 이렇게 아픈 적은 처음이야.

B 나도 그래. 그래도 보람은 있었어. 새해를 맞는 방법으로는 최고였거든.

음주 08 I would love a cocktail to take the edge 피로가 풀리도록 칵테일 한 잔 주세요

A Can I get you something from the bar before dinner?

B Well, **I would love a cocktail to take the edge off.** It was a tough day at the office.

A A dry martini would certainly help you relax.

B Sounds perfect.
Ask the bartender to throw in a couple of extra olives.

A 저녁 식사 전에 바에서 뭐 좀 갖다 드릴까요?

B 피로가 풀리도록 칵테일 한 잔 주세요. 회사일이 힘들었거든요.

A 산뜻한 마티니 한 잔이면 분명 편안해지실 거예요.

B 좋아요.
바텐더에게 올리브 몇 개만 좀 더 넣어달라고 해주세요.

음주 09 Should we order another round? 한 잔씩 더 할까?

A **Should we order another round?** You know, one for the road?

B Sure. Isn't it your turn to buy?

A It's yours. The booze here tastes a little watered down. I'm hardly even buzzed.

B I agree. So that's two double shots of Jack with two beer chasers.

A 한 잔씩 더 할까? 마지막 딱 한잔 어때?

B 그래. 네가 살 차례 아니냐?

A 네 차례야. 여기 술에 물을 좀 탔는지 취하지도 않아.

B 맞아. 그럼 더블샷을 넣은 잭 두 잔에다가 입가심으로 마시는 맥주를 두 잔 더 시키자.

음주 10 I already feel a little tipsy — 나 벌써 좀 취한 거 같아

A I've only had one drink but **I already feel a little tipsy.**

B You're a cheap date. Besides, I told you not to drink on an empty stomach.

A You're right. The alcohol went right to my head. I need to sit down.

B And you need to pace yourself. Don't have more than one drink an hour.

A 술을 한 잔 밖에 안 마셨는데 벌써 좀 취한 거 같아.

B 너 빨리 취하는구나. 게다가 내가 빈 속에 술 마시지 말라고 했잖아.

A 네 말이 맞아. 술 마시니 정신이 없네. 좀 앉아야겠어.

B 술 마시는 속도를 알아서 조절해야지. 한 시간에 한 잔 이상 마시지 마.

음주 11 You're three sheets to the wind. — 너 고주망태가 됐어

A You look like **you're three sheets to the wind.**

B What did you say?

A I said you look drunk. Your face is all red and you're slurring your words.

B You're right. I think I've had one too many. Can you call me a cab?

A 너 고주망태가 된 거 같아.

B 뭐라고?

A 너 취한 거 같다고 했어. 얼굴이 전부 벌겋고 말도 꼬이잖아.

B 맞아. 너무 많이 마신 거 같아. 택시 좀 불러 줄래?

음주 12 Would you like to see a wine list? — 와인 메뉴 보시겠어요?

A **Would you like to see a wine list?**

B Could you please recommend some good wines?

A 와인 메뉴 보시겠어요?

B 좋은 와인 좀 추천해주시겠어요?

CHAPTER 06

파티에서

파티에서 01 You look really sharp in that suit! 너 그 정장 입으니 너무 잘 어울린다

A **You look really sharp in that suit!**

B Thanks. You look like a million bucks as well.

A Well, thanks for saying that.

I was a bit worried this might be too loud.

B Not at all! It's just eye-catching enough.

A 너 그 정장 입으니까 너무 잘 어울린다!

B 고마워 너도 정말 멋진데.

A 그렇게 말해줘서 고마워.

나는 좀 야하지 않나 걱정했거든.

B 천만에! 근사하기만 한데 뭐.

파티에서 02 She must have crashed the party. 저 여자 파티초대도 안 받았는데 그냥 왔나봐

A Thank you so much for coming to my party.

Are you having fun?

B Oh, yes. Big time! It's a great party. Oh, no. Look who just walked in, Mary Jane Smith. Did you invite her as well?

A Are you kidding me?

She must have crashed the party. What a gut!

B I know. Talking to her is like pulling teeth.

Anyway, I gotta go. Catch you latter.

A 파티에 와 줘서 너무 고마워.

파티 재미있어?

B 그럼, 너무 재미있어! 정말 대단한 파티인데. 이런, 저기 지금 방금 들어온 애 봐. 메리 제인 스미스다. 너 저 애도 초대했어?

A 장난하니?

저 애 초대도 안 했는데 그냥 왔나 봐. 뻔뻔하기도 해라.

B 글쎄 말이야. 쟤랑 얘기하는 건 곤욕이라니까.

어쨌거나 나 가야겠다. 다음에 보자.

파티에서 03 Things got a little out of hand at the party. 파티가 약간 걷잡을 수 없이 돌아갔어

I'm just wondering if you got home safely last night. **Things got a little out of hand at the party** and I guess I was a little too drunk to see you off after the third round. But what's the point of going to a year-end party without getting loaded, right? Anyway, I hope you had a great time and you're all ready for a brand new year.

네가 어젯밤에 집에 잘 갔는지 궁금하다. 파티가 약간 격해져서, 3차 이후 너무 취해서 널 배웅할 수 없었어. 그래도 송년회 때 좀 취하기도 하고 그러는 거 아니겠어? 어쨌든, 어제 좋은 시간이었기를 바라고, 새해 잘 맞길 바란다.

파티에서 04 What are you all dressed up for? 무슨 일로 정장을 다 차려입었어?

A **What are you all dressed up for?**

B I have a formal party to attedn tonight.

It's our company promotion party.

A You should try this necklace then.

It would go with your dress nicely.

B Wow, it does. Thanks a lot.

A 무슨 일로 다 차려 입었어?

B 오늘 밤에 정장차림 파티가 있거든.

우리 회사 홍보파티야.

A 그럼 이 목걸이 한번 해봐.

네 드레스랑 잘 어울릴거야.

B 진짜 그러네. 정말 고마워.

파티에서 05 He had a whale of a time at the party! 그는 파티에서 최고의 시간을 보냈지!

A Did John enjoy the reunion party on Saturday?

B **He had a whale of a time!**

He met all of his old friends and they talked for hours.

A I'm glad he enjoyed himself.

I know he was worried that it might be boring.

A 존이 토요일 동창회에서 좋은 시간 보냈대?

B 최고의 시간을 보냈지!

예전 친구들 모두 만나서 오랜 시간 얘기했어.

A 즐거웠다니 다행이다.

혹시 지루할까봐 걱정하던데.

파티에서 06 Let's put the lights on the tree first 우선 트리에 조명부터 달자

A Help me with the decorations.

Let's put the lights on the tree first.

B Wow. How did the lights get tangled like this?

It looks like a giant ball of yarn.

A You start untangling the lights and I'll get the ornaments out of the box.

B Ask Mom for help.

She can get the strings of popcorn ready.

A 장식 좀 도와줘.

우선 트리에 조명부터 달자.

B 저런, 조명 줄이 어쩌다 이렇게 엉켰어?

큰 실 뭉치 같잖아.

A 넌 엉킨 줄부터 풀어. 난 장신구를 상자에서 꺼낼게.

B 엄마한테 도와달라고 하자.

팝콘을 실에다 쉽게 다실 수 있어.

파티에서 07 What if someone tries to talk with me? 누가 나한테 말 걸려고 하면 어쩌지?

A There are a million people here I don't remember.
What if someone tries to talk with me?

B That's why everyone is wearing these name-tags.

A Right. I can just read the nametag.

B Hey, do you recognize that guy? I think it's Tom, but he's put on a lot of weight.

A 이름이 기억 안 나는 사람들이 여기 너무 많아.
누가 나한테 말 걸려고 하면 어쩌지?

B 그래서 다들 이 이름표를 달고 있는 거야.

A 그렇구나. 이름표를 읽기만 하면 되겠네.

B 야, 저 남자 알아보겠어? 톰인 거 같은데 살이 많이 쪘네.

파티에서 08 Just bring yourself. 그냥 몸만 와

Hi, this is Susan Brown who happened to meet you at Carl's promotion party last week. I jumped for joy when I heard that you went to the same high school as me. No wonder you looked familiar to me. Well, my husband and I are going to throw a party at our place this Saturday and I would love for you to come to our party. **Just bring yourself.** We will love to see you. E-mail me back if you're interested. Take it easy.

안녕, 나 지난 주 칼의 승진 파티에서 우연히 만났던 수잔 브라운이야. 나 네가 나랑 같은 고등학교 출신이란 걸 들었을 때 진짜 기뻤다. 어쩐지 네가 낯이 익더라. 그나저나 이번 주 토요일에 남편하고 나하고 우리 집에서 파티를 열 예정인데 너도 왔으면 좋겠어. 그냥 몸만 오면 돼. 우린 너 꼭 보고 싶어. 만약에 관심 있으면 이메일로 알려줘. 잘 있어.

파티에서 09 Look at the expression on his face 쟤 얼굴 표정 좀 봐

A I'm sure this is him.
This time it's not going to bo another false alarm.

B Turn out the lights. As soon as he turns them on, we'll yell "Surprise!"

A "Surprise!" I bet you didn't expect this, did you, Tom?

B Wow! **Look at the expression on his face.**
He looks like he's about to fall over.

A 이제 그 애가 확실해.
이번엔 틀림없을 거야.

B 불을 꺼. 주인공이 불을 켜면 바로 "서프라이즈!"라고 함께 소리치자.

A "서프라이즈!" 깜짝 파티는 생각도 못했을 거야, 그렇지 톰?

B 와! 쟤 얼굴 표정 좀 봐.
놀라서 쓰러지려고 해.

파티에서 10 So far only fifteen have RSVP'd. 지금까지 15명만 연락이 왔어

A How many people are you expecting to show up at the party?

B I invited twenty people, but **so far only fifteen have RSVP'd.**

A I'm sure more people will end up coming, and some people will bring dates.

B In that case, you should get a cake big enough for twenty-five people.

A 파티에 몇 명이 올 거라고 예상하니?

B 20명을 초대했는데 지금까지 15명만 연락이 왔어.

A 결국엔 사람이 더 많이 올 거야. 게다가 애인을 데려오는 사람도 있을 거고.

B 그럼 25명은 족히 먹을 수 있는 큰 케이크를 사야겠네.

파티에서 11 Everyone gets dressed up in costumes 모두들 정장을 차려입다

A There's a midnight showing of The Rocky Horror Picture Show. Want to go?

B Are you serious? That's the movie where **everyone** in the audience **gets dressed up in costumes.**

A Sure. It's lots of fun.

B Doesn't sound like fun to me.

A 심야 영화로 '록키 호러 픽쳐 쇼'를 하는데, 보러 갈래?

B 진심이니? 관객들 모두 정장을 하고 보는 영화야.

A 물론이야. 아주 재미있어.

B 나는 재미없을 것 같다.

파티에서 12 This is a rockin' party! 이 파티 끝내주는데!

A **This is a rockin' party!**

B I'm so glad you came.
You're my favorite person here.

A Thanks for all the beer.

A 이 파티 끝내주는데!

B 네가 와서 너무 좋다.
넌 여기서 내가 제일 좋아하는 사람이야.

A 맥주 고맙다, 야.

파티에서 13 I'll light the candles. 내가 촛불을 켤게

A **I'll light the candles** and put them on the cake.

B Then I'll turn off the electric lights, so that the cake will look very bright.

A 내가 촛불을 켜서 케이크에 꽂을게.

B 그러면 나는 전깃불을 끌게.
그래야 케이크가 빛나니까.

파티에서 14 Let's hit the dance floor. 춤추러 나가자

A **Let's hit the dance floor.**

B I don't know how to dance.

A That's okay. I'll show you how.

A 춤추러 나가자.

B 어떻게 춤추는지 모르는데.

A 괜찮아. 내가 어떻게 하는지 보여줄게.

CHAPTER 07

식당에서

식당에서 01 What do you feel like eating? 뭐 먹고 싶어요?

A Well, Jess. Shall we continue talking over dinner? **What do you feel like eating?**

B Well, I know a great Italian restaurant just around the corner. Are you okay with Italian?

A A place nearby sounds great since I'm starving now, not to mention the fact that Italian food is one of my favorites.

A 근데요 제스, 우리 저녁 먹으면서 얘기하는 것이 어떨까요?

B 음, 제가 여기 바로 옆에 좋은 이탈리아 식당을 알거든요? 이탈리아 음식 괜찮아요?

A 바로 옆이라니 너무 좋은데요. 이탈리아 음식은 제가 좋아하는 음식 중에 하나이기도 하지만 제가 지금 배가 엄청 고프거든요.

식당에서 02 It's maybe just a bit beyond my means. 이거 내가 사기엔 좀 비싼 것 같아

A This is a perfect Christmas present for my mom.

B Are you sure you can afford it? It looks quite pricey.

A **It's maybe just a bit beyond my means** but this will make her so happy.

A If you say so, but don't be surprised if she returns it just like late year.

A 이거 우리 엄마 크리스마스 선물로 딱인데.

B 살 수 있겠어? 많이 비싸 보이는데.

A 내가 사기엔 좀 비싸긴 하지만 엄마가 받으시면 많이 좋아하실 것 같아.

B 네가 그렇게 말한다면야, 근데 작년처럼 선물 물리셔도 놀라지 마라.

식당에서 03 I love drumsticks. 닭다리를 아주 좋아해

A Wait! How can I get a whole chicken into this little pan?

B We're just cooking boneless, skinless chicken breasts. I've already cut them into strips.

A **I love drumsticks....** Hey why no skin?

B Drumsticks are dark meat, but for this dish we only use white meat.

A 잠깐만! 이 작은 프라이팬에 치킨을 통째로 어떻게 올리지?

B 뼈를 바르고 껍질을 벗긴 닭가슴살만 요리할 거야. 이미 조각으로 잘라놓았어.

A 난 닭다리를 아주 좋아하는데…. 왜 껍질은 안 되는 거니?

B 닭다리는 색이 검잖아. 이 요리에는 흰 살코기만 사용돼.

식당에서 04 How hot is the kung pao chicken? 쿵파오 치킨 맵니?

A **How hot is the kung pao chicken?**

B Not too spicy.

A 쿵파오 치킨이 맵니?

B 그리 맵지 않아.

식당에서 05 Your eyes may be bigger than your stomach. 너 식탐이 많은 것 같다

A What's good here, Jess?

B Well, last time I came here I tried the pasta and pizza. They tasted as good as I expected.

A It won't hurt to follow what the expert is saying. Why don't we get 2 pizzas and 2 pastas? Oh, and a salad.

B Joshua, **Your eyes may be bigger than your stomach.** You might need a doggy bag.

A 여기 뭐 잘해요 제스?

B 글쎄요, 전에 여기 왔을 때 파스타하고 피자를 먹어봤는데요, 예상한 대로 맛있었어요.

A 전문가 말씀을 들어야겠죠. 우리 피자 2개 파스타 2개 시킬까요? 아, 샐러드도요.

B 조슈아, 너무 많이 시키는 것 같아요. 나중에 남은 음식 싸달라고 해야 될지도 모르겠어요.

식당에서 06 We'd like another bowl of rice, please. 한 그릇 더 주세요

A Have you eaten all of the rice?

B Yes, and **we'd like another bowl of rice, please.**

A 밥 다 드셨어요?

B 네, 한 그릇 더 주세요.

식당에서 07 I usually go with spaghetti. 난 보통 스파게티를 주문해

A **I usually go with spaghetti.**

B I know, but maybe you should try something else.

A 난 보통 스파게티를 주문해.

B 아는데, 이번엔 다른 거 먹어봐.

식당에서 08 Under what name, please? 어떤 분 성함으로 할까요?

A Chez Michel. Good afternoon.

B Hello. I would like to make a reservation for tomorrow-lunch for six people. Do you have any quiet rooms? It's a business lunch.

A Yes, of course. We can reserve one of our private rooms for your group. **Under what name, please?**

B Jack Frost, for six.

A Very good. We'll see you then. Goodbye, Mr. Frost.

B Goodbye.

A: 체즈 마이클입니다. 안녕하세요.

B 안녕하세요. 여섯 사람용 점심 예약을 하려고 합니다. 조용한 방 가능할까요? 비즈니스차 식사하는 겁니다.

A 물론이죠. 개인실을 예약해 드리겠습니다. 어떤 분 성함으로 할까요?

B 잭 프로스트로 여섯 명요.

A 좋아요. 그때 뵙겠습니다. 안녕히 계세요. 프로스트씨.

B 안녕히 계세요.

식당에서 09 Put it on my account, please. 외상으로 달아놓으세요

A What do I owe you?

B $723.

A **Put it on my account, please.**

B Sorry, I can't.

A OK. Is financing available?

B Yes, it is.

A 얼마를 내야 하죠?

B 723달러요.

A 외상으로 달아주세요.

B 미안하지만 안 되겠는데요.

A 좋아요. 월부도 가능합니까?

B 네, 가능합니다.

식당에서 10 Can I take your order? "주문하시겠습니까?"

A **Can I take your order?**

B I'd like the cheeseburger combo, with a salad instead of French fries, please.

A Do you want everything on your burger?

B Hold the onions, please.

A 주문하시겠습니까?

B 치즈버거 콤보 주시고요. 감자튀김 대신 샐러드로 주세요.

A 버거에 토핑 다 넣어드릴까요?

B 양파만 빼주세요.

식당에서 11 You are very fussy about what you eat. 입이 매우 까다롭군

A You don't seem to be enjoying your meal.

B No, I'm not.

A I guess **you are very fussy about what you eat,** aren't you?

B Yes, I am.

A No wonder you are so skinny.
I have a great appetite. I eat like a pig.

B No wonder you are overweight.

A 입맛이 없나 보구나.

B 아냐.

A 너 입이 까다롭지,
그렇지 않니?

B 그래.

A 그러니까 네가 그렇게 말랐지.
난 식욕이 왕성해서 아주 잘 먹지.

B 그러니까 살이 쪘지.

식당에서 12 Is anyone saving room for dessert? 디저트 먹을 사람?

A **Is anyone saving room for dessert?**

B No, I'm stuffed. I can't eat another bite.

A 디저트 먹을 사람?

B 아니, 난 배불러. 한입도 더 못 먹겠다고.

식당에서 13 Can I get some extra coleslaw? 콜슬로 좀 더 주실래요?

A Will that be all?

B **Can I get some extra coleslaw?**

A Yes, but it cost extra.

A 이제 다 주문하셨나요?

B 콜슬로를 좀 더 주실래요?

A 예, 그런데 돈을 더 내셔야 해요.

■ 콜슬로와 콘샐러드(corn salad)는 패스트푸드점에서 인기있는 사이드 메뉴.

식당에서 14 I think the bill is wrong. 계산서가 잘못 나왔어요

A Waiter, **I think the bill is wrong.** We didn't order an appetizer platter.

B Oh, I'm terribly sorry. I'll fix that right away.

A 이봐요, 계산이 잘못 나왔어요. 우린 전채요리는 주문하지 않았어요.

B 아, 정말 죄송합니다. 바로 고쳐드리겠습니다.

식당에서 15 I'll bring you a doggy bag. 포장해 드리겠습니다

A Are you finished with your meal, ma'am?

B Yes, can I get the leftovers wrapped up?

A **I'll bring you a doggy bag, ma'am.**

A 식사 다 하셨습니까, 손님?

B 네. 남은 것 싸주실 수 있나요?

A 포장해드리겠습니다, 손님.

식당에서 16 Can we get separate checks? 계산서는 따로 끊어주시겠어요?

A Will that be all for your orders?

B **Can we also get separate checks?**

A Sure.

A 주문하신 것은 이게 다죠?

B 계산서는 따로 끊어주시겠어요?

A 알겠습니다.

식당에서 17 You can dice the onions. 양파 좀 잘게 썰어

A Can I help with dinner?

B Sure. **You can dice the onions.**

A 저녁 만드는 데 내가 뭐 도와줄까?

B 그래. 양파 좀 잘게 썰어.

식당에서 18 I had my fill. I'm stuffed. 많이 먹어서 배가 터질 지경입니다

A We have plenty of chicken soup. Eat your fill.

B I will.

-Later-

A Would you like more chicken soup?

B No, thank you. **I had my fill. I'm stuffed.**

A 치킨수프가 많이 있으니까 실컷 먹어.

B 그렇게 할게.

–얼마 뒤–

A 치킨수프 더 먹을래?

B 아니. 잔뜩 먹어서 배가 터질 지경이야.

식당에서 19 How is everything? 뭐 더 필요한 게 있으신가요?

A **How is everything, sir?**

B My steak is a little undercooked. Could you take it back to the kitchen?

A I'm sorry. I'll have the cook put it back on the grille for a few more minute.

A 더 필요한 게 있으신가요?

B 제 스테이크가 약간 덜 익었어요. 더 익혀주시겠어요?

A 죄송합니다. 더 익혀달라고 하겠습니다.

식당에서 20 I'm about to burst. 배가 터질 것 같아요

A Can I get you anything else? Would you like to see the dessert menu?

B No, thank you. **I'm about to burst.** I couldn't eat another bite. But, I'll have a cup of coffee, please.

A Certainly. I'll brew a fresh pot and bring you out a cup as soon as it's ready.

A 뭐 다른 걸 가져다 드릴까요? 디저트 메뉴 보시겠어요?

B 아, 됐어요. 배가 터질 것 같아요. 더는 한 입도 못 먹겠어요.

A 알겠습니다. 커피가 준비되는 대로 가져다 드릴게요.

CHAPTER 08

학교에서

학교에서 01 I'm on the verge of flunking out of school 퇴학당하게 생겼어

A **I'm on the verge of flunking out of school.**

B How did you let it get to this point?

A I don't know. Once my grades started slipping, I just stopped caring.

B Well, you need to resolve to do better. Or, you'll be a dropout.

A 퇴학당하게 생겼어.

B 어쩌다 이 지경이 됐니?

A 모르겠어. 점수가 한 번 내려가기 시작하니까 신경도 안 썼어.

B 그럼 성적 올릴 결심을 해야지. 안 그러면 낙제할 거야.

학교에서 02 All my hard work finally paid off. 열심히 공부한 성과가 드디어 나왔어

A **All my hard work finally paid off.** Check out my latest grades!

B Wow. You've really jumped to the head of the class. Congratulations.

A Thanks. Now I can finally take a break and relax a little bit. I've earned it.

B Not too much, though. You don't want to slide back into your old bad habits.

A 열심히 공부한 성과가 드디어 나왔어. 이번 점수를 봐!

B 우와. 정말 반의 상위권으로 올랐구나. 축하해.

A 고마워. 이제 드디어 좀 쉬면서 편히 지낼 수 있겠다. 그만큼 했으니까.

B 그래도 너무 많이 쉬지는 마. 자칫하면 이전의 나쁜 습관으로 다시 빠질 거야.

학교에서 03 I'm living off campus this year 올해는 캠퍼스 밖에서 지낼 거야

A **I'm living off campus this year.** I couldn't deal with all the noise at the dorms anymore.

B But how can you afford it on top of tuition?

A I can't I had to apply for a student loan.
I really hope I qualify

B I'm sure you'll get the money.

A 올해는 캠퍼스 밖에 집을 얻어서 지내려고. 기숙사의 소음을 더 이상 참아낼 수가 없어.

B 그런데 수업료에 집세까지 어떻게 감당하려고?

A 감당할 수 없어서 학자금 대출을 신청했어. 대출 자격이 되면 정말 좋을 텐데.

B 돈을 꼭 대출 받을 수 있을 거야.

학교에서 04 I'm bound to be late | 나 분명히 지각할거야

A How often do the buses run?

B It depends on traffic but normally every 10 minutes or so.

A Well, **I'm bound to be late** if the bus doesn't come soon.

B Don't worry. In case the bus comes late, you can always get a cab as an alternative.

A 버스가 얼마나 자주 와?

B 교통상황에 따라 다르지만 보통 한 10분에 한 대 와.

A 음, 버스가 금방 오지 않으면 나 분명히 지각할 거야.

B 걱정하지 마, 버스가 만약 늦게 오면 대신 항상 택시를 탈 수 있잖아.

학교에서 05 I need to earn two foreign-language credits to meet my degree requirements. | 학위 요건을 충족하려면 외국어 과정 2학점을 추가 이수해야 해

A **I need to earn two foreign-language credits to meet my degree requirements.**

B Ouch! That doesn't sound like fun at all!

A 학위 요건을 충족하려면 외국어 과정 2학점을 추가 이수해야 해.

B 이런! 진짜 재미없겠다!

학교에서 06 I brown-bagged it today. | 나 오늘 도시락 싸왔어

A Hey, do you want to go get some lunch?
I want to try the new restaurant next door.

B Sorry, **I brown-bagged it today.** Maybe we can do it tomorrow.

A Sounds good to me.

A 점심이나 먹으러 갈래?
옆에 새로 생긴 레스토랑에 가보고 싶은데.

B 미안, 난 오늘 도시락 싸왔어.
내일 가자.

A 그래, 좋아.

학교에서 07 He flunked out of school. 지난 학기 말에 학교에서 제적당했어

A I haven't seen Will around campus lately.

Is he still enrolled here?

B Didn't you hear?

He flunked out at the end of last semester!

A I guess he spent too much time partying, and not enough time studying.

A 학교에서 윌을 못 본 지 오래됐네.

걔 아직 여기 다녀?

B 못 들었어?

지난 학기 말에 학교에서 제적당했어.

A 공부는 얼마 안 하고 너무 파티만 했나 보구나.

학교에서 08 I pulled an all-nighter studying for the test! 시험 공부하느라 밤 샜어

A Wow-you look terrible this morning! Are you okay?

B I'm exhausted. **I pulled an all-nighter studying for the test!**

A I hope you have enough energy to stay awake

A 야, 너 오늘 아침 진짜 안 좋아 보인다. 괜찮은 거야?

B 피곤해 죽겠어. 시험 공부하느라 밤을 샜어.

A 시험 보는 동안 깨어있을 체력이 남아 있길 바라.

학교에서 09 Have you thought about joining a sorority? 여성 동아리에 가입하는 거 생각해봤어?

A I feel like all I do is study. I have no social life.

B **Have you thought about joining a sorority?**

it's like a campus club only for girls.

A But I've heard it's hard to get in

B Well.... they don't let just anyone in, but once you're in, it's for life.

A 내가 하는 건 공부뿐인 것 같아. 사회생활이 없어.

B 여성 동아리에 가입하는 거 생각해봤어?

여학생들만을 위한 교내 클럽 같은 거야.

A 그런데 거기 들어가기가 힘들다고 들었어.

B 글쎄, 아무나 들어가진 못하겠지만 일단 들어가면 평생회원이 되지.

학교에서 10 I need to drop a class
수업을 취소해야 돼

A This line hasn't moved in hours.

B I just hope I can get to the front before the end of the day. The Records Office closes at six.

A I'm here to pay tor my classes. What about you?

B **I need to drop a class.**

It conflicted with another one.

A 몇 시간째 줄이 움직이질 않네.

B 일과 끝나기 전에 앞에까지 갈 수 있어야 할 텐데.
학적과는 6시에 문을 닫거든.

A 나는 등록금 내러 여기 왔는데, 너는 왜 왔니?

B 수강 신청 하나를 취소해야 돼서. 다른 수업과 겹치거든.

학교에서 11 It's an honors level class
그건 우등생들이 듣는 수업이야

A Have you heard of Professor Wilson's Asian History class?

B **It's an honors level class.**

Only the top history students can get in.

A I asked Dr. Wilson and he said I could audit the class if I wanted to.

B Wow. You won't get any credit, but you'll learn a lot.

A 윌슨 교수님의 아시아 역사 수업에 대해 들어본 적 있니?

B 우등생들이 듣는 수업이잖아.
최고의 역사학도들만 들어 갈 수 있어.

A 윌슨 교수님께 여쭤봤는데 내가 원하면 청강할 수 있다고 하셨어.

B 우와. 학점은 못 따도 배울 게 많이 있을 거야.

CHAPTER 09

비즈니스

비즈니스 01 What day suits you best?

어느 날이 가장 적당해?

A Hello? This is Joshua Thomson, a friend of Michael. Can I speak to Jess Covey?

B This is she. You must be calling me for the blind date Michael was talking about.

A That's right.
I'm wondering **what day suits you best?**

B Well, my schedule is flexible.

A 여보세요? 전 마이클 친구인 조슈아 톰슨인데요. 제스 코베이 씨 있습니까?

B 제가 제스 코베인데요. 마이클이 말하던 소개팅 때문에 전화하셨군요.

A 맞아요.
약속 날짜로 언제가 가장 적당하신지 물어보려고요.

B 글쎄요, 제 스케줄은 조정이 가능하니까 좋으실 대로 하세요.

비즈니스 02 Can we put off our plans until next week?

우리 약속 다음 주로 미루면 안 될까?

A Hello, This is Jess. Is Joshua there?

B Hi, Jess. How nice to hear your voice on the phone. What's up?

A I'm terribly sorry, but **can we put off our plans until next week?** Something came up unexpectedly at work.

B Not a problem. Let me know when you settle things.

A 여보세요. 전 제스인데요. 조슈아 있나요?

B 안녕하세요, 제스. 전화로 목소리 들으니 너무 반가워요. 무슨 일이에요?

A 정말 미안한데요, 우리 약속 다음 주로 미루면 안 될까요? 갑자기 회사에서 일이 생겨서요.

B 문제 없어요. 정리 되면 저한테 알려주세요.

비즈니스 03 What is on your agenda tomorrow?

내일 스케줄이 어떻게 돼요?

A Hello. Joshua. This is Jess.
I'm calling to ask **what is on your agenda tomorrow?**

B Nothing special. Shall we meet up?

A Sure. I'm sorry about all the hassles I caused the other day.

B No worries.
Just don't go back on your word this time.

A 여보세요, 저 제스에요.
내일 스케줄이 어떤지 궁금해서 전화했어요.

B 특별한 일은 없는데요. 우리 내일 만날까요?

A 좋죠. 전에 약속 깨고 번거롭게 해 드려 죄송해요.

B 걱정마세요.
이번에 약속 깨지 않으시면 돼요.

비즈니스 04 I want my money working for me 돈을 잘 굴리고 싶어요

A I'd like to earn as much interest as possible. **I want my money working for me.**

B In that case, you need a term deposit.

A But once the money is in one of those, I can't touch it, right?

B Yes. But if you lock it up for six months or more, you earn a really good rate

A 가능한 한 많은 이자를 받고 싶어요. 돈을 잘 굴리고 싶네요.

B 그런 경우라면 정기예금이 필요하겠군요.

A 하지만 일단 돈을 거기에 넣으면 뺄 수 없는 거죠?

B 네. 그렇지만 6개월 이상 묶어두시면 이자가 아주 높아질 거에요.

비즈니스 05 You should use a big down payment 계약금을 많이 내셔야 합니다

A To lower your monthly payments, **you should use a big down payment.**

B I heard that I only need five percent of the value of the house.

A True.... but we don't recommend doing it that way.

B I don't want to put everything into the down payment. I still need money for taxes.

A 월부금을 줄이기 위해서는 계약금을 많이 내셔야 합니다.

B 듣기로는 집값의 5퍼센트만 내면 된다고 하던데요.

A 맞습니다. 하지만 그 방법은 추천해드리지 않습니다.

B 돈을 전부 계약금에 쏟고 싶지는 않아요. 세금 낼 돈도 필요하거든요.

비즈니스 06 I'm sorry I have to decline your order 죄송하지만 귀사의 주문을 받을 수가 없습니다

A I'd like to place an order for 30,000 units of model No. K-1 right away.

B **I'm sorry I have to decline your order** because our factory is already fully occupied with other orders at the moment.

A How long a wait will it be till you can process my order?

B I believe we could start on it later this week.

A K-1 모델 3만 개를 지금 즉시 주문하고 싶은데요.

B 주문을 받을 수 없어 죄송하군요. 현재 저희 공장이 이미 다른 주문들로 꽉 차 서요.

A 얼마나 기다리면 주문을 받을 수 있겠어요?

B 이번 주말부터는 시작할 수 있을 것 같습니다.

비즈니스 07 What are you terms? 거래조건이 어떻게 됩니까?

A I'll order this item. But first, **what are your terms?**

B When you established the letter of credit, make it so that the delivery date is a minimum of two months and a maximum of three months from the date of opening.

A That's kind of long but, okay.

A 이 제품들을 주문하겠어요. 그러나 우선 거래 조건이 어떻게 됩니까?

B 신용장을 개설할 때 납기는 개설일자로부터 최소 2개월에서 3개월로 해주십시오.

A 좀 길긴 하지만 그렇게 하죠.

비즈니스 08 I gave you my word 약속 드렸잖아요

A We've got to have that shipment no later than October 30.

B Don't worry. **I gave you my word.**

A If it arrives later than that, we'll be too late for the Christmas season.

B You can count on me 100%

A 그 선적은 늦어도 10월 30일까지는 도착해야 합니다.

B 걱정하지 마세요. 약속을 드렸잖아요.

A 만약 물건이 그보다 늦게 도착한다면 크리스마스 시즌을 놓치게 됩니다.

B 저를 100% 믿으셔도 좋습니다.

비즈니스 09 It's got a one-your warrantly 이것은 1년 품질 보증이 되어 있어요

A Excuse me, sir could you help me? I am looking for a fax machine for my office

B Yes of course, please follow me. May I show you the deluxe model? At $799 it's a bargain

A It's very nice, but it's pretty expensive.

B Well, in that case, let me suggest this machine at $249. It has a speakerphone, copier, and speed dialer.

A I like that model. **It's got a one-year warranty.** Wrap it up. I'll take it.

A 실례하지만, 도와주시겠습니까? 제 사무실용 팩스를 찾고 있어요.

B 네 물론이죠, 이쪽으로 오세요. 고급 사양은 어떠세요? 799불이면 헐값이죠.

A 아주 좋은데, 너무 비싸군요.

B 글쎄, 그렇다면 249불짜리 팩스를 권해 드릴게요. 스피커폰, 복사기, 단축 다이얼 기능이 있어요.

A 그 모델로 할게요. 이건 1년 품질 보증도 되어 있네요. 포장해 주세요. 그걸로 살게요.

비즈니스 10 That's pushing it. 무리한 요구입니다

A I'd like to place an order for this model. But a lot depends on timing. I mean, when can you make shipment?

B Well, if you place an order now, the shipment can be made in January.

A Too late. How about December?

B **That's pushing it**, but we'll try our best.

A 이 모델을 주문하고 싶지만 때를 맞춰 줄 수 있느냐에 달렸습니다. 내 말은, 언제 선적해 줄 수 있느냐는 거죠.

B 지금 주문하시면, 글쎄요, 1월에 선적이 될 수 있겠는데요.

A 너무 늦네요. 12월엔 안 될까요?

B 무리한 요구입니다만, 최선을 다해보죠.

비즈니스 11 What would you suggest? 어느 정도 해드리면 되겠습니까?

A Due to the delay, my customers wouldn't accept the goods at the contracted amount, but demanded a discount.

B Okay, we can offer you some savings too, then. **What would you suggest?**

A Two dollars on every unit.

B We can accept that on our end.

A 지연되는 바람에 저희 고객들이 계약 단가로는 물건을 인수하지 못 하겠다며 할인을 요구했습니다.

B 좋습니다. 할인을 해 드리지요. 어느 정도면 되겠습니까?

A 개당 2달러씩 할인해 주세요.

B 좋습니다.

비즈니스 12 How long should we make the contract for? 계약 기간은 얼마로 할까요?

A Okay, I think you can go ahead and make up the contract.

B Good. **How long should we make the contract for?**

A Ordinarily, we make our contracts for a period of one year, with an option to extend for an additional year upon a verbal agreement of both parties.

A 자, 계약서를 우선 작성하는 것이 좋겠습니다.

B 좋습니다. 계약 기간은 얼마로 할까요?

A 일반적으로 1년 계약을 합니다. 쌍방의 구두 합의에 따라 추가로 1년 연장하는 걸 옵션으로 해서요.

비즈니스 13 The stock market is going south. 증권 시장이 내림세에 있습니다

A How did the dow do today?

B It fell almost 40 points to 3645.27.

A Really? I'm in trouble, big trouble.

B I told you not to buy in this bear market.

A I only bought the blue chip stocks.

A 오늘 증권 시세는 어때요?

B 거의 40포인트 내려 3645.27이 됐어요.

A 정말요? 난 큰일났네요. 정말 큰일이에요.

B 주가가 내림세에 있는 지금은 사지 말라고 말했잖아요.

A 난 우량주만 샀을 뿐인데요.

비즈니스 14 The stock market has been rather bearish lately. 요즘 주식 시장이 좀 약세야

A **The stock market has been rather bearish lately.**

B I know. I'm losing my shirt because of some bad investments!

A I'm glad I didn't follow your investment advice last month!

A 요즘 주식 시장이 좀 약세야.

B 그러게 말이야. 잘못된 투자 몇 번에 알거지가 돼가고 있어.

A 지난달에 네 말 따라서 투자하지 않은 게 정말 다행이다.

비즈니스 15 I'd better pass this time 다음 기회로 하시죠

A Do you feel like dropping in somewhere for a few drinks?

B Well, maybe **I'd better pass this time**, it's getting a little late.

A I know a place nearby that's very casual and relaxing.

B Okay, you've talked me into it.

A 잠깐 들러 술 한 잔 하는 게 어때요?

B 글쎄요. 다음 기회로 미루는 게 낫겠어요. 늦었잖아요.

A 가볍고 편안하게 한 잔 할 수 있는 장소를 아는데요.

B 좋아요. 당신 말대로 하죠.

비즈니스 16 I'd like to transfer $5,000 — 5000달러를 이체하고 싶습니다

A **I'd like to transfer $5,000** from my savings account into my checking account.

B No problem. Can I have your account numbers?

A Sure, my savings account number is 374-56-90182, and my checking is 901-23-04959.

A 5000달러를 제 저축계좌에서 당좌예금 계좌로 이체하고 싶은데요.

B 알겠습니다. 계좌번호를 주시겠습니까?

A 네. 제 저축계좌는 374- 56-90182번이고 당좌예금 계좌는 901-23-04959번이에요.

비즈니스 17 How much is the monthly rent? — 한 달 임대료는 얼마죠?

A **How much is the monthly rent?**

B $1,500 per month.

A Oh, that's a lot of money. Maybe we need to look for a house with a cheaper rent.

A 한 달 임대료는 얼마죠?

B 한 달에 1,500달러입니다.

A 상당히 비싸네요. 임대료가 더 싼 집을 찾아봐야 할 것 같습니다.

비즈니스 18 Let's put it in writing and sign it. — 그것을 문서화해서 서명합시다

A Now I think we've been able to come to an agreement.

B Yes, all the problems have been ironed out, as far as we can see.

A Right. So **let's put it in writing and sign it.**

A 이젠 계약을 해도 될 것 같습니다.

B 그렇군요. 저희가 보기에도 모든 문제점들이 조정된 것 같습니다.

A 맞습니다. 그렇다면 문서화해서 서명을 합시다.

비즈니스 19 Do you really think you can beat that price? — 가격을 더 낮출 수 있다고 생각하세요?

A What are you asking for this model?

B I'll give you my best price:$3t a unit?

A Oh, come on. You must be kidding.

B why? **Do you really think you can beat that price?**

A 이 모델은 얼마입니까?

B 내가 해줄 수 있는 최상의 가격은 개당 35달러입니다.

A 자 농담 마시고요.

B 왜요? 가격을 이것보다 더 낮출 수 있다고 생각하시나요?

비즈니스 20 He is a bit green.

그는 비즈니스는 아직 초짜야

A I don't know how I am going to finish this project this week.

B Why don't you ask John? He's a sharp guy.

A True, but **he's still a bit green** when it comes to business.

A 이번 주까지 과연 이 프로젝트를 끝낼 수 있을지 모르겠어.

B 존에게 물어보지 그래? 똑똑한 사람이 잖아.

A 그렇기는 한데 비즈니스는 아직 초짜야.

비즈니스 21 We need to have a catchy jingle for our new commercial.

새 광고에 주목을 끌만한 CM송이 필요해

A **We need to have a catchy jingle for our new commercial.**

B It should be something upbeat, but not too silly of childish.

A I agree. We want it too be catchy, but not annoying.

A 새 광고에 주목을 끌만한 CM송이 필요해.

B 좀 신나면서도 유치하거나 우습지는 않은 것으로 말이야.

A 맞아. 주목을 끌되 너무 자극적이지는 않아야 해.

비즈니스 22 The stock market has been very bullish lately.

요즘 주식 시장이 아주 강세야

A **The stock market has been very bullish lately.**

B I know. My portfolio value has risen 23% in the last six weeks!

A I wish I had some extra money to invest right now.

A 요즘 주식 시장이 아주 강세야.

B 그러게 말이야. 내 포트폴리오 가치는 지난 6주간 23%나 올랐어!

A 지금 투자할 여윳돈이 있으면 좋을텐데.

CHAPTER 10

인간관계, 성격

인간관계, 성격 01 I have a soft spot for people like her. 나는 그녀 같은 사람에게 약해

A How do you get along with Susan so well?
She seems to be so moody.

B True. But she had a really bad childhood and I can't help but care for her.

A Well, I don't know how you do it.
She drives me crazy.

B I guess **I just have a soft spot for people like her.**

A 너 어떻게 수잔이랑 그렇게 잘 지내?
걔 너무 변덕스러운 것 같은데.

B 맞아. 그렇지만 그 애 아주 힘든 유년기를 보냈거든. 그래서 내가 그 애를 돌봐줄 수 밖에 없어.

A 글쎄, 네가 어떻게 그렇게 할 수 있는지 모르겠다.
난 걔 때문에 미치겠던데.

B 내가 그런 사람들에게 약한 것 같아.

인간관계, 성격 02 She is such a know-it-all. 쟤 정말 잘난 척 심해

A Look! There goes Kevin and Sue.

B I wonder why Kevin goes out with Sue.
She is so annoying.

A You're right. **She is such a know-it-all** and always looks down on everyone.

B I don't understand what Kevin sees in her.

A 저것 봐! 케빈하고 수 지나간다.

B 난 케빈이 왜 수하고 사귀는지 모르겠어.
수 정말 짜증나.

A 맞아. 쟤 정말 잘난 척 끝내주고 항상 모든 사람을 무시해.

B 케빈이 저 애 뭘 보고 좋아하는지 정말 이해가 안가.

인간관계, 성격 03 We are not meant to be together. 우리는 서로 잘 맞는 상대가 아니야

Hi, thanks for understanding how I feel about things. I should have come clean about everything a lot earlier. Like I said before, it's nothing you did wrong. It's just that as time went on I realized that **we were just not meant to be together.** I'm sorry to let you down by saying this but I'm sure you will be better off without me. Anyway, I hope we can still be good friends.

안녕, 내 마음을 이해해 줘서 고마워. 내가 진작에 모든 것을 다 털어놓았어야 했는데. 전에도 얘기했듯이 넌 잘못한 게 아무것도 없어. 그냥 우리가 시간이 지나면서 우리가 서로 잘 맞는 상대가 아니라는 것을 깨달았어. 미안해. 이렇게 말하고 널 실망시켜서. 그렇지만 나 없으면 넌 더 잘 살 거야. 어쨌든 우리가 계속 좋은 친구로 남았으면 좋겠다.

인간관계, 성격 04 We have one thing in common. 우린 한 가지 공통점이 있네

A So, Jess. I've heard that you are a writer. What are you writing about?

B Well, I write mostly about food, you know, recipes, restaurants and all that jazz. What do you do, Joshua?

A I'm a movie critic. I write for a weekly movie magazine.

B Funny that **we have one thing in common**; cutting down people around us.

A 그래서 제스, 듣기로는 작가라고 하던데, 어떤 글을 쓰시죠?

B 글쎄요, 전 거의 음식에 대해 써요. 그러니까 요리법이나 식당 등에 관해서요. 조슈아는 무슨 일을 하세요?

A 전 영화 평론가예요. 주간 영화 잡지에 글을 싣고 있어요.

B 재밌게도 우리 한 가지 공통점이 있네요. 주변 사람들 깎아내리는 일을 한다는 거요.

인간관계, 성격 05 They were like fish out of water. 그들은 잘 어울리지 못했다

The costume party we went to turned out to be a blast. I chose to be Elvis Presley, wearing tight white jeans and white boots. It was a little awkward at first, but I soon got comfortable after mingling with people. In fact, I think the people who forgot to wear costumes were the real **fish out of water**. Funny, huh?

우리가 갔던 가장 파티 정말 재미있었어. 난 엘비스 프레슬리처럼 꽉 끼는 하얀색 바지에 하얀색 부츠차림으로 갔지. 처음엔 좀 어색했는데 사람들이랑 어울리면서 곧 괜찮아졌어. 사실, 잊어버리고 70년대 복장을 안 입은 사람들이 오히려 물 떠난 물고기같이 어색했던 것 같아. 웃기지?

인간관계, 성격 06 We are not speaking the same language. 우린 서로 말이 안 통해요

A Let's wrap up this meeting. It's just going nowhere.

B You're right. We're all getting worn-out and I don't even think **we are speaking the same language** anymore.

A Why don't we meet up another time after we calm down and clear our heads?

B I guess we should.

A 이 회의 마무리 합시다. 도대체 결론이 나지 않네.

B 맞아요. 모두 점점 지쳐서 이젠 말도 통하지 않는 것 같아요.

A 좀 진정하고 머리나 식힌 후에 다시 모이는 게 어때?

B 그래야 할 것 같아요.

인간관계, 성격 07 He must have pigged out a lot. 걔 진짜 많이 먹고 살았나 보다

A Get a load of the guy over there. He looks kind of familiar to me.

B Who? Andrew Chan? Boy, he's gained so much weigh. What's up with him?

A He sure has. **He must have pigged out a lot.** But he still looks cute, though.

B Uh oh. He is coming this way! We should say hi.

A 저기 저 남자 좀 봐. 저 남자 어디서 많이 본 것 같은데.

B 누구? 앤드류 찬? 맙소사, 정말 살쪘네. 도대체 무슨 일이지?

A 진짜 그러네. 정말 많이 먹고 살았나봐. 그래도 아직 잘생겼네.

B 이런. 지금 여기로 온다. 우리 인사해야겠다.

인간관계, 성격 08 Are you seeing anyone these days? 너 요새 사귀는 사람 있어?

A Hey, Jess. **Are you seeing anyone these days?**

B Not that I recall. No. Why do you ask?

A I know someone who would get along with you perfectly. He is caring and funny, not to mention that he's drop-dead gorgeous.

B Sound like a lady's man, but it wouldn't hurt to meet him. Set me up with him. I'm pretty mush free next week.

A 제스 너 요새 사귀는 사람 있어?

B 내가 아는 한 없어. 왜 물어봐?

A 너한테 완벽하게 어울릴 만한 사람을 알거든. 그 사람 자상하고 재밌어. 물론 엄청 잘 생기기도 했고.

B 여자 꽤나 만나고 다닐 남자 같다. 그래도 만나본다고 나쁘진 않겠지. 소개시켜줘봐. 나 다음 주엔 꽤 한가해.

인간관계, 성격 09 She's got a lot of willpower 그 애는 의지력이 아주 강해

A The key to sticking to a resolution is having a support network.

B It'll be easier to follow through on my plans if I have a group of friends helping me out.

A Right, because you can encourage one another.

B Perfect. I'll ask Betty to help me.

` **She's got a lot of willpower.**

A 결심을 지키는데 중요한 것은 도와주는 사람들이 주변에 있냐는 거야.

B 나를 도와주는 친구들이 있으면 계획을 끝가지 지키는 게 더 쉬울 거야.

A 맞아, 서로 격려해줄 수 있으니까.

B 좋아. 베티에게 도움을 청해야겠어. 그 애는 의지력이 아주 강하거든.

인간관계, 성격 10 It's hard to stay motivated 평정심을 유지하기가 어려워

A Have you kept your resolution to lose weight?

B Not really. I was very motivated for the first couple of days, but….

A I know. **It's hard to stay motivated,** but if you keep at it, you'll see result.

B I hope so. Nowdays, every time I look in a mirror I feel guilty.

A 체중 감량 결심은 잘 지켜지고 있니?

B 그렇지만은 않아. 처음 며칠간은 결심이 대단했는데….

A 알아. 처음 결심을 유지하긴 어렵지만 하다 보면 효과가 나타날 거야.

B 그랬으면 좋겠어. 요즘 거울을 볼 때마다 죄책감이 들거든.

인간관계, 성격 11 Your eyes may be bigger than your stomach. 너 식탐이 많은 것 같다

A What's good here, Jess?

B Well, last time I came here I tried the pasta and pizza. They tasted as good as I expected.

A It won't hurt to follow what the expert is saying. Why don't we get 2 pizzas and 2 pastas? Oh, and a salad.

B Joshua, **Your eyes may be bigger than your stomach.** You might need a doggy bag.

A 여기 뭐 잘해요 제스?

B 글쎄요, 전에 여기 왔을 때 파스타하고 피자를 먹어봤는데요, 예상한 대로 맛있었어요.

A 전문가 말씀을 들어야 겠죠. 우리 피자 2개 파스타 2개 시킬까요? 아, 샐러드도요.

B 조슈아, 너무 많이 시키는 것 같아요. 나중에 남은 음식 싸달라고 해야될지도 모르겠어요.

인간관계, 성격 12 I'd like to take you out to lunch for all the help you've given me. 저를 도와주신 감사의 표시로 점심을 대접하고 싶은데요

A **I'd like to take you out to lunch for all the help you've given me.**

B You don't have to do that. But thanks.

A 저를 도와주신 감사의 표시로 점심을 대접하고 싶은데요.

B 그럴 필요까지는 없어요. 어쨌든 고마워요.

인간관계, 성격 13 Did you bump into him recently? 최근에 그와 우연히 만났니?

A Do you remember Mike Smith from high school? He just got married.

B Mike Smith? I haven't heard that name in ages. **Did you bump into him recently?**

A Not really. I stumbled across his blog last night.

B I guess blogs are the new way of staying in touch.

A 고등학교 동창인 마이크 스미스 기억나? 결혼했더라.

B 마이크 스미스? 그 이름은 들어본 지 꽤 됐는데. 최근에 우연히 만난 거야?

A 그런 건 아니고 어젯밤에 그 애 블로그를 우연히 발견했어.

B 블로그가 연락을 유지하는 새로운 수단인 거 같아.

인간관계, 성격 14 I'm actually head over heels in love with you. 실은 너한테 푹 빠졌어

A I know I'm supposed to play it cool, but **I'm actually head over heels in love with you.**

B Really? Then, I can admit I'm really into you, too.

A So, what is it that you like about me the most? My good looks, right?

B Actually.... You remind me of the expression, "Love is blind."

A 냉정해야 되는 건 알지만, 실은 너에게 푹 빠졌어.

B 정말? 그럼, 나도 너한테 관심이 많다는 거 고백할게.

A 근데 나의 어떤 점이 가장 좋아? 잘생긴 얼굴?

B 실은 너를 보면서 생각나는 말이 있어. '사랑은 맹목적이다'라는 말.

인간관계, 성격 15 You could hang out with them there 여기서 그분들과 놀아 드리는 게 어떨까요

A It's my first time volunteering.

B Some of the residents are already in the Day Room, watching TV. If you like, **you could hang out with them there.**

A I just watch TV with them?

B If they want, but a lot of them love card games.

A 봉사활동은 처음 해봐요.

B 여기 사는 어르신들이 휴게실에서 TV를 보고 계세요. 괜찮으면 가서 그분들과 놀아드리는 게 어떨까요.

A 그분들과 TV만 같이 보면 되나요?

B 그분들이 원하시면요. 하지만 대부분 카드게임을 좋아하세요.

인간관계, 성격 16 He's gone too far. 그 사람 너무했군요

A I hear that Michael Bang is in jail. Is that true?

B Yes, it's true.

A What did he do this time?

B He stole the test paper and the entire hard drive before beginning of midterm.

A He did? **He's gone too far.**

B He sure has.

A 마이클 방이 감옥에 갔다는데 사실이니?

B 응, 사실이야.

A 이번엔 또 무슨 일을 저질렀니?

B 중간고사 시작 전에 시험지와 하드 드라이브 전체를 훔쳤다는군.

A 그랬다고? 너무 심했군.

B 그러게 말이야.

인간관계, 성격 17 I am done with him. 그 사람과는 완전히 끝났어요

A Why do you have a long face?

B I no longer see her.

A You mean you have split with her?

B Yes, **I am done with her.**

A That's too bad.

B Where is my new better half?

B 나 그녀를 더 이상 만나지 않기로 했어.

A 그녀와 완전히 결별했다는 거야?

B 응, 그녀와는 이제 끝났어.

A 저런. 안됐구나.

B 새로운 나의 반쪽은 그 어디에 있을까?

인간관계, 성격 18 We're in the same boat. 우리 한 배를 탔어

A Adrian, can you tell me where you are with your work?

B Okay. I have only a couple of more modules to cover.

A Wow, You're really fast. I'd better speed up to keep up with you.

B Take your time. Your portion is way more complicated than mine.

A But it's better we're on the same track as partners.

B **We're in the same boat** and I'll help you whenever you need me.

A 애드리안, 네 일 진도 얼마나 나갔어?

B 한 두 부분만 더 하면 돼.

A 와, 너 진짜 빠르다. 너랑 진도를 맞추려면 서둘러야겠어.

B 천천히 해. 네 부분이 내 것보다 훨씬 복잡하잖아.

A 하지만 우린 파트너니까 진도를 맞추는 게 좋아.

B 우린 한 배를 탔으니까 필요할 때면 언제든 내가 널 도울게.

인간관계, 성격 19 You look kind of low. 기분이 우울해 보여요

A What's wrong? **You look kind of low.**

B Does it show that much?

A Yes, because your eyes are puffy.

B Actually I was crying. My grandmother's death made me upset.

A Perk up!

A 무슨 일 있으세요? 기분이 안 좋으신가 봐요.

B 그렇게 보이세요?

A 네, 눈이 부은 것 같아요.

B 실은 울었거든요. 할머니의 부음 때문에 기분이 안 좋아요.

A 힘내세요!

인간관계, 성격 20 You'll be hearing from my lawyer. 당신을 고소하겠소

A What do you mean you owe me nothing?
You must pay me the security deposit back.

B I'm not going to pay you back, because you've done a lot of damage to my property.

A That's not true. That was normal wear and tear.

B No, it's not.

A OK, if you don't may me $10,000 within a week, **you'll be hearing from my lawyer.**

A 저에게 줄 돈이 하나도 없다니 무슨 소리에요?
보증금을 돌려주셔야 하잖아요.

B 내 재산을 많이 파손시켰으니 보증금을 돌려 줄 수 없습니다.

A 그건 사실이 아니에요. 정상적으로 닳은 거잖아요.

B 아니요, 그렇지 않아요.

A 좋아요. 일주일 내로 1만달러를 갚지 않으면 고소하겠어요.

인간관계, 성격 21 Both of us bring home the bacon. 저희는 맞벌이 부부입니다

A Kenny, what do you do for a living?

B I am a junior high school teacher.

A Does your wife work, too?

B Yes, we are a two-paycheck couple. **Both of us must bring home the bacon** to make the mortgage payments on our house.

A 케니씨, 직업이 어떻게 되세요?

B 저는 중학교 교사입니다.

A 부인도 일하시나요?

B 네, 저희는 맞벌이 부부입니다. 주택대출금을 납부하기 위해서 둘 다 일해야 하거든요.

인간관계, 성격 22 Between you and me

아무에게도 말하지 마라

A In fact, I'm the only reason we made this sale.
I worked night and day on this project.

B Did anyone else help you?

A Well, **between you and me**, right now no one else is qualified here.

B Really? I thought they were all qualified when I hired them.

A 사실 나 때문에 이 제품이 성공리에 판매된거지 뭐.
내가 밤낮으로 일했거든.

B 널 도와준 사람은 아무도 없었고?

A 이거 아무한테도 말하지 마. 지금 여기 아무도 자격을 갖춘 사람이 없어.

B 정말? 내가 그 사람들 뽑았을 때는 모두 적임자라고 생각했었는데.

인간관계, 성격 23 You're way off base.

네 생각은 완전히 틀렸어

A Regina says she is engaged to marry.

B Really? Who is the lucky guy?

A I thought you were.

B No, I am not. If you thought I was going to marry her, **you were way off base.**

A But you love her, don't you?

B I like her very much, but I'm not in love with her.

A 레지나가 약혼했다고 그러던데.

B 그래? 행운아가 누구야?

A 난 너로 생각했는데.

B 아니, 난 아냐. 내가 그 여자랑 결혼할 걸로 알았다면 크게 잘못 안 거야.

A 그렇지만, 넌 그녀를 사랑하잖아.

B 매우 좋아하지만, 사랑에 빠져 있지는 않지.

인간관계, 성격 24 Could you fix me up with her?

내게 그녀를 소개해주시겠어요?

A Does your sister have a boy friend?

B Why? Are you attracted to her?

A If she hasn't got any boy friend, **could you fix me up with her?** Actually I have a crush on her.

B I am not sure if you are her type. But I will ask her when she is available.

A Thanks man.

A 네 여동생 남자 친구 있니?

B 왜? 그녀에게 관심 있어?

A 남자 친구 없으면 소개해줄래? 실은 나 그녀에게 반했어.

B 네가 그녀 타입인지는 모르겠다. 언제 시간이 나는지 물어볼게.

A 고마워, 친구.

인간관계, 성격 25 He's full of beans. 그는 매우 신이 나 있다

A Didn't Andrew make it? I haven't seen him recently.

B Andrew? He went on a trip to Japan. I bumped into him going to the airport this morning.

A Really? He must be having some fun now.

B Sure. He deserves it. He studied really hard this year.

A Yeah. **All kids are full of beans** after final exams.

B Definitely. Look back on us. We used to be the same

A 앤드루는 안 왔나? 요즘 통 못 보겠네.

B 앤드루? 일본으로 여행 갔잖아. 오늘 아침에 우연히 봤는데 공항으로 가는 길이던데.

A 정말? 지금 한참 즐겁겠네.

B 그럼. 당연히 그래야지. 올해 정말 열심히 공부했잖아.

A 맞아. 애들이 기말고사 끝내고 신나는 건 당연하지.

B 그렇지. 우리 때를 생각해 봐. 우리도 그랬어.

인간관계, 성격 26 He's such a brat. 그는 아주 버르장머리가 없어

A I was with my sister's kid yesterday. **He's such a brat.**

B Don't be so judgmental. Maybe he's just stubborn. You know, hardheaded.

A You're right. Besides, I'm sure it's just a phase. He'll grow out of it.

A 어제 조카와 함께 지냈는데, 그 녀석 아주 버르장머리가 없어.

B 그렇게 판단하지 마. 어쩌면 그저 고집이 센 걸지도 모르니까. 똥고집 있잖아.

A 네 말이 맞아. 게다가, 딱 그럴 시기인 것 같아. 크면 괜찮아지겠지.

인간관계, 성격 27 It's like I'm rubbing their noses in it 내가 그 애들의 기분을 상하게 할 것 같아

A I'll take you to a nice coffee shop.

B Just promise me that we won't go to that place on Third.

A But I thought you loved it there.

B I do, but some of my friends work there. They don't have boyfriends, so if I show up with you, **it's like I'm rubbing their noses in it.**

A 분위기 좋은 커피숍에 가자.

B 3번가에 있는 그 커피숍에는 가지 않겠다고 약속해줘.

A 너 거기 정말 좋아하잖아.

B 좋아하긴 하는데 친구들이 거기서 일해. 그 애들은 남자친구가 없어서 내가 너랑 가면 기분 나빠할 거 같아.

인간관계, 성격 28 I'm here to sub for him. 그 사람 대신 (일하러) 나왔어요

A Can I help you?

B Hi. My name is Kenny. My friend NBC is sick, so **I'm here to sub for him.**

A What? NBC studio?

B Oh, sorry. NBC stands for Nam Bong-chul, not the NBC studio in Manhattan.

A Oh, I see. It's so nice of you to stand in for NBC. He is not very ill, is he?

B No. A good day's rest should bring him back to work tomorrow.

A 도와 드릴까요?

B 안녕하세요? 저는 케니라고 합니다. 제 친구 NBC가 아파제가 대신 일하러 나왔습니다.

A 뭐라고요? NBC 스튜디오라고요?

B 미안합니다. NBC는 맨해튼에 있는 NBC 스튜디오가 아니라 남봉철을 뜻합니다.

A 아, 알겠어요. NBC를 대신해 일하러 나왔다니 반갑군요.
그 친구 많이 아픈 건 아니죠?

B 아니요. 하루 푹 쉬면 내일 일하러 나올 수 있을 겁니다.

인간관계, 성격 29 You're such a bleeding-heart. 너는 마음이 너무 여려

A What took you so long to come home?
You're supposed to be home like an hour ago.

B Sorry, mom. I came home on foot.

A You walked home? What happened?

B I saw a pauper and his poor little girl at the subway station. They looked so abject and I accidentally gave them all the money I had.

A Oh, **you're such a bleeding-heart**, sweetheart.

B You wouldn't have passed over them either.

A 왜 이렇게 오래 걸렸어?
평소보다 한 시간이나 늦게 왔잖아.

B 죄송해요, 엄마. 집까지 걸어오느라 그랬어요.

A 집까지 걸어왔어? 왜?

B 지하철역에서 한 걸인과 어린 딸을 봤는데 너무나 가엾어 그냥 제가 가진 돈을 다 줘버렸거든요.

A 넌 마음이 너무 여려 탈이야.

B 엄마도 보셨다면 아마 그냥 지나칠 수 없었을 거예요.

인간관계, 성격 30 I don't want to put you out. | 너한테 부담 주기 싫어

A Heading home? Do you want me to give you a ride?

B Thanks, but **I don't want to put you out.**

A It's okay. I'm going past your place anyway. Besides, I could use some good company.

B Thanks, I owe you a big one.

A 집에 가? 내가 차로 데려다 줄까?

B 고마워, 그렇지만 너한테 부담을 주기 싫은데.

A 괜찮아 어차피 너희 집 지나는 길인데 뭐. 게다가 너 있으면 지루하지 않아서 좋지.

B 고마워 이번에 크게 빚졌네.

인간관계, 성격 31 I'm no one's doormat anymore | 사람들한테 더 이상 고분고분하지 않을 거야

A Wow. Was that Bill you were gust talking with on the phone? I can't believe what you said to him.

B I surprised myself, too. But my resolution is to be tougher with co-workers. **I'm no one's doormat anymore!**

A You might want to take it slow. Remember, baby steps.

A 와. 너랑 전화통화 한 사람 빌이었니? 네가 그 사람한테 그렇게 말하다니 말도 안돼.

B 나도 내 자신한테 놀랐어. 내 결심은 직장동료에게 좀 더 강하게 하기야. 사람들한테 더 이상 고분고분하지 않을거야!

A 천천히 신중하게 해. 조금씩 바꿔가는 것도 잊지 말고.

인간관계, 성격 32 What would you do in my shoes? | 당신이 내 입장이라면 어떻게 하겠습니까?

A What do you think I am. a swindler or something?

B Don't raise your voice. I didn't call you a swindler.

A Why do you treat me like that?

B **What would you do in my shoes?** Put yourself in my place.

A I don't get it. What's the point?

A 당신은 나를 사기꾼쯤으로 생각하고 있지?

B 언성을 높이지 마세요. 나는 당신을 사기꾼이라고 하지 않았습니다.

A 왜 날 사기꾼처럼 대하지?

B 당신이 내 입장이라면 어떻게 하겠습니까? 입장을 바꿔놓고 봅시다.

A 무슨 소리인지 모르겠네. 요점이 뭐야?

인간관계, 성격 33 He's so full of himself. 걔는 자기가 가장 잘난 줄 알지

A What is mark's problem?

B **He's so full of himself.**

A 마크는 뭐가 문제야?

B 걔는 자기가 가장 잘난 줄 알지.

인간관계, 성격 34 I think he is crass. 내 생각에 걔는 무식해

A Is Jim mean?

B No. **I think he is crass.**

A That might explain it.

A 짐이 좀 못됐지?

B 아니. 내 생각에 걔는 멍청해.

A 그 말이 맞겠다.

인간관계, 성격 35 He really pissed me off. 개가 날 진짜 열받게 했어

A When he said that my girlfirend was ugly, **he really pissed me off.**

B I understand. What a mean thing to say!

A 개가 내 여자친구가 못생겼다고 했을 때 나 진짜 열받았어.

B 이해된다. 어떻게 그런 말을 할 수가!

인간관계, 성격 36 Philately is a relaxing hobby. 우표 수집은 마음을 편안하게 해주는 취미지요

A I need to relieve all the stress in my life. What would you recommend?

B **Philately is a relaxing hobby.** So is RC car driving.

A 일상에서 받는 스트레스를 모두 풀어야겠어요. 추천할 만한 것이 있나요?

B 우표 수집은 마음을 편안하게 해주는 취미지요. 무선조종 자동차 운전도 그렇고요.

인간관계, 성격 37 I was sort of jealous. 난 좀 질투가 났어

A When he received that important job and I didn't, **I was sort of jealous.**

B You shouldn't feel that way. You're a good person, even if you didn't receive the job.

A 그 사람은 번듯한 직장을 잡았는데 나는 그러지 못했을 때, 좀 질투가 났지.

B 그렇게 생각하지 마. 그 직장에 들어가지 못 했어도 넌 아주 훌륭한 사람이야.

인간관계, 성격 38 She's aged very well. 그 연세로 안 보이셔

A It was a pleasure to meet your mother last week. What a lovely lady!

B Thanks. Actually, today is her 80th birthday.

A I had no idea she was 80! **She's aged very well.**

A 지난주에 네 어머니 만나서 너무 좋았어. 정말 좋은 분이신 것 같아.

B 고마워. 실은 오늘이 어머니 팔순 생신이야.

A 팔순이나 되셨다고는 생각도 못했어! 그 연세로 안 보이셔.

인간관계, 성격 39 He's the black sheep of the family. 그 애는 가족의 애물단지야

A I heard from John last week. Apparently he's in India studying Hinduism.

B Yeah, his parents can't understand why he has spent so much time there.

A Well, **he always was the black sheep of the family.**

A 지난주에 존이랑 얘기했어. 인도에서 힌두교 공부 중이라더라.

B 그래. 그 애 부모님도 그 애가 왜 거기서 그렇게 오래 지내는지 이해 못 하셔.

A 그 애는 항상 가족의 애물단지잖아.

인간관계, 성격 40 Where do you see yourself in five years? 5년 뒤 당신은 어떤 모습일 것 같습니까?

A **Where do you see yourself in five years?**

B I would like to keep growing in a company that challenges me.

A Excellent. We are looking for employees with a long term commitment to the company.

A 5년 뒤 당신은 어떤 모습일 것 같습니까?

B 제 능력을 시험할 수 있는 회사에서 성장해 나가고 싶습니다.

A 좋습니다. 저희는 장기간 근무할 직원을 찾고 있습니다.

인간관계, 성격 41 I wouldn't give her the time of day. 걔랑 상대 안 할 거야

A After the way Sarah talked about me yesterday, **I wouldn't give her the time of day!**

B She must have said some terrible things about you.

A You have no idea! And they were all untrue!

A 어제 사라가 나에 대해 그런 식으로 말하다니. 걔랑 상대 안 할거야!

B 너에 대해 아주 나쁜 말을 한 모양이구나!

A 말도 마! 게다가 모두 다 거짓말이야!

인간관계, 성격 42 There's some bad blood between us. 불화가 좀 있었어

A Do you have any siblings?

B Yes, I have a brother, but we're not close.

A Why not? Did you have some trouble in the past?

B Yeah, **there's some bad blood between us.**

A 넌 형제가 있어?

B 응. 오빠가 있는데 가깝니는 않아.

A 왜? 예전에 좀 문제가 있었어?

B 응. 불화가 좀 있었어.

인간관계, 성격 43 I could set you up on a blind date 내가 소개팅을 주선해 줄 수 있을 것 같아

A **I could set you up on a blind date.** I have several eligible friends.

B That would be great! Why didn't you mention that before?

A I didn't realize you were looking for a relationship!

A 내가 소개팅 주선해 줄 수 있을 것 같아. 괜찮은 친구가 여럿 있거든.

B 그럼 좋지! 전에는 왜 얘기 안 했는데?

A 네가 만날 사람 찾고 있는지 몰랐지!

인간관계, 성격 44 We don't see eye to eye. 의견이 맞지 않아

A I just had a marathon meeting with Mr. Kim.

B Oh, really? What was the problem?

A It's our hiring policy. He and **I just don't see eye to eye** on our benefits package.

A 지금까지 미스터 김과 마라톤 회의를 했어.

B 그래? 뭐가 문제였는데?

A 고용방침 때문이야. 복리후생제도에 대해 의견이 맞지 않아.

인간관계, 성격 45 My wife takes care of the bills. 돈은 집사람이 관리해

A Oh no, my credit card is maxed out again.

B I don't know how you survive. You are terrible with money.

A Thank goodness **my wife takes care of the bills.**

A 이런, 신용카드 한도가 또 초과됐네.

B 네가 어떻게 버티는지 모르겠다. 돈 관리 정말 못한다.

A 돈을 집사람이 관리해서 정말 다행이야.

인간관계, 성격 46 He's finally coming of age. 이제 철이 들었어

A I'm so proud of my son. He recently started his own business.

B Is that so? It seems like just yesterday he was in college.

A **He's finally coming of age.**

A 내 아들이 정말 자랑스러워. 최근에 자기 사업을 시작했거든.

B 그래? 대학 다닐 때가 엊그제 같은데 말이야.

A 이제 철이 들었어.

인간관계, 성격 47 He's the breadwinner. 그가 혼자 벌어

A John was complaining that it's been hard to make ends meet.

B Yeah, since his wife had a baby, **he's been the breadwinner.**

A These days, it's hard to make ends meet with only one income.

A 존이 생활비 맞추기가 어렵다고 불평하더라.

B 그러게, 부인이 아이를 낳은 후로 그가 혼자 벌잖아.

A 요즘은 한 사람 수입으로 생활하기가 쉽지 않지.

인간관계, 성격 48 He's sort of a loner. 그는 혼자 있어

A Who's that guy?

B He's in our class, but **he's sort of a loner.**

A We should go say "Hi!" to him.

A 쟤 누구야?

B 우리 반인데 보통 혼자 있는 편이야.

A 우리 쟤한테 인사하자.

■ loner는 혼자 지내는 것을 좋아하는 사람을 가리킵니다. 이 표현은 "He tends to keep to himself."와 같은 의미입니다.

인간관계, 성격 49 I was in a mood. 기분이 그냥 그래서

A Why didn't you talk to anyone at the party?

B Oh, **I was in a mood.**

A 왜 파티에서 아무하고도 말 안했니?

B 아, 기분이 그냥 그래서.

인간관계, 성격 50 He's a jolly guy. 걔는 기분 좋은 친구야

A I like Gus. **He's a jolly guy.**

B I think so, too.

A 나는 거스가 좋아. 걔는 기분 좋은 친구야.

B 나도 그렇게 생각해.

■ 누군가 jolly하는 말은 같이 있으면 happy하고 cheerful하다는 의미입니다. (=He's a happy fellow.)

인간관계, 성격 51 He has got a short temper. 그는 화를 잘 내거든

A Why did you say I should be careful around the boss?

B **He has got a short temper.**

A Thanks for the warning.

A 내가 왜 사장 앞에서 조심해야 한다는 거지?

B 화를 잘 내거든.

A 알려줘서 고마워.

인간관계, 성격 52 I am in bad condition. 컨디션이 안 좋아

A I don't feel well. I have a headache.

B I am very tired today. **I am in bad condition.**

C I am upset because I failed my exam yesterday.

A 몸이 안 좋아. 두통이 있어.

B 오늘 너무 피곤하네. 컨디션이 안 좋아.

C 어제 시험을 망쳐서 기분이 안 좋아.

인간관계, 성격 53 I like him, but he's so naive. 그 사람이 좋긴 한데 너무 순진하단 말야

A **I like him, but he's so naive.**

B Yes. He's got a lot to learn.

A 그 사람 좋긴 한데 너무 순진하단 말야.

B 그래. 걔는 많이 배워야 돼.

인간관계, 성격 54 He's very family-oriented. 아주 가정적인 사람이야

A My husband is taking the kids to the zoo today.

B Wow, he's a really dedicated father.

A Yes, he's great. **He's very family-oriented.**

A 남편이 오늘 애들 데리고 동물원에 가.

B 와, 정말 헌신적인 아버지네.

A 응, 최고야. 아주 가정적인 사람이야.

인간관계, 성격 55 No spring chicken.

더 이상 영계가 아니라고

A Wow. I am exhausted today. I stayed out until 3 a.m. last night with some old college buddies.

B 3 a.m.? That's it? You used to be a real party animal.

A Yeah, but that was years ago. I'm **no spring chicken.**

A 와, 오늘 정말 피곤하다. 어제 예전 대학 친구들을 만나서 새벽 3시까지 놀았거든.

B 3시? 겨우? 너 파티광이었잖아.

A 그건 예전 얘기지. 나는 더 이상 영계가 아니라고!

인간관계, 성격 56 I don't think we were a good match.

서로 잘 안 맞는 것 같아

A Hey Brian, how was your blind date with Jane?

B Well, she was very pretty, but **I don't think we were a good match.** We don't have anything in common.

A 브라이언, 제인하고 한 소개팅 어땠어?

B 정말 예쁘기는 한데 서로 잘 안 맞는 것 같아. 공통점이 하나도 없어.

인간관계, 성격 57 He's a brown-noser.

그는 아첨꾼이야

A Have you seen how Kim is acting? He's desperately trying to impress th boss!

B **He's a brown-noser!**

A I know-he's even volunteered to pick up the boss's laundry for him.

A 김씨 하는 거 봤어? 상사에게 잘 보이려고 아주 난리던데!

B 그는 아첨꾼이야!

A 맞아. 자진해서 상사 세탁물까지 찾아다 준다니까!

CHAPTER 11

교통

교통 01 I locked myself out of the car. 나 차에다 열쇠 두고 잠갔어

A I'm completely scatterbrained.
I locked myself out of the car again.
B Did you get your car key back?
A Fortunately, I know the number of a locksmith.
B If you are that absentminded, you should always carry a spare key in your wallet.

A 나 진짜 정신없다.
또 차에다 열쇠를 두고 잠갔어.
B 열쇠 다시 찾았어?
A 다행이 열쇠 수리공 전화번호를 알고 있어.
B 그렇게 정신이 없으면 열쇠 하나 더 만들어서 항상 지갑에 넣고 다녀야겠다.

교통 02 Pull over as soon as you can 되도록 빨리 차를 한쪽으로 세워

A I think that the officer in the police car wants you to pull over. He's flashing his lights.
B I guess he saw me make that illegal U-turn.
A Maybe it's about something else. But, **pull over as soon as you can.**
B Right. I don't want him to think I'm trying to start a high-speed car chase.

A 순찰차 안에 있는 경찰관이 차를 세우라는 것 같아.
B 내가 불법 유턴한 걸 본 거 같아.
A 다른 거 때문일지도 몰라. 그래도 되도록 빨리 차를 한쪽으로 세워.
B 그래. 우리가 과속 추월 경쟁을 하려 했다고 생각하지 않았음 좋겠다.

교통 03 Parking is going to be murder 주차하기가 아주 힘들 거예요

A **Parking is going to be murder.**
B I'm sure they have a giant lot; we'll be fine.
A Listen. We're going to get three early and take the best spot, right beside the exit.
B Right. It's a long walk to the gate, but then really easy to leave on the way home.

A 주차하기가 아주 힘들 거요.
B 주차장이 넓어서 괜찮을 거예요.
A 잠깐만요. 일찍 가서 출구 바로 옆 제일 좋은 자리에 차를 댑시다.
B 그래요. 입구까지는 한참 걸어야 하지만 귀가 길은 아주 쉽겠네요.

교통 04 We need short-term parking | 단기주차로 해야겠다

A We'll only be gone for a few days, so I guess **we need short-term parking.**

B Short-term is for less than a day. We need long-term.

A This is so complicated! Why didn't we just take a cab to the airport?

B Because taxis can be expensive. With the flat rate, parking is only about ten bucks a day.

A 며칠만 다녀올 거니까 단기주차로 해야 할 거 같아.

B 단기주차는 하루 미만을 말하는 거야. 우리는 장기주차를 해야 돼.

A 이거 너무 복잡하다! 공항까지 택시 탈 걸 그랬나?

B 택시는 비싸잖아. 균일요금이라서 주차비는 하루에 10달러 정도 밖에 안 해.

교통 05 The parts you can't see are called blind spots. | 보이지 않는 곳을 사각지대라고 합니다

A The rearview mirror is too small. I can't see everything behind me.

B **The parts you can't see are called blind spots.**

A Isn't it dangerous if I can't see all the cars behind me?

B Don't worry. You can see them in the side-view mirrors.

A 백미러가 너무 작아서 뒤에 안 보이는 게 많네요.

B 보이지 않는 곳을 사각지대라고 합니다. 모든 차에 다 있죠.

A 뒤에 오는 차를 다 볼 수 없으면 위험하지 않나요?

B 걱정 마세요. 사이드미러로도 뒤에 오는 차를 볼 수 있어요.

교통 06 That guy's facing some stiff fines | 저 남자 엄청난 벌금을 낼 거야

A Did you see that guy? he jumped right over the turnstile without paying.

B A gate jumper. Don't sorry, though, the transit police will catch him.

A Well, it's not like it's a serious crime. The subway's not expensive.

B Sure, but nowadays the transit police are very strict. **That guy's facing some stiff fines.**

A 저 남자 봤어? 요금을 안 내고 개찰구 위로 뛰어넘어갔어.

B 불법 개찰자인데, 걱정 마. 교통경찰이 저 사람을 잡을 거야.

A 심각한 범죄는 아닌 거 같네. 지하철 요금이 비싼 것도 아니니까.

B 그렇긴 한데, 요즘 교통경찰은 아주 엄해. 저 남자는 엄청난 벌금을 낼 거야.

교통 07 You almost rear-ended it. | 추돌할 뻔했어요

A You're too close to the red car in front of you.

B But if I leave too much space, another car will try to get in front of me.

A Watch out! You almost hit that red car. **You almost rear-ended it.**

B It stopped so suddenly. I guess I should stay a bit back.

A 앞에 있는 빨간색 차와 너무 붙었어요.

B 그런데 차간 거리를 너무 많이 두면 다른 차가 앞에 끼어들려고 해요.

A 조심해요! 저 빨간색 차를 칠 뻔했어요. 추돌할 뻔했다고요.

B 저 차가 갑자기 멈췄어요. 좀 거리를 떼야겠군요.

교통 08 He pulled out in front of me without even signaling! | 저 사람이 신호도 없이 내 앞으로 끼어들었어

A Did you see what that guy just did? **He pulled out in front of me without even signaling!**

B That's really dangerous. I wish people would use their indicators when changing lanes.

A And they should shoulder-check, too.

A 저 사람 봤어? 신호도 없이 내 앞으로 끼어들었어!

B 정말 위험하네. 차선을 바꿀 때 사람들이 깜빡이를 켜야할 텐데.

A 그리고 고개를 돌려서 옆쪽도 잘 살펴야 해.

교통 09 Buying a car would cost me an arm and a leg. | 차 사려면 너무 비싸

A Talking three different busses to work is killing me.

B Why don't you buy a car then?

A **Buying a car would cost me an arm and a leg.**

B I'm sure if you shop around you can find a car that is within your means.

A 버스 두 번씩 갈아타고 출근하기 힘들어 죽겠어.

B 차를 한 대 사는 게 어때?

A 요즘에 차 사려면 기둥 뿌리 뽑히잖아.

B 돌아다녀 보면 네 예산에 맞는 차를 분명히 찾을 수 있을거야.

교통 10 It gets much steeper here. | 여기 점점 가팔라지네

A **It gets much steeper here.**

B This will tire us out.

A At least it will be downhill on the way home.

A 여기 점점 가팔라지네.

B 우린 완전히 기진맥진해질 거야.

A 그래도 집으로 가는 길은 내리막길이야.

교통 11 My car got rear-ended. | 내 차가 뒤에서 받혔다고

A My car is in the shop again.

B When are you going to start driving more carefully?

A But this time it wasn't my fault! **My car got rear-ended.**

A 내 차가 또 정비소에 들어갔어.

B 넌 언제쯤 주의를 하며 운전할래?

A 이번엔 내 잘못이 아니야. 내 차가 뒤에서 받혔다고.

교통 12 They closed a lane of traffic up ahead. | 앞에 길 하나를 막았어

A We are moving at a snail's pace.

B **They closed a lane of traffic up ahead.**

A Everything always bottlenecks when drivers have to merge.

A 완전히 달팽이 속도로 움직이네.

B 앞에 길 하나를 막았어.

A 차가 합류되는 지점에는 늘 병목현상이 있게 마련이지.

교통 13 How long will the next bus be? | 다음 버스가 올 때까지 얼마나 오래 기다려야 하나요?

A **How long will the next bus be?**

B About ten minutes.

A Really? How often do the buses run on this route?

B Every 20 minutes or so.

A That's not too bad.

A 다음 버스가 오려면 얼마나 걸릴 것 같습니까?

B 약 10분요.

A 그래요? 이 노선의 버스들은 얼마나 자주 다닙니까?

B 약 20분마다 다닙니다.

A 그렇게 나쁜 편은 아니군요.

교통 14 It's got a lot of pickup. 이 차는 아주 빠릅니다

A What makes this car so special?

B **It's got a lot of pickup.**

A I like fast cars.

A 이 차는 뭐가 특별한가요?

B 이 차는 가속이 아주 좋습니다.

A 저는 빠른 차를 좋아해요.

■ 차를 운전할 때 속도를 내는 것을 영어로 pickup이라고 합니다.

CHAPTER 12

속담

속담 01 Time and tide will wait for no man. 시간은 사람을 기다려주지 않는다

Hey, Jess. It's me, Michael. I was wondering if you are still interested in the blind date I mentioned the other day. I have talked to my friend, Joshua about you and he is really dying to see you. I was thinking you guys will meet each other this Friday evening. Drop me a line if you are okay with it. I have a hunch that you guys will make a good couple. **Time and tide will wait for no man.**

제스, 나 마이클이야. 네가 아직도 전에 내가 말한 소개팅에 관심이 있는지 궁금해. 내 친구 조슈아한테 네 얘길 했더니 보고 싶어 난리야. 내 생각엔 너희들 이번 주 금요일에 서로 만났으면 좋겠는데 만약에 괜찮으면 연락해 줘. 너희 둘 잘 될 것 같은 예감이 들어. 시간은 사람을 기다려주지 않아.

속담 02 A man is known by the company he keeps. 친구를 보면 그 사람을 알 수 있다

Hey, Michael. It's me, Jess. Thanks for setting me up with Joshua. Actually I'm not fond of meeting strangers, but I'm going to give it a shot. I'm sure he will be good natured like you just like in the saying **"A man is known by the company he keeps."** I'll be in touch after the date.

마이클, 나 제스야. 조슈아랑 소개팅 주선해 준 것 고마워. 사실 나 낯선 사람들 만나는 것 좋아하지 않지만 그래도 한 번 도전해 보려고. '친구를 보면 그 사람을 알 수 있다'는 속담도 있듯이 그 사람도 분명히 너처럼 성격이 좋을 거야. 데이트 끝나고 어떻게 됐는지 알려줄게.

속담 03 Friends and wine improve with age. 친구와 와인은 오래될수록 좋다

Michael, It's Jess. I had a great time with joshua thanks to you. He was so funny, pleasant and down-to-earth. I hope things are going to work out with him. Anyway I'm happy that we are still good friends. You've been my bosom friend ever since high school. Just like the saying goes **"Friends and wine improve with age."**, let's keep our friendship forever.

마이클, 나 제스야. 덕분에 죠슈아랑 정말 좋은 시간을 보냈어. 그 사람 진짜 재밌고 유쾌해. 그리고 현실적이기도 하고. 나 그 사람이랑 잘 됐으면 좋겠어. 그나저나 우리가 아직 친한 친구라는 것이 기쁘다. 넌 고등학교 때부터 나의 가장 친한 친구잖아. '친구와 와인은 오래될수록 좋다'는 속담처럼 우리 우정 평생 지키자.

속담 04 There's light at the end of the tunnel | 고생 끝에 낙이 있다

A Keeping this resolution to do better in school is nearly killing me.

B Really? What is the hardest part?

A No matter how much I study, there's always another test just around he corner.

B **There's light at the end of the tunnel.** keep your eye on the prize: graduation.

A 학교 성적을 올리겠다는 결심을 지키느라 거의 죽을뻔했어.

B 그래? 어떤 게 가장 어려웠어?

A 아무리 공부를 많이 해도 시험이 끊일 새가 없더라고.

B 고생 끝에 낙이 오는 법이야. 네가 받을 상을 생각해. 졸업 말이야.

속담 05 The icing on the cake. | 금상첨화

A It sounds like you got a really good deal on your car.

B But that's not it. There's more.

A What more could there possibly be?

B Well, **the** real **icing on the cake** is that my dad is going to pay for the whole thing.

A 너 차 정말 싸게 잘 산 것 같아.

B 그게 전부가 아니야. 또 있다니깐.

A 또 뭐가 있는데?

B 음, 진짜 금상첨화인 것은 바로 우리 아빠가 돈을 전부 내주실 거라는 거지.

속담 06 Curiosity killed the cat | 너무 많이 알려고 하면 다친다

A Come on. Tell me what's in the bag.

B No way. It's a secret.

A I just have to know what's in there.

B You know what they say. **Curiosity killed the cat.**

A 야, 가방 안에 뭐가 있는지 말 좀 해봐.

B 절대 안 돼. 비밀이야.

A 난 거기 뭐가 들었는지 알아야만 하겠어.

B 너 사람들이 하는 말 알지? 너무 많이 알려고 하면 다친다니까.

속담 07 Everyone has a skeleton in his closet. 털어서 먼지 안 나는 사람 없다

A Michael Bang has said that he is running for Congress.

B Really?

I don't think he is qualified to be a lawmaker.

A Why not?

B He is dirt, didn't you know that?

A Well, **everyone has a skeleton in his closet.**

A 마이클 뱅이 국회의원으로 출마한대.

B 정말? 그 친구는 국회의원이 될 자격이 없는데.

A 왜?

B 그 친구는 쓰레기 같은 인간이야. 몰랐어?

A 글쎄, 털어서 먼지 안 나는 사람은 없어.

속담 08 The opera's never over fill the fat lady sings. 사람 팔자 시간문제다

A I hear that Kenny made a fortune in the garbage hauling business. Is that true?

B Yes, that's true.

A As I know, he was down and out after filing for bankruptcy.

B Right. But he didn't throw his hands. He began to haul garbage, and made over a million dollars.

A Really? Well, **the opera's never over till fat lady sings.**

A 케니가 쓰레기 수거사업에서 큰돈을 벌었다는데 사실이니?

B 응. 맞아.

A 나는 케니가 파산신고를 하고는 완전히 망한 것으로 알고 있거든.

B 맞아. 그러나 포기하지 않고 쓰레기수거를 시작해서 1백만 달러 이상을 벌었데.

A 정말? 음. 사람 팔자 시간문제로군.

속담 09 Nobody likes a back-seat driver! 뒤에서 감 놔라 배 놔라 하는 거 좋아하는 사람 없어

A You should have filled up with gas at the last gas station.

B And, are you sure that this is the fastest way to get to the restaurant?

A Hey, **nobody likes a back-seat driver!**

A 이전 주유소에서 기름을 넣었어야지.

B 그리고 이게 식당가는 가장 빠른 길 맞아?

A 야, 뒤에서 감 놔라 배 놔라 하는 거 좋아하는 사람 없어!

속담 10 Time is on your side. 시간이 해결해 줄 거야

A I don't know if I should sell my apartment now, or wait for the prices to rise.

B Prices are sure to go up over the next year, so you should wait. **Time is on your side.**

A You're probably right.

A 아파트를 지금 매도해야 할지 가격이 오를 때까지 기다려야 할지 모르겠네.

B 매매가는 내년에도 고공행진일 테니 기다려봐. 시간이 해결해 줄 거야.

A 네 말이 맞는 거 같아.

속담 11 It runs in the family. 피는 못 속인다

A I heard your daughter won a prize at the science fair.

B Yes. I'm very proud of her. She worked so hard on her project.

A Well, I guess **it runs in the family.**

B Yeah, she gets it from her mother!

A 네 딸이 과학전람회에서 상 탔다며.

B 응, 너무 자랑스러워. 연구 과제를 진짜 열심히 준비했거든.

A 피는 못 속이나 보네.

B 맞아. 엄마를 닮아서 그래.

속담 12 Clean up your act. 행동 조심해라 점잖게 행동해라

A **Clean up your act,** Steven. I'm afraid you're giving your family a bad name.

B If I'm giving my folks a bad reputation, that's none of your business.

A No wonder they say you are the black sheep of your family.

B Look, Kenny! Mind your own business, will you?

A 스티븐, 행동 좀 조심해라. 네 집안 망신을 시키고 있잖아.

B 내가 집안 망신을 시킨다고 해서 네가 상관할 바는 아니잖아.

A 사람들이 너를 집안의 말썽꾸러기라 부르는 것도 무리가 아니군.

B 이봐 케니! 넌 네 일이나 신경 쓰지 그래?

CHAPTER 13

미용실에서

미용실에서 01 You've got split ends. 머리카락 끝이 갈라졌네요

A **You've got split ends.** I can fix that by trimming your hair all the way around your head.

B Thank you. You're a skilled and attentive hair stylist.

A 머리카락 끝이 갈라졌네요. 제가 전체적으로 다듬어 드릴게요.

B 감사합니다. 실력도 있고 정말 세심하시네요.

미용실에서 02 That haircut suits you. 그 헤어스타일 너한테 딱인데

A I look very different with this haircut.

B But it seems to reflect your personality. **That haircut suits you.**

A 이 머리 스타일을 하니까 나같지 않은데.

B 근데 네 분위기에 잘 맞는 것 같아. 그 헤어스타일 너한테 딱인데.

미용실에서 03 I'd like a trim. 조금만 다듬어주세요

A Do you want me to cut your hair in an entirely new style?

B No, **I'd like a trim.**

A 혹시 머리를 잘라서 헤어스타일을 확 바꾸고 싶으세요?

B 아니오, 그냥 다듬어 주세요.

미용실에서 04 I'd like a sensible haircut. 저는 보수적인 헤어스타일이 좋아요

A I could shave one side of your head, if you want.

B No! **I'd like a sensible haircut.**

A 원하시면 제가 머리 한쪽을 밀어드릴 수 있는데요.

B 됐어요! 저는 보수적인 헤어스타일이 좋아요.

미용실에서 05 I usually wear my hair up. 저는 보통 머리를 위로 묶고 다녀요

A **I usually wear my hair up.**

B But you have beautiful hair. You should let it fall down your neck and back.

A 저는 보통 머리를 위로 묶고 다녀요.

B 하지만 손님 머리는 너무 아름다워요. 그냥 목이랑 등으로 흘러내리게 하세요.

미용실에서 06 Give me a buzz. 기계로 짧게 밀어주세요

A Do you want me to keep your hair long?

B No, **give me a buzz.**

A 머리를 길게 놔둘까요?

B 아니요, 기계로 짧게 밀어주세요.

미용실에서 07 Do you think I'd look better with bangs? 앞머리를 가지런히 자르는 게 더 나은 것 같니?

A **Do you think I'd look better with bangs?**

B I generally don't like them. They look too square.

A Really? But I had bangs when we first met.... And you said you liked them.

B I lied. I was so happy when you grew them out.

A 앞머리를 가지런히 자르는 게 더 나은 것 같니?

B 난 대체적으로 앞머리 있는 걸 안 좋아해. 너무 고리타분해 보이잖아.

A 그래? 하지만 우리 처음 만났을 때 난 앞머리가 있었어. 네가 좋다고 했고.

B 거짓말했어. 네 앞머리가 자라니까 정말 좋더라.

미용실에서 08 Please hold your head still. 머리를 움직이지 마세요

A Wow! I have to turn around to look at this woman who just walked in.

B **Please hold your head still.**

A 와! 방금 들어온 여자를 보려면 고개를 돌려야 하는데.

B 머리를 움직이지 마세요.

CHAPTER 14

전화에서

전화에서 01 Please hold. 끊지 말고 기다리세요

A Thank you for calling e-bay. How may I help you?

B Yes. I just bought a scanner from your online shopping network, and I have a question about my bill.

A I'll connect you to the billing department, sir. **Please hold.** (Seconds later) I am sorry, sir. But all the lines are busy at the moment. Would you hold until the next representative becomes available?

A 이베이입니다. 전화 주셔서 감사합니다. 어떻게 도와드릴까요?

B 네. 얼마 전에 온라인 쇼핑 네트워크에서 스캐너를 구입했는데 청구서에 관해 질문이 있어서요.

A 대금 결제부로 연결해드리겠습니다. 끊지 말고 기다리십시오. (잠시 후) 죄송합니다만 지금 모든 선이 통화 중입니다. 다음 상담 직원을 기다리시겠습니까?

전화에서 02 Could you put me through? 전화 연결 부탁해요

A Acme manufacturing, may I help you?

B Yes, please. this is Otto Kunstler from Swiss Trading Associates calling for Tom jones is in?

A Do you know which Department Mr. Jones is in?

B I think he's in Marketing. Could you look it up for me?

A No trouble. Hmm, it looks like he's in advertising

B Thank you. **Could you put me through, please?**

A 애크미 제조 회사입니다. 제가 도와드릴 일이 있을까요?

B 네, 저는 스위스 무역협회의 오토 쿤슬러인데 톰 존스씨와 통화하고 싶습니다.

A 톰 존스씨가 어느 부서에 계신지요?

B 마케팅 부서에 계신다고 알고 있어요. 확인해 주시겠습니까?

A 물론이죠. 음, 그 분은 홍보부에 계시네요.

B 감사합니다. 전화 연결 부탁드립니다.

전화에서 03 His extension is 1818. 그의 내선 번호는 1818입니다

A How can I reach George Bush?

B **His extension is 1818.** In the future you can use that number to dial straight to his office.

A 조지 부시와 통화하려면 어떻게 해야 하나요?

B 그의 내선 번호는 1818입니다. 앞으로는 그 번호를 돌리면 바로 그분 사무실로 연결됩니다.

전화에서 04 I'm just calling to say hi. 그냥 안부 전화한 거야

A Hi, Tommy.

B Hi, Steve. is anything the matter?

A No, not at all. **I'm just calling to say hi.**

A 안녕, 타미.

B 안녕, 스티브. 무슨 일 있니?

A 아니, 없어. 그냥 안부 전화한 거야.

전화에서 05 I'll have him get back to you. 바로 연락하라고 할게요

A Hello, may I please speak to Bruce?

B Sorry, he's asleep, **I'll have him get back to you.**

A All right, thank you.

A 여보세요, 브루스 좀 바꿔주실래요?

B 미안하지만 자고 있거든요. 나중에 연락하라고 할게요.

A 알겠습니다, 고마워요.

전화에서 06 Can you hold, please? 잠시만 기다려주실래요?

A Hello, may I please speak to Mr. Williams?

B Yes. **Can you hold please?**

A Yes, I'll hold.

A 여보세요, 윌리엄스 씨 좀 바꿔주시겠어요?

B 예, 잠시만 기다려주실래요?

A 그러죠, 기다릴게요.

■ 전화를 끊지 말고 잠시만 기다려달라고 할 때 사용하는 표현으로, "Just a moment.", "Wait a minute!"보다 더 많이 쓰인다.

전화에서 07 The reception is pretty poor. 수신이 잘 안 돼

A I can't hear this station well.

There is a lot of static, which hurts my ears.

B Yes, **the reception is pretty poor.**

Let's listen to another station instead.

A 이 방송을 잘 들을 수가 없어.

잡음이 너무 많아서 귀가 아플 지경이야.

B 맞아, 수신이 잘 안돼.

차라리 다른 방송 듣자.

■ 요즘은 이런 경우가 거의 없지만 라디오의 수신 음질이 안 좋을 때 poor를 씁니다.

전화에서 08 The lines seem to be mixed up. | 전화가 혼선이 된 것 같습니다

A Is this Soongsil University?

B Yes, it is.

C No. You have the wrong number.

A **The lines seem to be mixed up.**

I'll hang up and call again.

B All right.

A 숭실대학교입니까?

B 네, 그렇습니다.

C 아니요. 잘못 거셨습니다.

A 혼선이 된 것 같군요.

끊었다 다시 걸죠.

B 그렇게 하세요.

전화에서 09 I'm sorry I'm calling at this late hour. | 이렇게 늦게 전화를 걸어 죄송합니다

A Hi, Kenny, how are you? This is Tom.

I'm sorry I'm calling at this late hour.

B It's Okay. What's the matter with you?

A Bad news.

I hope I'm not calling at a bad time.

B No, not at all.

A 안녕, 케니, 잘 지냈니? 나 탐이야.

늦은 시간에 전화 걸어 미안해.

B 괜찮아. 무슨 일이야?

A 나쁜 소식인데.

내가 좋지 않은 때에 전화를 하는 건지 모르겠다.

B 아니, 괜찮아.

전화에서 10 I'm calling from a pay phone. | 공중전화로 전화하는 거야

A Hi, Sandy. **I'm calling from a pay phone.** Could you give me the directions to your house again?

B Yes, turn left on Elm Street and then turn right on Oak Street.

A 안녕, 샌디. 공중전화로 전화하는 건데, 너희 집 가는 길 좀 다시 알려줄래?

B 그래, 엘름 가에서 좌회전한 다음에 오크 가에서 우회전하면 돼.

11 No one by that name lives here. 여기 그런 사람 없는데요

A Hi, is Michael there?

B **No one by that name lives here.**

What number were you calling?

A I was calling 351-5081.

I must have the wrong number.

A 안녕하세요. 마이클 있나요?

B 여기 그런 사람 없는데요. 몇 번으로 전화하셨죠?

A 351–5081로 했는데, 제가 전화를 잘못 걸었나 봐요.

CHAPTER 15

우편

우편 01 Can you have it sent by express mail? 속달 우편으로 보내주시겠어요?

A Did you bring a sample of model No. 65-K with you?

B Oh my god. It completely slipped my mind.
I'm sorry about that

A No problem. **Can you have it sent by express mail?**

B Sure thing. I'll get on the phone right away and have the company rush it off.

A 모델 65-K 의 견본을 갖고 오셨나요?

B 이럴 수가 있나. 깜빡 잊어버렸습니다.
죄송합니다.

A 그럴 수도 있죠. 속달로 보내주실 수 있죠?

B 물론입니다. 당장 회사에 전화를 걸어 빠리 보내도록 하겠습니다.

우편 02 I'll have it rushed off to you. 서둘러 보내드리겠습니다

A How soon will you send me the contract for the order of Cell-phones we talked about yesterday?

B I'll have our president sign it first, and sed it on to you by the 15th at the latest. So, after your boss signs off on it, please return one of the originals to me. We need it very urgently so we can order the raw materials.

A In that case, **I'll have it rushed off to you.**

A 오늘 상담했던 휴대전화 주문에 대한 계약서를 언제쯤 보내 주시겠습니까?

B 먼저 사장님의 서명을 받은 다음 늦어도 15일까지 보내 드리겠습니다. 그러나 귀사 사장님의 서명을 받은 뒤 원본 중 한 부를 제게 보내 주십시오. 원자재 주문용으로 매우 급하게 필요하니까요.

A 그러시다면, 서둘러 보내 드리겠습니다.

우편 03 We have priority mail and overnight express mail. 특급 우편과 속달 우편이 있습니다

A I would like to send this package to LA.
What kind of service do you recommend?

B I recommend **priority mail or overnight express mail.**

A How long does each take?

B Overnight express arrives within 24 hours and priority takes about 2 to 4 days.

A 이 소포를 LA로 보내고 싶은데요.
어떤 서비스를 권해 주시겠어요?

B 특급 우편 또는 속달 우편을 권합니다.

A 각각 얼마나 시간이 걸려요?

B 속달 우편은 24시간 이내, 특급 우편은 2~4일 정도 걸립니다.

우편 04 I'm getting too many flyers in my mailbox 우편함에 광고지가 너무 많이 와요

A **I'm getting too many flyers in my mailbox.**

B There is nothing we can do about that here.

We're not the ones delivering them.

A You're not? But then who is?

B Different companies. If you don't want flyers, put a "No Flyers" sticker on your mailbox.

A 우편함에 광고지가 너무 많이 와요.

B 저희는 어떻게 할 방법이 없습니다.

우체국에서 보내는 게 아니거든요.

A 여기서 보내는 게 아니라고요? 그럼 누가 보내나요?

B 다른 회사들이요. 광고지를 받지 않으려면 '광고지 사절' 스티커를 우편함에 붙이세요.

우편 05 The mail is always slow around the holidays 우편물 배송이 연휴 때는 항상 느려져

A Have you made your list yet?

B List? Oh, you mean my Christmas list. Sure. I already gave it to Mom.

A Why would you give it to her?

I'm mailing mine directly to the Big Man at the North Pole.

B I hope it gets there in time.

The mail is always slow around the holidays.

A 목록 만들었니?

B 목록? 아, 크리스마스 선물 목록 말이지? 그럼, 벌써 엄마께 드렸지.

A 왜 엄마한테 드려?

난 북극에 있는 산타할아버지한테 직접 우편으로 보냈어.

B 늦지 않게 도착해야 할 텐데.

우편물 배송이 연휴 때는 항상 느려지잖아.

CHAPTER 16

축제, 관람, 체험

축제, 관람, 체험 01 Did you get the right tickets?

티켓 제대로 끊었어요?

A **Did you get the right tickets?**

B I think so…. It's really complicated.

A Well, there are five of us, two adults and three kids. And we need ticktets that cover the entrance fees and unlimited redes.

B Let me double-check.

A 티켓 제대로 끊었어요?

B 그런 것 같아요. 정말 복잡하더라고요.

A 성인 둘, 애들 셋, 모두 다섯 명이에요. 그리고 입장료와 자유이용권이 포함된 티켓이어야 해요.

B 다시 확인해볼게요.

축제, 관람, 체험 02 They might really like the merry-go-round

아이들이 회전목마를 정말 좋아할 거 같아요

A Let's take the kids on the Ferris wheel.

B Or, **they might really like the merry-go-round.**

A But they might not want to go on te kiddie rides.
Maybe they've outgrown them.

B We could try the bigger rides.
You'll have to take them on, though. I'm too afraid!

A 아이들을 페리스 관람차에 태웁시다.

B 아니면 회전목마도 정말 좋아할 거 같아요.

A 근데 애들이나 타는 건 안 타려고 할 거예요.
그런거 타기엔 이제 컸으니까요.

B 더 큰 놀이기구를 타도 되겠네요.
그럼 당신이 애들 데리고 타요. 난 너무 무서워요!

축제, 관람, 체험 03 There's a shuttle bus that runs all the time

항시 운행하는 셔틀버스가 있어

A How are we supposed to get all these bags all the way over there?

B Don't worry.
There's a shuttle bus that runs all the time.

A Great. Where does it pick us up?

B That's the best part. It just drives up and down the lot looking for people.

A 이 가방을 어떻게 다 저기까지 가져가지?

B 걱정 마.
셔틀버스가 수시로 다녀.

A 그거 좋은데. 어디서 타는 거야?

B 제일 좋은 게 그거야. 오고 가다가 사람을 보면 태워주지.

축제, 관람, 체험 04 Is this ride scary? 이 놀이기구 무서운가요?

A Are you all ready? Remember to keep your arms and legs inside the ride at all times.

B OK. Hey, **is this ride scary?**

A Well.... there's a big drop and then the loop deloop.

B Sounds good. Can you just check the safety bar one more time?

A 준비 다 되셨나요?
팔다리는 항상 안쪽에 두셔야 합니다.

B 알겠어요. 이봐요. 이 놀이기구 무서운가요?

A 글쎄요. 크게 한 번 낙하한 다음 공중회전을 하죠.

B 재미있겠네요. 안전바를 한 번 더 확인해주실래요?

축제, 관람, 체험 05 It'll make a great souvenir 멋진 기념품이 될 거에요

A Look over there by the drink stand.
Isn't that Charlie the Mouse?

B Sure. Look over there, kids.
It's your favorite character, Charlie.

A Look at all the kids kicking the poor guy.

B Let's go over and get our picture taken with him.
It'll make a great souvenir.

A 저쪽 음료수매점 옆에 좀 봐요.
저거 마우스 찰리 아니에요?

B 맞아요. 얘들아 저기 좀 봐라.
너희가 좋아하는 캐릭터 찰리야.

A 아이들 모두 불쌍한 찰리 아저씨를 발로 차고 있네요.

B 저기 가서 찰리와 사진 찍어요. 멋진 기념이 될 거에요.

축제, 관람, 체험 06 What are the hours of operation? 개관 시간이 어떻게 되죠?

A **What are the hours of operation?**

B The museum is open from 9AM to 6PM, Monday through Saturday.

A That's too bad.
I was hopping to see the exhibit on Sunday.

A 개관 시관이 어떻게 되죠?

B 박물관은 월요일부터 토요일까지 오전 9시에서 오후 6시 사이에 엽니다.

A 아쉽네요.
일요일에 전시회를 보려고 했는데.

축제, 관람, 체험 07 I'm getting goosebumps

소름, 닭살 돋다

A This movie is so scary

B Hey, this isn't scary at all.

This movie is for little kids!

A No, it's not oh no! That monster is horrible!

I'm getting goosebumps!

B That "monster" is just a cute little elf!

What's the matter with you? You should try to relax. It's not real. it's just a movie!

A but how can you be so sure?

Maybe this is a documentary and you don't even know it.

B No more of such nonsense!

How can this be a documentary?

A 이 영화 너무 무서워.

B 이봐 전혀 무섭지 않아.

이 영화는 어린이들이 보는 영화라고.

A 아니야. 그렇지 않아. 저 괴물 너무 무서워. 나 소름 돋은 거 봐.

B 저 "괴물"은 그저 귀여운 꼬마 요정일 뿐이야.

너 괜찮니? 진정해 저건 사실이 아니야 영화일 뿐이라고.

A 하지만 어떻게 확신해?

어쩌면 이건 다큐멘터리고 내가 그것을 모르고 있을지도.

B 이상한 소리 좀 그만 해!

이게 어떻게 다큐멘터리가 될 수 있니?

축제, 관람, 체험 08 I'm so pumped to see Death Purge live

데스펄지의 라이브 공연을 보다니 정말 설렌다

A It's the night of the big concert.

I'm so pumped to see Death Purge live.

B I heard they put on a really great show.

There're tons of dancers.

A I heard the bass player spits fire from his mouth.

B Awesome. Don't forget to bring your camera!

A 오늘 밤 멋진 공연이 펼쳐져.

데스펄지의 라이브 공연을 보다니 정말 설렌다.

B 굉장한 쇼가 펼쳐진대.

댄서들도 많이 나오고.

A 베이스 연주자가 입에서 불을 뿜는 쇼도 선보인다고 하더라.

B 멋지다. 카메라 가져오는 거 잊지마!

축제, 관람, 체험 09 Do you have a student discount?

학생할인 되나요?

A I would like a ticket for the Smithsonian, please.

B That will be $23, please.

A **Do you have a student discount rate?**

I'm an international student on vacation.

A 스미스소니언 입장권 하나 주세요.

B $23입니다.

A 학생할인 되나요? 여행 중인 국제학생인데요.

축제, 관람, 체험 10 I don't want to be in the nose bleed section

제일 높이 있는 맨 뒷자리에 앉고 싶지 않아

A So, which tickets should we get? Front row, center?

B Aren't those a bit expensive?

A We could get something a bit further back.

But I want to be close enough to really see the band.

B I know.

I don't want to be in the nose bleed section.

A 자, 어느 자리로 표를 살까? 앞쪽 줄, 가운데?

B 거기는 좀 비싸지 않을까?

A 좀 더 뒤쪽 자리를 사야 할 것 같아. 하지만 밴드가 보일 정도는 돼야 하는데.

B 그러게. 제일 뒤쪽 높이 있는 자리에 앉고 싶진 않아.

축제, 관람, 체험 11 It must be wall to wall people in there.

저기 안에 사람들로 발 디딜 틈이 없을 거야

A Look at all the cars!

It must be wall to wall people in there.

B What did you expect?

There are a lot of big sales going on.

A Do you think we'll be able to find a place to park? Do you see any empty spots?

B There's one over there. See it?

Grab it before someone else.

A 저 차들 좀 봐!

쇼핑몰에 사람들로 발 디딜 틈이 없을 거야.

B 당연한 거 아니야?

대대적인 세일들을 하고 있잖아.

A 주차할 곳을 찾을 수 있을까?

빈 공간 보이니?

B 저기 하나 있다. 보이지?

축제, 관람, 체험 12 Those gorillas sure make a racket

저 고릴라들은 화가 난 게 분명해

A Let's go to the monkey house.

B It's just around the corner. Can you heart that?

Those gorillas sure make a racket.

A I can hear one beating his chest.

B Maybe someone looked at them wrong.

Making direct eye contact is a sigh of aggression.

A 원숭이 우리로 가보자.

B 모퉁이를 돌면 바로 있어. 저 소리 들려?

고릴라들이 화가 난 게 분명해.

A 가슴을 치는 소리가 들리네.

B 누가 고릴라를 잘못 쳐다봤나 봐.

눈을 똑바로 마주치면 공격을 하겠다는 뜻으로 알거든.

축제, 관람, 체험 13 Sound the alarm!

비상벨을 울려!

A Holy cow! That bird escaped from its cage.

Sound the alarm!

B The peacock? Don't worry.

It's allowed to roam free.

A Aren't the zookeepers worried that it'll run away?

B Why would it ever want to leave?

It's more than happy to hang out and steal food from the kids here.

A 저런! 저 새가 새장에서 나왔어.

비상벨을 울려!

B 공작새 말하는 거야? 걱정 마.

자유롭게 돌아다니도록 나둔 거야.

A 공작새가 도망갈까 봐 사육사들은 걱정이 안 되나?

B 왜 도망가고 싶겠어?

어슬렁거리며 여기 온 아이들 음식이나 뺏어먹는 게 더 좋을 텐데.

CHAPTER 17

공항에서

공항에서 01 The runways are a bit backed up. 활주로에 비행기들이 좀 밀려있습니다

A The captain has just informed us that there will be a slight delay.

B Excuse me, but why the delay? Is something wrong?

A Not at all. It's just that **the runways are a bit backed up,** because it's the busy season.

B Oh. Well, I hope it's our turn soon.

A 기장은 비행기 이륙이 약간 지연될 거라고 알려왔습니다.

B 실례지만, 왜 지연된 건가요? 뭐가 잘못됐나요?

A 아닙니다. 활주로에 이륙할 비행기들이 좀 밀려있을 뿐입니다. 성수기잖아요.

B 아, 그럼 우리 차례가 빨리 왔음 좋겠네요.

공항에서 02 How many bags will you be checking? 가방은 몇 개 부칠 건가요?

A **How many bags will you be checking,** sir?

B None. I only have this one carry-on suitcase.

A I'm sorry, sir.
That suitcase is too large for carry-on.
I'm afraid you'll have to check it.

A 가방을 몇 개 부칠 건가요?

B 없어요. 들고 탈 가방 하나만 있습니다.

A 손님, 죄송합니다만 그 가방은 가지고 타기엔 너무 큽니다. 부쳐야겠습니다.

공항에서 03 They are not allowed in. 그것들은 반입이 허용되지 않습니다

A Oh, Mr. Kim, When I go to the US, is it possible to take some dried laver with me?

B Oh, sure. Any type of agricultural products that are dried are okay, but otherwise **they are not allowed in,** because they're afraid it may spread disease among farm crops in the US.

A 아, 김 선생님, 미국에 갈 때 마른 김을 좀 갖고 들어가도 될까요?

B 아, 물론이죠. 마른 농산물이면 무엇이든 괜찮지만 그렇지 않으면 반입이 허용되지 않습니다. 미국 내의 농작물에 질병을 전파시킬지도 모르기 때문이죠.

공항에서 04 Can you put me on the standby list? 대기자 명단에 올려줄 수 있나요?

A I'm sorry ma'am, there are no seats available on that flight.

B **Can you put me on the standby list?**

I need to get to Washington as soon as possible.

A Certainly, ma'am. Please check back at 6:30

A 죄송합니다만 그 비행기는 만석입니다.

B 대기자 명단에 올려줄 수 있나요?

워싱턴으로 가능한 한 빨리 가야 하거든요.

A 알겠습니다. 6시 30분에 다시 확인해주세요.

공항에서 05 Is this a direct flight? 이 비행기 직항인가요?

A **Is this a direct flight?**

B No, ma'am. There is a stopover in Honolulu.

A Do I need to catch a connecting flight?

B No, ma'am. You don't need to get off the plane.

A 이 비행기 직항인가요?

B 아니요, 손님. 호놀룰루에서 한 번 경유합니다.

A 비행기를 갈아타야 하나요?

B 아니요. 갈아타실 필요 없습니다.

공항에서 06 It's just under the limit. 중량 초과를 겨우 면했어요

A Pleas place the first bag on the scale.

B Here we go!

It's the smallest one, so I'm sure it'll be fine.

A **It's just under the limit.**

I'll have to attack a "HEAVY" sticker to it.

B Uh oh. I better rearrange some of this stuff.

I dont's want to pay any excess baggage fees.

A 첫 번째 가방을 저울 위에 올리세요.

B 자 여기요!

가장 작은 거라서 분명 괜찮을 거예요.

A 중량 초과를 겨우 면했어요.

'과중' 스티커를 붙이겠습니다.

B 이런. 짐들을 다시 정리해야겠어요.

무게 초과비용을 내고 싶지는 않아요.

CHAPTER 18

단어

단어 01 tattletale 고자질쟁이

A I wouldn't mention that to Gloria if I were you.

B Why not? She seems a very sympathetic person.

A No, not at all. I know from experience that she's a real **tattletale**.

B Really? Well, if that's the case, I'll take your advice.

A 내가 너라면 그걸 Gloria에게 말하지 않을 텐데.

B 왜? 그녀는 인정 있는 사람인 것 같던데?

A 아니, 전혀. 내 경험으로는 그녀는 고자질쟁이야.

B 정말? 그렇다면 너의 충고를 받아들일게.

단어 02 bylaw (이사회의 구조와 해야 할 일을 정해 놓은) 내규·규칙·정관

A Did you see the minutes of the last board meetings? They **bylaws** were re-vised to reflect the company's new mission and vision.

B the board has developed an ambitious strategic plan. I agree with the new focus.

A The problem is that the board did not have a quorum when the vote was held.

A 지난번 이사회 회의록 봤어? 회사의 새로운 임무와 이상을 반영하도록 내규가 수정됐어.

B 이사회에서 야심차게 전략적인 계획을 만들어 냈지. 나는 새로 중점 둔 부분에 동의 해.

A 문제는 투표가 실시되었을 때 이사회는 정족수를 채우지 못했다는 거야.

단어 03 overstaffed 과잉인원의

A Volume we're now **overstaffed** at sales levels.

B I know. We have a lot of people sitting around doing nothing.

A The problem is that we don't know how to do with them.

B Yeah, it's turning into a real morale problem.

A 판매량이 떨어지고 있는 지금 필요이상으로 판매 직원이 많네요.

B 알고 있습니다. 아무 일도 하지 않고 빈둥대는 사람이 너무 많아요.

A 문제는 그들을 어떻게 처리해야 할지 모른다는 점이죠.

B 네. 이제는 근로의욕에 관한 문제가 되고 있어요.

단어 04 brainstorm 여러 가지 착상을 모으다, 논의해 보다

A The chairman of the board convened an emergency meeting to discuss the president's sudden resignation from the company.

B I heard the board **brainstormed** for hours about how to handle the situation.

A One member even made a motion to dissolve the company. They tabled that motion indefinitely.

A 이사회 의장이 사장님의 갑작스런 사임을 논의하기 위해서 긴급회의를 소집했어.

B 이사회에서 그 사태를 어떻게 다룰지에 대해 몇 시간 동안 브레인스토밍을 했다던데.

A 한 이사는 심지어 회사를 해산시키자는 제안까지 했어. 이사들은 그 제안을 무기한으로 연기했지만.

단어 05 downsize 감원하다

A Hello, Mrs. Seymour. How are you?

B Never better. And you?

A I was **downsized** in April, and I've been looking for work ever since.

B That's a shame.
I'll try my best to find the right job for you!

A 여보세요, 세이모어양. 안녕하세요?

B 아주 좋아요. 안녕하셨어요?

A 저는 4월에 직장에서 해고돼 그때부터 계속 일자리를 찾고 있었어요.

B 유감이네요.
당신한테 맞는 일을 찾도록 최선을 다 할게요.

단어 06 savvy 실용적인 지식

A Did you see how Tom got us free drinks at the bar? What a smooth talker!

B I know. He's got a lot of **savvy**. He knows how to make things happen.

A I could really use a friend like that.

A 술집에서 우리가 공짜 술을 얻어 마실 수 있게 톰이 어떻게 하는지 봤죠? 톰은 말주변이 참 좋아요!

B 맞아요. 그는 수완이 아주 뛰어나요. 그는 일이 되게 만드는 법을 알고 있어요.

A 톰 같은 친구가 있으면 정말 좋겠네요.

단어 07 cubicle 칸막이 방

A I heard they gave you a new desk.
You're moving up in the world.
B It's nothing. really. I don't have an office, yet.
It's just a new **cubicle.**
A I know that. But It's beside the window.
It's a cubicle with a view!

A 회사에서 새 책상을 사줬다면서요.
승진하신 거군요.
B 정말 별거 아니에요. 아직 사무실도 없어요.
그냥 칸막이 방 하나 새로 생긴 거에요.
A 알아요. 하지만 창문 옆이잖아요.
전망 좋은 칸막이 방이요!

단어 08 facelift 주름 제거 수술

A I think it's Botox. Look!
She can barely smile!
B No way. It was a **facelift.**
Just look at how tight the skin is over her cheeks.
A Nope. Definitely Botox.
I can tell. See how her forehead never moves?

A 보톡스 주사를 맞은 것 같아요. 봐요!
저 여자 잘 웃지도 못하잖아요!
B 아니에요. 주름 제거 수술을 받았어요.
양 볼의 피부가 팽팽한 것 좀 봐요.
A 아니라니까요. 분명 보톡스예요.
제가 알아요. 이마가 전혀 안 움직이는 거 보이죠?

단어 09 Dicey 불확실한

A Do you have any information relating to the O'Brian Company?
B No. Why do you want to know about the company?
A A friend of mine says I can make a lot of money if I buy stock in O'Brian.
B I wouldn't if I were you.
The chances for success are **dicey.**

A 오브라이언 회사에 관한 정보가 좀 있나요?
B 아니오. 그 회사에 관해 왜 알고 싶어하시죠?
A 제 친구가 오브라이언 주식을 사면 돈을 많이 벌거라고 해서요.
B 저라면 안 살 겁니다.
이윤을 낼 수 있을지 여부가 불확실하잖아요.

단어 10 informercial — 홈쇼핑 광고

A Are you positive that the **informercial** will work?

B Sure. An informercial is most effective way of seeling products because it lead consumers to believe everything they see.

A Yeah. But the problem is its cost, It's incredivly expensive compared to a newspaper ad.

B We have no option though.
We have to make it happen within a few months.

A 홈쇼핑 광고가 정말 효과가 있을까?

B 그럼. 홈쇼핑 광고는 소비자가 보는 대로 믿게 만들기 때문에 가장 효과적인 판매 전략이야.

A 그래. 하지만 비용이 문제야.
신문 광고에 비해 너무 비싸.

B 하지만 다른 방법이 없잖아.
우린 몇 달 내로 승부를 봐야 해.

단어 11 get-together — 모임

A I guess I'll be seeing you this Saturday.

B Saturday? Oh, no. Did we get called into work this weekend?

A Work? No, I'm talking about the **get-together** at the boss's house. It's this weekend. Sounds like you forgot all about it.

A 이번 주 토요일에 봐요.

B 토요일이요? 이런. 이번 주말에 회사에 출근하라는 통보를 받았던가요?

A 회사요? 아뇨, 사장님 댁에서 열리는 모임 얘기하는 거예요. 이번 주말이잖아요. 까맣게 잊고 있었나 보군요.

단어 12 cataract surgery — 백내장 수술

A Tom goes in for his **cataract surgery** on the fifteenth.
He's really looking forward to it.

B Really? If I were him, I'd be totally scared.
An operation.... on my eye!

A It's routine surgery.
We're not expecting any complications.

A 톰은 15일에 백내장 수술을 받아요. 그는 수술을 몹시 고대하고 있어요.

B 정말이에요? 나라면 완전히 겁먹었을 텐데.
수술을… 눈에 하는 거잖아요!

A 일상적인 수술이에요.
합병증 같은 건 없을 거예요.

단어 13 dress code — 복장 규정

A I need to talk with Jim about the company **dress code.** He's not wearing appropriate clothes for the office.

B Just make sure you choose your words carefully. You don't want to offend him.

A I know. I'll make it clear I'm not attacking him personally.

A 회사 복장규정에 관해 짐과 이야기를 해야겠어요. 회사 옷차림이 적절하지 않아요.

B 단어 선택을 신중하게 하세요. 그가 기분 상하지 않게요.

A 네. 인신공격을 하기 위한 게 아니라는 걸 분명히 해둘게요.

단어 14 strong coffee — 진한 커피

A Are you OK? You look like a zombie.

B I wish I were dead. I am so hung over. I need to have some **strong coffee.**

A Here's my secret hangover cure: Drink lots of water and go back to sleep.

A 당신 괜찮아요? 꼭 산송장 같아요.

B 차라리 송장이 낫겠어요. 술이 아직도 안 깼어요. 진한 커피를 좀 마셔야겠어요.

A 제가 숙취 해소 비법을 알려드릴게요. 물을 잔뜩 마시고 다시 잠자리에 들어요.

단어 15 stocky — (체격이) 다부진, 다리가 굵은

A I hear short summer dresses are all the rage this season. Have you bought any yet?

B What? Just look at my legs! I'm too **stocky** for short dresses.

A Oh. I see what you mean. Oh well. There's always fall!

A 이번 여름에는 짧은 원피스가 유행이라고 들었어요. 당신은 아직 안 샀어요?

B 뭐라고요? 제 다리 좀 보세요! 짧은 원피스 입기에는 다리가 너무 굵잖아요.

A 아, 무슨 말인지 알겠어요. 어쩔 수 없죠. 가을은 항상 오는 법이니까요.

단어 16 step out — 잠깐 자리를 비우다, 잠시 나가다

A I'm looking for Jim Fowler. Is he available now?

B Oh, I', sorry. He just **stepped out** for a few minutes.

A Where can I find him? It's urgent.

A 짐 파울러를 찾고 있는데요. 지금 계세요?

B 아, 죄송하지만 방금 잠시 자리를 비우셨어요.

A 어디 가면 짐을 만날 수 있을까요? 급하거든요.

단어 17 coop up — 가두다

A Didn't you go snowboarding last year?

B I did. I also broke my leg on the first day and spent the rest of the vacation **cooped up** in the hospital.

A In that case, I guess you won't be doing that again this year.

A 작년에 스노보드 타러 가지 않으셨어요?

B 그랬죠. 첫 날 다리가 부러져서 남은 휴가 내내 병원에 틀어박혀 지냈어요.

A 그럼 올해는 스노보드 타러 안가겠네요.

단어 18 (one's) portfolio — 자산 알람표

A My fund manager recommends that I diversify my investment **portfolio** because I have all my money in one stock.

B That makes sense. If one stock decreases in value, another is likely to increase, and you'll break even.

A Which stocks are profitable?

A 제 투자담당자가 투자 자산 구성을 다양화하라고 권고하네요. 제가 하나의 주식에만 투자하고 있거든요.

B 일리가 있는 말입니다. 만약 한 주식의 주가가 떨어져도 다른 건 오를 수 있으니까요. 그러면 손해는 안 볼 겁니다.

A 어떤 주식이 수익성이 있나요?

단어 19 Temp — 임시직 직원

A Henry, do you have a number for the Globe H.R.?

B Sure. Are we short handed?

A One of the receptionists called in sick this morning. We'd better get a **temp** to help out for a day.

B Which of the receptionists is it?

A It's Clara. She sounded awful on the line.

B Okay. I'll work on it.

A 헨리, 글로브 인력 회사 전화 번호 알지?

B 그럼. 왜? 사람이 더 필요해?

A 안내 직원 한 명이 아파서 결근한대. 오늘 하루 일할 임시 직원을 구해야겠어.

B 안내 직원 누구?

A 클라라. 전화 목소리가 많이 아픈 것 같았어.

B 알았어. 바로 알아볼게.

단어 20 Scuttlebutt — 소문

A There's something weird today. Everyone seems to have butterflies in their stomachs.

B There are good reasons for it.

A What's going on?

B Didn't you hear? The **scuttlebutt** is all around that an enormous scale of layoff is being planned.

A 오늘 뭔가 이상하네. 다들 매우 불안해 보여.

B 그럴 만도 하지.

A 무슨 일이야?

B 못 들었어? 대대적인 정리해고가 있을 예정이라는 소문이야.

단어 21 Utility Bill — 납부서

A Hello, I'm calling from the Public Utilities Commission.
Is this Ms.Monroe's resident?

B That's right.
Is there something that I need to be informed of?

A Your record shows that you owe us $75.
Did you get your **utility bill** yet?

B Oh, yes. I completely forgot about the bill.
I'll wire the money as soon as possible.

A 여보세요, 공익설비 위원회인데요.
몬로양 댁인가요?

B 네, 맞는데요.
제가 알아야 할 사항이 있나요?

A 예, 몬로양 기록에 75달러 미납금이 있어서요. 고지서는 받으셨나요?

B 아, 네. 제가 받아 놓고 잊고 있었어요.
제가 되도록 빨리 송금하겠습니다.

단어 22 Cram — 벼락치기 공부를 하다

A I can't wait to get this mid-term over with.
I've done nothing but study for the last 20 hours.
B I just reviewed some of the chapters last night.
I never **cram** for tests.
A Well, whatever works for you. In my case,
I usually do better when I study everything the night before.

A 이번 중간고사가 빨리 끝났으면 좋겠어. 지난 20 시간 동안 공부 말고는 아무것도 못했어.
B 난 어젯밤에 몇 챕터를 훑어봤어. 난 벼락치기는 절대 안 하거든.
A 글쎄, 너한테 맞는 공부 방법이 있지. 나 보통 전날 밤에 모조리 공부하면 성적이 잘나와.

단어 23 Wind chill factor — 풍속냉각지수(체감 온도)

A How cold is it right now? It feels like it's minus ten, at least.
B Let me see.... According to my smartphone, it's only minus five.
A But that's without the wind. **Wind chill factor**, it's got to be much colder.

A 지금 날씨가 얼마나 추운 거예요? 적어도 영하 10도는 되는 것 같아요.
B 어디보자…. 스마트폰으로 검색해보니 영하 5도 밖에 안 되는데요.
A 하지만 그건 바람이 안 불었을 때 얘기고요. 체감온도는 훨씬 더 춥다고요.

단어 24 soap opera — (텔레비전, 라디오의) 연속극

A ... and then I told Brian he had better watch out, because....
B You know, you should really avoid all the office politics.
It's going to get you into trouble.
A Sure, it might. But, it's like watching a **soap opera**.
I can't help myself.

A 그리고 나서 브라이언에게 조심하는 게 좋겠다고 말했어요. 왜냐하면….
B 있죠, 사내 정치 문제들은 정말 관여하지 않는 게 좋겠어요. 곤란한 상황에 처하게 될 거에요.
A 네, 그럴지도 모르죠. 하지만 마치 연속극을 보는 것 같아요. 저도 어쩔 수가 없어요.

단어 25 bank loan — 은행 대출금

A The company is on the brink of bankruptcy.
We need cash, fast

B Have we tried to get extensions on our **bank loans**?
Can they give us an extra thirty days?

A We asked, and they turned us down flat.
We're going to need to find more investors.

A 회사가 파산 직전에 있어요.
지금 당장 현금이 필요해요.

B 은행에 대출금 연장 신청했어요?
30일 더 연장해줄 수 있대요?

A 요청해봤는데 한마디로 거절당했어요.
우린 더 많은 투자자들을 찾아야 할 거예요.

단어 26 blurry — 흐릿한

A Any other symptoms? How's your vision?

B Sort of **blurry**, but usually only in the mornings.
Is it something serious, doc?

A Hard to tell. We'll have to run some more tests.
You'll need to stay in the hospital overnight.

A 다른 증상이 있나요? 시력은 어떠세요?

B 좀 흐릿한데 보통 오전에만 그래요.
심각한 건가요, 선생님?

A 아직 알 수 없어요. 몇 가지 검사를 더 해봐야 할 것 같아요. 병원에 하루 입원하셔야 돼요.

단어 27 freckle — 주근깨

A The weather's been beautiful theses last few weeks.
I've been going to the beach a lot.

B Well, I can't stand all this sunny weather.
Look at my face! It's covered in **freckles**.

A Oh, my. It looks like you need a better hat and some stronger sunscreen. SPF 50 at least, I'd say.

A 요 몇 주 동안 날씨가 참 좋아요.
바닷가에 여러 번 갔다 왔어요.

B 음, 전 햇빛이 쨍쨍 나는 이런 날씨는 정말 싫어요.
제 얼굴 좀 보세요! 온통 주근깨투성이에요.

A 저런, 챙이 더 넓은 모자와 더 강력한 선크림이 필요할 것 같아요. SPF 지수가 적어도 50은 되어야 해요.

단어 28 second-choice school — 2지망 학교

A Have you heard anything from the universities yet?

B I got into my safety school, but I'm still waiting for an answer from Harvard.

A Well, at least you know you got into your **second-choice school.**

A 대학에서 아직 연락 없었어요?

B 안전하게 하향 지원한 대학은 합격했는데, 아직 하버드대에서 연락 오기를 기다리고 있어요.

A 음, (하버드에서) 떨어지더라도 2지망한 학교에는 갈 수 있겠네요.

단어 29 hospitalized — 병원에 입원한

A ... and then we realized he was having a heart attack! We called an ambulance right away.

B It sounds like your quick thinking saved his life. Good for you.

A Well, it was nothing, really. He's still **hospitalized**, but should be released next week.

A … 그러다 그가 심장마비를 일으켰다는 걸 알아차렸어요! 우린 바로 구급차를 불렀죠.

B 당신의 빠른 판단이 그의 목숨을 살린 것 같네요.
잘하셨어요.

A 사실 대단한 일은 아니었어요. 그는 아직 병원에 입원해 있지만 다음 주에 퇴원할 거예요.

단어 30 volley — 받아치다

A How did Mr. Schnell do at the conference?

B He gave a great speech and then answered a lot of questions.

A Did he have any problems answering the questions?

B Not at all. he **volleyed** all the questions everyone asked.

A 회의에서 쉬넬 씨 어땠어요?

B 멋진 연설을 하고 여러 질문에 답변도 했죠.

A 질문에 답변할 때 문제는 없었나요?

B 전혀요. 모든 사람들의 질문을 다 잘 받아쳤어요.

단어 31 scratch 동등한

A I'm going to open a business with Allen.

B So who is going to be the majority partner?

A Neither of us. We are going to be **scratch** partners.

B It's good that you'll both have equal shares.

A 앨런과 사업을 시작하려고 해.

B 그럼 누가 주도권을 갖게 되는 거지?

A 둘 다 아니야. 동등한 조건으로 파트너가 되는 거거든.

B 둘이서 동등하게 출자하는 거라면 좋을 거 같은데.

단어 32 walk-in 예약하지 않고 가는 손님 [환자]

A Good evening, sir. Do you have a reservation?

B I'm sorry, I don't. I didn't realize you'd be so busy on a Tuesday.

A I'm sorry, but all the tables are booked; we can't accommodate **walk-ins**.

A 안녕하세요. 예약이 되어 있으신가요?

B 예약 안 했어요. 화요일에 사람이 많을 거라 생각 못했어요.

A 죄송하지만, 모든 테이블이 다 예약이 되어 있어요. 예약 없이 그냥 오시는 분은 받을 수 없어요.

단어 33 deadwood 쓸모없는 사람, 짐만 되는 사람

A No, thanks. We don't need any more line managers.

B We're talking about a capable manager.

A Look, we have enough **deadwood** as it is.

B I think she would be an invaluable asset to our company.

A 아니오, 괜찮습니다. 관리자는 더 이상 필요하지 않습니다.

B 제가 말씀드리는 사람은 유능한 관리자입니다.

A 보세요. 지금도 쓸모없는 사람들이 넘치고 있어요.

B 그녀라면 우리 회사에 매우 귀중한 인재가 될 텐데요.

단어 34 shoestring operation / budget 영세운영자금, 예산

A They're asking for payment in advance this time.

B Yeah, they're a typical **shoestring operation**.

The company has been and continues to run on a shoestring budget.

A Well, what do you think?

A 그들이 이번에도 선불을 요하고 있어.

B 그래, 그들은 전형적인 영세업체야.

그 회사는 소자본으로 운영해 왔고 지금도 그래.

A 그럼, 어떻게 할까?

단어 35 Interest 이자, 금리

A Rising **interest** rates are a result of rising inflation.

B Was it the other way around?

A It's really hard to determine which is the cause and which is the effect.

B Either way, I'm getting out of the stock market and putting my money into bonds.

A 금리가 상승하는 건 물가 상승률이 높아졌기 때문입니다.

B 그 반대 아닌가요?

A 사실 무엇이 원인이고 무엇이 결과인지를 결론짓기는 어렵습니다.

B 어느 쪽이든, 나는 주식투자를 그만두고 채권에 투자할 겁니다.

단어 36 corny 시시한

A I'd like to tell a few jokes now.

B That's okay. You don't have to do that.

A Why? Don't you like any of my jokes.

B Your jokes are too **corny**.

And I've heard them all too many times.

A 재밌는 얘기 몇 개 해줄게.

B 됐어. 그러지 않아도 돼.

A 왜? 내 얘기가 싫으니?

B 네 얘긴 너무 시시해. 다 너무 많이 들어본 얘기들이야.

단어 37 peachy 훌륭한

A You look really happy these days.

B Oh, yeah. Everything in my life is totally **peachy.**

A Really? Well, I'm glad to hear that things are going well.

B Me, too. It's about time things in my life got better.

A 너 요즘 굉장히 기분 좋아 보인다.

B 아, 맞아. 요즘은 내 인생의 모든 일이 정말 잘 풀리는 것 같아.

A 그래? 음, 다 잘 되고 있다니 기쁘다.

B 나도 그래. 이젠 내 형편도 더 좋아질 때가 됐지 뭐.

단어 38 daily temperature range 일교차

A Don't forget to take a jacket with you, Bill.

B But it's really sunny out. I don't need a jacket in this weather.

A The **daily temperature range** is still quite wide. It's cold in the evenings.

A 빌, 재킷 꼭 챙겨 가요.

B 하지만 밖이 정말 화창해요. 이런 날씨에는 재킷 안 입어도 돼요.

A 일교차가 여전히 심하잖아요. 저녁에는 아직 추워요.

CHAPTER 19

숙어

숙어 01 A glutton for punishment — 고된 일도 마다 않는 열정적인 사람

A Okay. Let's call it a day and we can reconvene again tomorrow.

B Mr. Reeves, with all with respect, I think that this is not a good place to leave things. We haven't finalized the terms of the Tresco merger.

A Well, I never realized you were such a glutton for punishment!

A 오늘은 여기까지 하고, 내일 다시 모이도록 하죠.

B Reeves씨, 외람된 말씀이지만, 일을 남겨놓고 가는 건 좋지않을 것 같은데요. Tresco 합병 계약조건을 마무리 못했어요.

A 글쎄, 당신은 정말 고된 일을 마다하지 않는군요.

숙어 02 State-of-the-art — 최첨단 기술을 사용한

A What is this for?

B It lets you bring data together from multiple systems into one reliable, high-end networked storage system.

A Sounds wonderful. Your company must be proud of the equipment.

B That's right. It's **state-of-the art.**

A 이것은 무슨 용도로 쓰이나요?

B 정보를 복합체계로부터 하나의 확실하고 네트워크화 된 고급 저장장치로 모으게 합니다.

A 훌륭하네요. 당신 회사가 이 장비에 자부심을 갖겠네요.

B 맞습니다. 이 장치는 최첨단 기술을 사용했거든요.

숙어 03 All told — 모두 합해서

A I heard you were great at the presentation yesterday. Good for you!

B Thanks. I owe you a lot.

A Don't mention it. How many people were there?

B There were 35 guests coming, **all told.**

A 35? That's quite a number. Weren't you nervous at all?

A 어제 발표 아주 잘했다며?
너무 잘됐다!

B 고마워, 네 덕분이야.

A 그런 말 마. 몇 명이나 왔어?

B 총 35명.

A 35명? 꽤 많이 왔네. 그런데 안 떨렸어?

숙어 04 Set the stage for ~ | ~의 발판을 마련하다

A You look awfully exhausted. Did you have another sleepless night?

B I just couldn't get a wink of sleep. I may go to a therapist or something.

A I suppose you're under too much pressure with the ongoing project. Isn't that why you're suffering insomnia?

B Definitely. But you know what? If it goes well, this project can **set the stage for** my whole career in the future.

A 너 너무 피곤해 보인다. 어제도 못 잤어?

B 한숨도 못 잤어. 아무래도 치료를 받아야 할까봐.

A 이번 프로젝트 때문에 네가 지나치게 스트레스를 받는 것 같아. 그래서 불면증도 생긴 거 아냐?

B 맞아. 그런데 그거 알아? 이번 프로젝트가 잘되면 내 일은 앞으로 탄탄대로가 될 거야.

숙어 05 let me see if ~ | ~를 (확인해)보다

A Go ahead, ma'am.

B My business address is 2795 West Laurence, Chicago, same zip code.

A Okay. **Let me see if** I got that correct. Your business address is 2795 West Laurence, Chicago, zip code 60637.

B Yes, that's right.

A 말씀하세요, 손님.

B 제 사무실 주소는 시카고 웨스트 로렌스가 2795번지이고 우편번호는 같아요.

A 알겠습니다. 맞게 입력했는지 확인해 보겠습니다. 사무실 주소는 시카고 웨스트 로렌스가 2795번지이고 우편번호는 60637이요.

B 네, 맞아요.

숙어 06 Got in a fender-bender | 접촉사고를 당하다

A My mother **got in a fender-bender** last week.

B My goodness! Is she okay?

A Yeah, she is fine.

A 어머니께서 지난주에 접촉사고를 당하셨어.

B 이런, 괜찮으셔?

A 응 괜찮으셔.

숙어 07 Got the boot　해고되다

A Do you want to grab a cup of coffee?

B I'd love to, but I can't.

A There's a coffee shop right across the street.

B I really can't. Ever since I **got the boot** from my job, money has been tight.

A Don't worry about it, Edward. Coffee is on me.

A 너 커피 한잔 할래?

B 그러고 싶은데, 그럴 수 없어.

A 길 건너에 커피점이 생겼어.

B 정말 안 된다니까. 회사에서 해고된 이후로 경제 사정이 좋지가 않아.

A 걱정하지 마, Edward. 커피는 내가 살게.

숙어 08 Let off steam　화를 가라앉히다

A What are you doing after work?

B I'm going karaoke singing.

A Why? You can't even sing.

B I know. But it's a great way to **let off steam.**

A Can I join you?

B Sure. Let's go!

A 일 끝나고 뭐 할 거야?

B 가라오케에 가서 노래 부를 거야.

A 왜? 너 노래 잘 못하잖아.

B 알아. 근데 스트레스 풀기에 좋거든.

A 같이 가도 돼?

B 그래, 같이 가자!

숙어 09 Take the plunge　과감히 ~을 하다

A Becky, do you really think shopping online is safe?

B For the most part, it's safe. There are people that try to steal money, but most of the sites are safe.

A How can I make sure that the site I'm using is safe?

B The best thing to do is to find other people who have shopped on the website.

A Thanks. I think I'll **take the plunge** and order something.

A Becky, 온라인 쇼핑이 정말 안전하니?

B 대부분은 안전해. 돈을 훔치려는 사람들이 있긴 하지만 대부분의 사이트는 안전해.

A 내가 사용하는 사이트가 안전한지 어떻게 확인하지?

B 가장 좋은 방법은 그 웹사이트에서 쇼핑을 했던 다른 사람들을 찾아보는 거야.

B 고마워. 내가 과감히 어떤 것을 주문해 봐야겠는걸.

숙어 10 put yourself in one's shoes
~의 입장이 되어 보다

A I know that many of you are unhappy with the recent changes. But **put yourselves in my shoes.**

B It's OK, Bill. We understand. You had no choice.

A Thank you. When the economy gets better, things will go back to normal.

A 최근 변화들에 대해 여러분 대다수가 불만스러워 하고 있다는 거 알아요. 하지만 제 입장이 되어 생각해보세요.

B 괜찮아요, 빌. 이해해요. 달리 방법이 없으셨겠죠.

A 고마워요. 경기가 호전되면 안정을 찾을 겁니다.

숙어 11 Be cramped for room
다닥다닥 붙어 있는

A Did you have a nice trip to Busan last weekend?

B It was awesome except that we **were cramped for room** in Leo's car.

A Didn't you drive your car?

B No. My wife needs a car every weekend to pick up all the groceries.

A Oh, so all of you guys were in on car?

A 주말동안 부산에 잘 갔다 왔어?

B 좋았지. 리오의 차 안에서 다닥다닥 붙어 있느라 힘들었던 것만 빼고는.

A 너는 차 안 가져갔어?

B 응. 주말에는 아내가 장을 보느라 차를 써야 하거든.

A 아, 그럼 너희 모두가 한 차에 탔던 거야? 진짜 불편했겠다.

숙어 12 Stick to
~를 고집하다

A How many cups of coffee did you have today?

B Well.... I didn't count. Four of five?

A Don't you think that's too much? Why don't you try some green tea instead?

B I tried before but didn't work. I'd rather **stick to** coffee especially when I'm working.

A Herbal tea keeps you awake. It's worth it for you to switch to herbal tea for your health.

A 오늘 커피 몇 잔이나 마셨어?

B 글쎄…. 세어보지는 않았는데. 네 잔이나 다섯 잔?

A 너무 많이 마시는 거 아냐? 커피대신 녹차를 마셔봐.

B 전에 시도해 봤는데 효과가 없더라고. 특히 일할 때는 커피가 좋은 것 같아.

A 차에도 각성 효과는 있어. 건강을 위해서라도 차로 좀 바꿔봐.

숙어 13 Do's and don'ts — 규칙들

A Gosh.... Are those flip-flops that you're wearing?

B Yeah. Aren't they cool? I bought them at the clearance sale last weekend.

A Have you lost your mind? We're not allowed to wear those to work.

B What? That's ridiculous.

A There are some **do's and don'ts** to follow in the office, dude.

A 맙소사…. 너 지금 끈 달린 샌들 신고 온거야?

B 응. 멋지지? 지난 주말 재고정리 세일 때 산거야.

A 너 미쳤어? 회사에서는 그런 걸 신으면 안되는 거 몰라?

B 뭐? 말도 안 돼.

A 회사에는 따라야할 규칙들이 있는 거야, 친구.

숙어 14 get a raw deal — 부당한 대우를 받다

A I understand he was forced into compulsory retirement.

B "Foreced" is too strong a word. I'd say he was eased out.

A Call it what you want, but I think he **got a raw deal.**

A 제가 이해하기에 그는 강제 퇴직을 강요당한 겁니다.

B 강요당했다는 말은 좀 지나치군요. 오히려 고통 없이 나간 것 같은데요.

A 그걸 뭐라고 표현하든 저는 그가 부당한 대우를 받았다고 생각합니다.

숙어 15 cold turkey — 딱 끊어버리는

A Hey, I heard that you quit smoking. Congratulations!

B Thanks. I haven't smoked once in over a week.

A So you quit **cold turkey**, huh?

B Yeah. It's been hard, but I think I've managed to kick that habit.

A 야, 너 담배 끊었다며? 축하한다!

B 고마워. 일주일 넘게 한 번도 안 피웠어.

A 한 번에 딱 끊은 거네?

B 응. 힘들긴 하더라.
하지만 그런대로 금연에 성공한 것 같아.

숙어 16 In hot water — 곤경에 처하다

A Is Kimberly at her desk?

B No, she didn't come yet.

A Since she always arrives late to work, she is **in hot water** with her boss.

B She is in big trouble!

A 킴벌리씨 출근하셨나요?

B 아니요, 아직 안 오셨어요.

A 킴벌리씨는 항상 늦어서, 사장님께 꾸중을 듣게 생겼어요.

B 큰일이군요!

숙어 17 Music to one's ears — 반가운 소식

A Why the long face?

B I've been working on this report all afternoon but no progress at all so far.

A You need to slow down. How about some beer after work? I'm buying.

B Sure. That's **music to my ears**.

A Okay. say sevenish?

B Sevenish is perfect.

A 왜 울상이야?

B 오후 내내 이 보고서에 매달려 있는데 전혀 진척이 없어.

A 천천히 해. 퇴근 후에 맥주 한잔 어때? 내가 살게.

B 좋지. 듣던 중 반가운 말이야.

A 그럼 일곱 시쯤 괜찮아?

B 일곱 시쯤 좋아.

숙어 18 Sleep on it — 결단을 다음날로 미루다, 하룻밤 자고 생각하다

A Hi, Kara. How are you doing?

B Fine. By the way, the job that you're offering me sounds really good, but I'd like to **sleep on it** before giving you my final decision.

A Oh, really? Do you need more time to think over?

B Right. It's more important to figure out if I will be able to handle all the re-quired tasks.

A 안녕, 캐라. 잘 있었어요?

B 네. 그런데, 제게 제안하셨던 일자리가 무척 좋아 보이지만, 최종 결정은 좀 미루고 싶어요.

A 아, 그러세요? 생각할 시간이 더 필요하세요?

B 네. 제가 필요한 업무들을 모두 소화할 수 있을지를 재보는 것이 더 중요하니까요.

숙어 19 Pass the hat around — 모금하다

A Did you check out the bulletin board this morning?

B Nope. What's on it?

A The union is going th raise some money to help Kenny's son.

B Oh, the boy with leukemia? It's the right time to **pass the hat around.**

A Yeah. If everyone in this company chips in, that'll be a huge help to Kenny.

A 오늘 아침 게시판 봤어?

B 아니, 뭐가 올라왔는데?

A 노조에서 케니의 아들을 위해 모금을 할 거래.

B 아 그 백혈병에 걸렸다는 아이? 바로 이럴 때 모금을 해야지.

A 응, 우리 회사 사람들이 전부 조금씩 보태면 케니에겐 큰 힘이 될거야.

숙어 20 Jump All Over Someone — 몹시 비난하다

A What's wrong with Joe?

B He's feeling bad because his boss **jumped all over him** this morning.

A Has Joe done something wrong?

B No, it seems his boss just has to loosen up when he talks to his employees.

A 조한테 무슨 일이 있나요?

B 오늘 아침 상사가 심하게 질책하는 바람에 기분이 안 좋아요.

A 조가 무슨 잘못이라도 했나요?

B 아니요, 그의 상사는 부하 직원들을 좀 더 부드럽게 대할 필요가 있는 것 같아요.

숙어 21 Lend someone a hand — 조력하다

A As you know, Mr Peterson wants some equipment for the meeting tomorrow.

B Yes, he wanted a whiteboard and an overhead projector.

A He told me to ask if you could bring them with you when you come.

B Would you mind **lending me a hand**?

A 아시다시피, 피터슨씨는 내일 있을 회의에 쓸 장비들을 원하십니다.

B 네, 화이트보드와 OHP가 필요하다고 하셨습니다.

A 당신이 회의에 (장비들을) 가지고 올 수 있는지 물어보라고 하셨어요.

B 도와주실 수 있으세요?

숙어 22 A bitter pill to swallow 가혹한 일

A Have you heard from Earl recently? What's he up to?

B I gave him a call a couple of times but he didn't answer. He must hang I there.

A Well.... I understand it's **a bitter pill** for him **to swallow** to get laid off like that.

B Sure. I hope he gets over it soon.

A Why don't we drop in on him? You know, just for a little cheering up.

A 요즘 얼 소식 들었어? 뭐하고 지내나?

B 전화는 몇 번 해봤는데 안 받던데. 잘 견디고 있겠지.

A 글쎄…. 그렇게 해고되는 게 그에겐 참 힘든 일이었을거야.

B 그럼. 어서 괜찮아졌으면 좋겠다.

A 우리 한번 그의 집에 들러볼까? 그냥 기운내라는 의미로.

숙어 23 One and only 단 하나뿐인

A I'm interested. You've been very devoted to the work, I guess.

B You know I have to. What else can the person on the edge do?

A Now you are dead serious.

B Absolutely. This is the **one and only** opportunity I've got for now.

A Go for it! The harder you try, the more you get.

A 진짜 감동적인데. 너 요새 정말 열심히 일하네.

B 내 처지 알잖아. 궁지에 몰린 사람이 어쩌겠어?

A 이번엔 정말 진지하네.

B 당연하지. 이번이 나에게는 유일무이한 기회야.

A 열심히 해 봐. 열심히 할수록 더 큰 수확을 얻을거야.

숙어 24 Keep One's Nose to the Grindstone 뼈 빠지게 일하다

A Hey, Josh. Pull up a chair and join me for a cup of coffee.

B Thanks, but I have to get these reports in by today.

A Won't you have enough time to finish the reports?

B If I **keep my nose to the grindstone**, I should be finished by the end of the day.

A 이봐, 조쉬. 이리 와서 커피 한 잔 하지.

B 고맙지만, 오늘까지 이 보고서들을 제출해야 해.

A 보고서 끝낼 시간이 충분히 있지 않아?

B 쉬지않고 하면, 오늘 안엔 끝낼 수 있을 거야.

숙어 25 keynote speaker | 기조연설자

A The **keynote speaker** gave me an interesting speech. Her presentation was the best I've ever seen.

B Not only did she give a lively presentation, but she also engaged the audience.

A If the audience asks a lot of questions during a presentation, the presentation is successful.

A 기조연설자가 흥미로운 연설을 했어. 그녀의 발표는 내가 본 중에서 최고였어.

B 활기에 넘칠 뿐만 아니라, 관객들을 끌어들이게 하는 발표였지.

A 만약 관객들이 많은 질문을 하면, 그 발표는 성공한 셈이지.

숙어 26 reach a consensus | 합의에 이르다

A Take a break and we'll reconvene in ten minutes.

B When we come back, we'll try to agree on the issues.

A Getting this group to come to an agreement will be almost impossible.

B I'm sure once we get to the crux of the disagreement, we'll be able to **reach a consensus.**

A 휴식을 취하고 10분 후에 다시 모입시다.

B 다시 모이면 그 쟁점에 대해 합의하도록 노력해 보자고.

A 이 그룹이 합의에 도달하도록 하는 건 거의 불가능할 것 같아.

B 일단 논쟁의 핵심을 찾으면, 합의에 이를 수 있을 거라고 확신해.

숙어 27 cut the cackle | 용건으로 들어가다

A We're running late, so let's **cut the cackle.**

B The first item of business is to approve the agenda for the meeting.

A We have a number of points to cover in a short period time.

B Once we identify the crux of the matter, we will be better equipped to come up with solutions.

A 시간이 없으니, 용건으로 들어가죠.

B 첫째 항목은 회의의 의제를 승인하는 것입니다.

A 짧은 시간 안에 다루어야 할 사항이 많군요.

B 일단 문제의 핵심만 파악하면, 해결책을 이끌어 낼 준비를 더 잘할 수 있을 겁니다.

숙어 28 fit the bill 요구를 충족시키다

A I hear an ad hoc committee has been formed to focus on recruitment of new board members.
B We need to recruit members who are dedicated to our mission.
A Please think about who you know who might **fit the bill**, such as your colleagues.
B I will make recommenda- tions for potential new members at the next meeting.

A 새로운 이사회 임원들의 채용에 전념할 특별 위원회가 구성되었다고 하더라.
B 우리의 임무에 헌신적인 멤버들을 채용할 필요가 있어.
A 아는 사람 중에 네 동료들처럼 요건을 충족시킬 만한 사람을 생각해봐.
B 다음 회의 때 가능성 있는 새로운 인물들을 추천할게.

숙어 29 get one's foot in the door 발을 들여놓다

A You will be graduating soon, won't you?
B Yes, I only have one semester to go.
A It's about time for you to prepare for job interview.
B Since I do not have any company experience, it will be hard for me to fine a good position.
A Workin as an intern is one way to **get your foot in the door** of a big corporation.

A 곧 졸업을 하겠네요.
B 네, 한 학기밖에 안 남았어요.
A 취업 면접 준비를 해야겠군요.
B 제가 직장 경력이 없어서 좋은 자리를 찾기는 어려울 것 같아요.
A 인턴으로 일을 시작하는 것도 큰 회사에 발을 들여놓을 수 있는 한 방법이죠.

숙어 30 lead time 준비기간

A There's not enough **lead time** to submit a concentrate proposal.
B I'll try to get the deadline extended.
A That would be helpful.
B I'll get you whatever resources you need.

A 구체적인 제안서를 제출하기엔 준비할 시간이 충분하지 않아요.
B 마감시한을 연장하도록 해봐야겠어요.
A 그렇게 된다면 도움이 되겠네요.
B 필요한 자료는 어떤 것이든 드릴게요.

숙어 31 If ever there was one　의심의 여지없이

A How was the dinner at the Plaza last night?

B Oh, it was a fine dinner **if ever there was one**!

A Was it that good?

B Absolutely. The food was excellent and the flowers on the table were so beautiful.

A Umm.... I envy you guys there. Did you have a chance to talk to the president?

A 어젯밤 플라자 호텔에서의 저녁식사는 어땠어?

B 의심의 여지없이 훌륭한 식하였지.

A 그렇게 좋았어?

B 그럼. 음식도 맛있었고 꽃장식도 무척 예뻤어.

A 음…. 거기 갔던 사람들이 부럽다. 회장님과 얘기도 나눠봤어?

숙어 32 Too Much On One's Plate　해야 할 일을 잔뜩 안고

A Mr. Swanson, did you hear about the new project?

B Yes, but I can't take on a new project. I already have **too much on my plate.**

A Is that so? We should put off our plan till next week.

B Right. I will need more time to finish the prior work.

A 스완슨씨, 새 기획에 관해 들어 보셨나요?

B 네, 하지만 제가 새 프로젝트를 맡긴 힘들어요. 해야 할 일이 너무 많거든요.

A 그러세요? 다음 주 까지 계획을 미뤄야 겠네요.

B 그래요. 전에 하던 일을 마무리할 시간이 필요해요.

숙어 33 fill an order　주문대로 완수하다

A Things are really beginning to move.

B It's about time.

A We've had to take on more skilled workers to **fill an orders.**

B That's music to my ears.

A 사업이 잘되기 시작했어.

B 그렇게 될 때가 됐지.

A 우리는 주문을 감당하기 위해 숙련된 노동자들을 더 고용해야만 했어.

B 즐거운 이야기군.

숙어 34 A Quick Buck — 쉽게 번 돈

A I've recently started a real estate business.

B How is it going?

A I'm not making much profit on this business yet.

B You'd better devote yourself to the business instead of trying to turn **a quick buck**.

A 최근 부동산 사업을 시작했어요.

B 잘 되어 가세요?

A 아직 큰 수익은 못 내고 있어요.

B 쉽게 이익을 내려고 하기보다, 이 사업에 심혈을 기울이는 게 나을거에요.

숙어 35 Get into hot water — 곤경에 빠지다

A How long have you been with BCM?

B This is my seventh year with the company.

A The company is not doing well, is it?

B I might have to start looking for a new job since our company is **getting into hot water**.

A BCM에서 근무한 지는 얼마나 되었나요?

B 7년째 일하고 있습니다.

A 회사 형편이 좀 어려운 것 같은데, 그렇죠?

B 회사가 곤경에 처하고 있어서 새로운 일자리를 찾아봐야 할 것 같아요.

숙어 36 set a long-range goal — 장기적인 목표를 세우다

A The **long-range goal** we **set** for our department need to be revised.

B You mean since we can't meet the short-range ones?

A Yes, that, and the fact that our competition has already achieved what we planned to do in five years.

A 우리 부서의 장기 목표는 수정돼야 해.

B 우리가 단기적인 목표를 달성할 수 없기 때문에 그러는거야?

A 그래. 그리고 우리의 경쟁사는 우리가 앞으로 5년 동안 하려고 계획한 것을 이미 달성했고.

숙어 37 Give shape to something — 분명히 표현하다

A You look so devastated. What're you up to now?

B I've been squeezing my head to come up with a solid idea for the next meeting and it's just not going well.

A What's giving you such a hard time?

B Something is obviously brewing in my mind and I just can't **give shape to it**.

A May I take a look at the memo?

A 되게 힘들어 보이네. 무얼 하는 중인데?

B 다음 회의에 낼 구체적인 아이디어를 짜내는 중인데 무척 힘드네.

A 뭐가 그렇게 어려운데?

B 머릿속에는 분명히 뭔가 있는데 말로 정확히 표현이 안 돼.

A 메모한 거 내가 봐도 돼?

숙어 38 With a bad grace — 마지못해서

A What happened to you and Henry? Did you guys have a fight?

B Not a fight. We had an argument and I was a little too harsh on him.

A That explains the awkward ambience between you two this morning.

B Yeah. You showed up at the exact moment he accepted my apology **with a bad grace**.

A Got it. You did apologize, though.

A 너랑 헨리 사이에 무슨 일이야? 싸웠어?

B 싸움은 무슨. 약간 논쟁이 있었는데 내가 좀 심한 말을 했거든.

A 그래서 오늘 아침 둘이 그렇게 어색한 분위기였구나.

B 응. 헨리가 마지못해 내 사과를 받아들일 때 딱 네가 나타났거든.

A 그랬구나. 그래도 사과는 했네 뭐.

숙어 39 as stubborn as a mule — 황소고집인

A Come on. Let's get going.

B I'm not going to do anything until you apologize.

A You are **as stubborn as a mule**. Stop being so childish!

B Hey, you did something bad, and now you need to apologize.

A 자 어서 가자니까.

B 네가 사과하기 전에는 아무것도 안 할 거야.

A 너 정말 황소고집이다. 제발 좀 애처럼 굴지 마!

B 야, 네가 잘못을 했으니까 네가 사과해야지.

숙어 40 have no heart — 용기가 없다

A I don't know why I should work overtime every day.

B Then go and tell your boss what you think.

A I'd like to, but what happens if I get fired?

B You **have no heart**. You hate your job. So what if you get fired?

A 난 왜 매일 야근을 해야 되는지 모르겠어.

B 그럼 너희 사장한테 가서 네 생각을 말해.

A 나고 그러고 싶어. 하지만 그러다 해고라도 당하면 어떡해?

B 너 참 용기 없다. 너 그 일 싫어하잖아. 해고당한들 뭐 어때서?

숙어 41 bet on the wrong horse — 잘못 짚다

A I hope that Wilson wins this match.

B Me, too. I'm counting on him to lead us to victory.

A Let's just hope we haven't **bet on the wrong horse**.

B I'm sure we haven't. I have total faith in Wilson.

A 윌슨이 이번 시합에서 이겼으면 좋겠어.

B 나도 그래. 난 그 친구가 우리 팀을 승리로 이끌어줄 거라고 믿어.

A 우리 예측이 빗나가지 않도록 빌기나 하자.

B 빗나갈 리가 없어. 난 윌슨을 전적으로 믿으니까.

숙어 42 hold one's horses — 진정하다

A Come on. Let's get going!

B What's the rush?

A We don't have any time to lose. We have to go now!

B **Hold your horses**. I'm not ready yet.

A 자, 어서 출발하자!

B 뭐가 그리 급해?

A 허비할 시간이 없단 말이야. 지금 가야 돼!

B 좀 진정해. 난 아직 준비가 덜 됐어.

숙어 43 a copycat — 남의 것을 그대로 베끼는 사람

A Hey, why are you looking at my homework?

B I want to write down the answers just the same as you.

A Don't be **a copycat**! Come up with your own answers!

B But I like the way that you answered them.

A 야, 너 왜 내 숙제를 보는 거니?

B 너랑 같은 답을 쓰려고.

A 따라하지 마! 네가 직접 답을 구하란 말이야!

B 하지만 네가 답해 놓은 방식이 마음에 들어서 그래.

숙어 44 be chicken-livered

간이 콩알만하다

A Let's go white water rafting this weekend.

B Sorry. You can count me out.

A Why do you always have to **be so chicken livered**?

B I'm not. It's just that rafting can be kind of dangerous, and I don't want to risk my neck.

A 이번 주말에 우리 래프팅 하러 가자.

B 미안해, 난 빼 줘.

A 넌 왜 만날 간이 콩알만해서 그러냐?

B 그런거 아냐. 그냥 래프팅은 위험하니까 괜히 목숨 걸기 싫은 것 뿐이야.

숙어 45 save one's breath

그런 말을 해봐야 소용이 없다

A I'm going to try to get Steve to change his mind.

B I wouldn't do that if I were you.

A Why do you say that?

B **Save your breath.** Once he makes up his mind, he never changes it.

A 스티브가 마음을 바꾸도록 설득을 해봐야겠어.

B 내가 너라면 그런 짓 안 해.

A 왜 그런 말을 하지?

B 해봐야 소용없으니까. 걔는 한 번 마음 정하면 절대 바꾸는 법이 없거든.

숙어 46 put out to pasture

은퇴시키다

A What do your parents do for a living?

B My mom is a doctor at the local hospital.

A How about your dad?

B He works at a company, but he's being **put out to pasture** because of his age.

A 너희 부모님은 뭘 하시니?

B 우리 엄마는 이 지역 병원에 의사로 계셔.

A 아버지는?

B 회사에 다니시는데, 연세가 있으시니까 곧 은퇴하실 거야.

숙어 47 catch up on

(밀린 일을) 만회하다

A Are you going somewhere at the end of this year?

B Sadly, no. I'll have to try to **catch up on** some work.

A I'm sorry to hear that. Let me know if there is anything I can do for you.

A 연말에 어디 가실 건가요?

B 아쉽게도 아무 데도 안 가요. 밀린 일을 좀 해야 하거든요.

A 안됐네요. 뭐든 제가 도와드릴 일이 있으면 알려주세요.

숙어 48 get sidetracked — 옆길로 새다

A Have you finished the report I asked for yesterday, Sam? I need it right away

B Sorry, Susan. I was working on it, but then the phone rang and I **got** a bit **sidetracked**.

A Sam, you need to learn to manage your time better. Now, get back to work on that report!

A 줄리, 그 서류 작업 제시간에 끝낼 수 있어요?

B 끝내야죠. 간신히 시간에 맞출 수 있을 것 같아요.

A 어쨌든 저한테도 알려주세요. 만약 마감일을 못 맞추게 되면 우리도 일정을 조정해야 하니까요.

숙어 49 going-out-of-business sale — 점포정리 세일

A There is a **going-out-of-business sale** at the mall.

B What kind of place is closing?

A I think it's a sporting goods store. You know, with shoes and stuff.

B We have plenty of shoes. It's not a deal if you're buying something you don't need.

A 샘, 내가 어제 부탁한 보고서 다 끝냈어요? 지금 당장 필요하거든요.

B 미안해요, 수잔. 작업하다가 전화벨이 울려서 잠깐 옆길로 샜어요.

A 샘, 시간 관리를 좀 더 효율적으로 다루는 법을 배워야겠어요. 자, 얼른 그 보고서부터 끝내요!

숙어 50 just under the wire — 마지막 순간에, 간신히

A Julie, are you going to have the paperwork done in time?

B I hope so. I think I can get it in **just under the wire.**

A Well, let me know. We need to adjust the schedule if you can't meet the deadline.

A 쇼핑몰에서 점포정리 세일을 한대요.

B 어느 가게가 문을 닫죠?

A 스포츠 용품 가게인 것 같아요. 있잖아요, 신발 같은거 파는 가게요.

B 우리 신발 많잖아요. 필요 없는 물건은 사봐야 싸게 사는 게 아니에요.

숙어 51 pass with flying colors — 우수한 성적으로 합격하다

A I heard you finally took the CPA exam. How did it go?

B All my hard work finally paid off. I **passed with flying colors.**

A Great. So I guess the company will promote you soon, too. Congratulations!

A 마침내 공인회계사 시험을 봤다면서요. 시험은 어땠어요?

B 그 동안 열심히 공부했던 보람이 있었어요. 좋은 성적으로 합격했어요.

A 잘됐네요. 그럼 회사에서도 곧 진급시켜주겠군요. 축하해요!

숙어 52 In the black — 수익이 있는

A It's amazing how well you've been doing.

B Yes, we've been **in the black** for two months in a row.

A What did you do to increase profit and cut losses?

B The supervisors in each department are well-trained and reliable.

A 그동안 경영을 아주 잘하셨네요.

B 예, 2개월 연속으로 많은 수익을 얻었지요.

A 어떻게 그렇게 수익을 올리고 손실을 막을 수 있었나요?

B 각 부서의 관리자들이 훈련이 잘 되어 있고 믿을 수 있는 사람들이기 때문이죠.

숙어 53 feel blue — 기분이 울적하다, 우울하다

A Why are you with the long face? Is anything the matter?

B I'm just **feeling** sort of **blue**. I guess it's just the Monday morning blues.

A I know how you feel. But look on the bright side; it's just another hour until lunch.

A 왜 시무룩한 표정을 하고 있어요? 무슨 일 있어요?

B 그냥 좀 기분이 우울해서 그래요. 그냥 월요병인 것 같아요.

A 어떤 기분인지 알겠는데 좋게 생각해요. 점심 시간이 한 시간 밖에 안 남았잖아요.

숙어 54 static on the line | 전화상의 잡음

A Can you hear that? I think there's some **static on the line**.

B It's just your microphone. Sit closer to the computer. Now try it.

A Oh, that's a lot better. This video conferencing is still all new to me.

A 들려요? 전화상에 잡음이 좀 있는 것 같아요.

B 당신 마이크 때문에 그래요. 컴퓨터에 좀 더 가까이 앉아봐요.

A 아, 훨씬 낫네요. 전 이 화상 회의가 아직도 낯설어요.

숙어 55 Get one's wires crossed | 혼돈되다

A Hi, Christina, How are you doing?

B Hi, Can I help you with something?

A Mr. Trident said there was a department meeting yesterday. Is that true?

B No, the meeting's tomorrow. I guess he **got his wires crossed**.

A 안녕하세요, 크리스티나. 잘 지내셨어요?

B 안녕하세요. 뭘 도와드릴까요?

A 트라이던트씨가 어제 부서 회의가 있었다고 하던데, 정말인가요?

B 아니에요. 회의는 내일 있어요. 아마 헷갈리셨나 봐요.

숙어 56 Be in and out | 들락날락하다

A We were supposed to get together today and talk about out problems, remember?

B No, I don't remember that. What were we going to discuss

A We need to have a casual meeting to find out how much progress we've made in preparing for the San Diego industrial Fair.

B I will **be in and out of** the office most of this afternoon, So I prefer to have the meeting in the morning.

A 오늘 다같이 모여서 우리의 문제점에 대해 의논하기로 한 것 기억하세요?

B 아니오, 기억이 안 나네요. 무엇에 관한 거였죠?

A 센디에이고 산업 박람회를 위한 준비가 어느 정도 진척이 되었는지 알아보기 위해 간단한 회의를 열어야 할 것 같아요.

B 오늘 오후엔 사무실과 밖을 들락날락하게 될 것 같아서, 아침에 회의를 했으면 좋겠네요.

숙어 57 Just so — 완벽한

A Whose stuff is this on my desk?

B Not mine. Must be Ryan's. He was around a while ago.

A Why is he doing this? I hate to see other people's belongings on my desk

B Easy. It's not that big a deal. Everything can't be **just so** as you wish.-

A Are you saying that I'm picky?

A 내 책상 위에 있는 이거 누구 거야?

B 내 건 아니야. 라이언 물건 같은데. 좀 전에 거기 있었거든.

A 도대체 왜 이러는 거지? 내 책상에 남의 물건이 있는 거 싫단 말이야.

B 진정해. 별일 아니잖아. 모든게 네가 원하는 대로 완벽할 순 없어.

A 내가 까다롭다는 얘기야? 난 그냥 지저분한 책상이 싫을 뿐이야.

숙어 58 Buzz around — 분주하게 돌아다니다

A Do you know who is working on the marketing plan for the next year?

B I have no idea. You'd better ask Ryan.

A Ryan? Where is he? He never seems to be in his office.

B He must be **buzzing around** the office building. He never stays still.

A What an outgoing person he is!

B Yeah, he's really fun to hang out with too.

A 내년 마케팅 계획은 누가 담당하는지 아세요?

B 모르겠는데. 라이언에게 물어봐.

A 라이언이요? 어디에 있죠? 언제나 자리에 없는 것 같던데.

B 아마 사무실 어딘가를 분주하게 누비고 다니는 중일 걸. 절대 얌전히 있는 법이 없거든.

A 매우 적극적인 사람이군요.

B 그럼, 함께 어울리기에도 아주 재밌는 친구지.

숙어 59 as nutty as a fruitcake — 완전히 미친

A What do you know about Julie?

B There's not too much I can tell you about her really.

A I've heard that she's **as nutty as a fruitcake**. You might want to be careful around her, Rick.

B Yeah, I've heard the same thing, too.

A 줄리에 대해서 뭐 아는 거 있어?

B 걔에 대해서는 사실 별로 해줄 말이 없는데.

A 정말 이상하다는 얘길 들었거든. 너도 조심하는 게 좋을거야, 릭.

B 그래, 나도 그런 얘기 들었어.

숙어 60 Bulk out — 분량을 늘리다

A Are you finished with quarterly report on the market analysis?

B Sort. Only a few more pages to go.

A Good. Let me take a look at that once you're done.

B Sure. The report will count up to no more than 10 pages. Do you think I'd better **bulk it out?**

A No, the length of the report doesn't make a difference as long as it has all the necessary information.

B Okay. I just want to make sure.

A 시장분석에 관한 분기 보고서는 끝냈어?

B 거의. 두어 페이지만 더 하면 돼.

A 좋아. 끝내는 대로 나에게 한번 보여줘.

B 응. 다 해도 총 열페이지가 넘지 않을 것 같은데, 분량을 좀 늘리는 게 좋을까?

A 아니. 필요한 정보만 다 있다면 분량은 중요한 게 아니잖아.

B 그래. 그냥 확실히 하고싶었어.

숙어 61 Shake up — 개혁을 단행하다

A I can't believe she's the new big boss lady. How old is she?

B Must be fifty something. But she looks quite young.

A Yeah. she certainly will bring lots of changes to this company.

B Isn't it good? This company definitely needs some **shaking up.**

A That goes without saying.

A 저 분이 새로 부임한 여사장이라니 믿을 수가 없어. 몇 살이지?

B 오십대라고 들었는데 꽤 젊어 보이네.

A 맞아. 회사에 엄청난 변화가 생기겠는걸.

B 잘됐잖아. 우리 회사는 정말 개혁이 필요해.

A 당연하지!

숙어 62 milk someone for information — 정보를 털어놓게 만들다

A How are you going to find it out?

B I'll try to **milk Percy for information.**

A Are you kidding? He won't tell you anything.

B Don't worry. I'll sweet-talk him until he tells me what I want to know.

A 그걸 어떻게 알아낼 거야?

B 퍼시한테서 정보를 빼내봐야지 뭐.

A 농담하니? 퍼시는 아무 말도 안 해줄걸.

B 걱정 마. 내가 알고 싶은 걸 말해 줄 때까지 살살 구슬리면 돼.

숙어 63 To get nowhere
아무 성과도 없다

A Did you hear that Jeremy got called to the carpet this morning?

B He did? Gee.... I wouldn't be surprised if he got sacked.

A What's that supposed to mean?

B Don't you know how much damage Jeremy had brought to this company?

A Even though he **got nowhere** with his work, he did try hard through.

B So what? Honey, this is a workplace. You get nowhere, you get fired.

A 제레미가 오늘 아침에 불려가 몹시 혼난 거 알아?

B 그랬대? 저런…. 하긴 제레미가 해고당했대도 놀랄 일은 아니지.

A 무슨 말이야?

B 제레미가 회사에 끼친 손해가 얼마나 심각하지 몰라서 그래?

A 일에 성과는 없었지만 열심히 했잖아.

B 그래서? 이봐, 여긴 회사야. 성과가 없으면 해고되는 거라고.

숙어 64 sink or swim
실패냐 성공이냐

A You don't get any training in this job

B In this company we are just thrown in at the deep end.

A It's a carefully considered **sink or swim** policy.
I think you all realize that.

A 여러분은 이 업무에 대해 전혀 직업훈련을 받지 않았군요.

B 이 회사는 우리가 경험이 없는 상태에서 일을 시작하길 요구하는 거지요.

A 이것은 면밀히 고려된 죽느냐 사느냐의 정책입니다.
여러분 모두가 이 점을 충분히 인식하고 있다고 생각합니다.

숙어 65 walk through
차근차근 설명하다

A I'm having trouble understanding this refund policy.
Can you **walk** me **through** it?

B Sure. Basically, you can get a refund within thirty days of your purchase.

A I see. Thanks for helping me with that.

A 이 환불 정책이 이해가 잘 안 돼요. 차근차근 설명 좀 해주시겠어요?

B 물론입니다. 기본적으로, 구입 후 30일 이내에 환불을 받으실 수 있습니다.

A 알겠어요. 도와주셔서 고마워요.

숙어 66 To lend an ear — 귀 기울이다

A Hey, folk. May I have an attention please?

B What is it, Mr. Green?

A I know you guys are very busy, but could you just **lend me your ear** for a minute?

C Sure, Mr. Green. We are all ears.

A Good. Thanks to your hard work for the past three months, I am honored to announce that each of you will be given a raise from next month.

A 잠깐만요, 여러분 저를 좀 주목해 주시겠어요?

B 무슨 일이죠? 그린씨?

A 여러분 모두 바쁜 건 알지만 잠시만 제 말에 귀 기울여 주세요.

C 그러죠, 그린씨. 우리 모두 경청하고 있어요.

A 좋아요. 지난 석 달간 열심히 일해 준 덕분에 여러분 모두 다음 달부터 봉급이 인상된다는 걸 알려드리게 돼 매우 기쁩니다.

숙어 67 To keep body and soul together — 가까스로 먹고 살다

A Why do you look so tired? Didn't get any sleep last night?

B I didn't get to sleep at all because of some paperwork.

A What? Did you bring your work home?

B No, I didn't. I'm moonlighting.

A Wow. How can you have time to do other work? I just can't imagine.

B I really have to. I'm barely able **to keep body and soul together** with this job.

A 왜 그렇게 피곤해 보여? 어제 못 잤어?

B 몇 가지 서류 업무 때문에 전혀 못 잤어.

A 뭐야? 집에까지 일을 갖고 간거야?

B 아니. 아르바이트로 다른 일을 하거든.

A 와, 어떻게 다른 일을 할 시간이 돼? 난 꿈도 못 꾸는데.

B 안 할 수가 없어. 이 일로는 겨우 먹고 살 만큼의 벌이도 안 되는 걸.

숙어 68 worth one's salt — 밥값을 하는

A Hiring Janice was the best thing I've ever done.

B I agree. She certainly is **worth her salt.**

A She made our profits go up by fifty percent.

B Let's just hope she doesn't decide to take a job with another company.

A 재니스를 고용하길 정말 잘했어.

B 맞아. 정말 제몫을 하는 직원이지.

A 우리 회사 수익을 50퍼센트나 올려 줬잖아.

B 이젠 재니스가 다른 회사로 옮길 생각 같은 건 하지 않도록 바랄 수밖에.

숙어 69 To make a typo　오타를 치다

A Oh my god, who the heck worked on this paper?

B I did Mr. Smith. Any problem with it?

A Look at all these **typos you made**. You didn't go over it before handing it in, did you?

B I'm terribly sorry, sir. I didn't have enough time to do it.

A I don't wanna see such sloppy work ever again. Got it?

B Absolutely. I'll work on it right away.

A 맙소사. 이 보고서는 도대체 누가 작성했죠?

B 전데요. 스미스씨. 무슨 문제가 있나요?

A 이 많은 오타를 좀 봐요. 나에게 넘기기 전에 검토도 안했나요?

B 죄송합니다. 시간이 모자라서요.

A 다시는 이런 성의 없는 보고서는 보고 싶지 않아요. 아시겠죠?

B 그럼요. 바로 시정하겠습니다.

숙어 70 To break even　이익도 손실도 없다

A How is our new magazine doing? Getting any better?

B Not at all. Its sales record is just about to hit the bottom.

A To be honest with you, I don't understand why the editor decided to publish this type of magazine.

B No one does. He will be just lucky **to break even** with this magazine

A 새로 창간한 잡지는 좀 어때? 좀 나아지고 있어?

B 전혀. 판매 수치가 바닥을 치기 직전이야.

A 솔직히 말해서 난 편집장이 이 잡지를 왜 출판하기로 했는지 이해가 안가.

B 그 누구도 이해 못 하지. 적자만 면해도 다행일걸.

숙어 71 grease someone's palms　뇌물을 먹이다

A How can I get you to change your mind?

B I'm sorry, but I've already decided.

A Not even if I offered to pay off some of your debts?

B Hey, don't try to **grease my palms** like that. I don't want to do anything against the law.

A 어떻게 하면 네 마음을 바꿀 수 있겠니?

B 미안하지만, 벌써 난 결정했어.

A 네 빚을 내가 좀 갚아준다고 해도 안 될까?

B 이봐, 그런 식으로 뇌물 먹이려고 하지 마. 난 법에 저촉되는 일은 하고 싶지 않아.

숙어 72 To step out — 자리를 비우다

A The Ashton, how may I help you?

B I'd like to speak to Mr. Murray, please.

A I'm afraid he just **stepped out**. Would you like me to have him return your call?

B Yes, please let him know Amanda Simpson wants to talk to him as soon as possible.

A Okay. And your number is…?

B He has it. Just tell him to give me a call

A 애슈턴사입니다. 무엇을 도와드릴까요?

B 머레이씨와 통화하고 싶은데요.

A 잠깐 자리를 비우셨는데요. 돌아오시면 전화 드리라고 전할까요?

B 예. 아만다 심슨이 가능한 한 빨리 통화하길 원한다고 전해주세요.

A 알겠습니다. 전화번호가 어떻게 되시나요?

B 머레이씨가 알아요. 그냥 저에게 전화하라고만 전해주세요.

숙어 73 reach me — 연락하다

A Is this his wife? I am working with your husband on a project with his company.

B Really? Nice to meet you. Mr. Kim.

A Would you mind telling him that I called? He can **reach me** at the Portsmith Hotel, Room 20. When is he expected home?

B I'm not sure when he'll be back. But I'll let him know you called.

A Thank you very much. I appreciate it. Bye.

B Bye now.

A 사모님이십니까? 저는 회사에서 남편분이랑 프로젝트를 함께 수행하고 있습니다.

B 아 그러세요! 김선생님 반갑습니다.

A 실례지만 제가 전화했다고 전해주시겠어요? 포스트밋 호텔 20호실로 연락하시면 됩니다. 언제쯤 들어오실까요?

B 저도 확실히 모르겠지만 전화하셨다고 전해드릴게요.

A 감사합니다. 안녕히 계세요.

B 안녕히 계세요.

숙어 74 back to the salt mines — 일을 하러 돌아가는

A Well, I guess that we have been at lunch long enough.

B Looks like it's **back to the salt mines** for us.

A I really wish we could hurry and finish this project.

B Me, too. It's too boring.

A 글쎄, 우리 점심을 너무 오래 먹은 것 같아.

B 슬슬 일하러 가야 할 것 같군.

A 서둘러서 이번 프로젝트를 얼른 끝냈으면 좋겠어.

B 그래, 맞아. 너무 지겨워.

숙어 75 bugging someone — 귀찮게 괴롭히다

A Do you know how to solve these problems?

B Go and ask Richard. He's good at math.

A I already tried, but he told me to stop **bugging him.**

B That's too bad. You should just wait until he has some time to help you then.

A 너 이 문제 어떻게 푸는지 아니?

B 리처드한테 가서 물어봐. 걔는 수학을 잘 하니까.

A 이미 물어봤는데 자기 귀찮게 하지 말래.

B 안됐다. 그럼 걔가 도와줄 시간이 날 때까지 그냥 기다려야지 뭐.

숙어 76 hang in there — 참고 견디다

A I don't know if I can finish all this work in time. They deadline is tomorrow.

B You'll be fine. Just **hang in there.** Don't give up yet.

A Thanks for encouraging me. All right. I can do it!

A 이 일을 다 제시간에 끝낼 수 있을지 모르겠어요. 마감일이 내일이에요.

B 잘할 수 있을 거예요. 조금만 더 힘내요. 아직 포기하긴 일러요.

A 격려해 줘서 고마워요. 알았어요. 난 할 수 있다고요!

숙어 77 face the facts　사실을 인정하다

A No. I refuse to admit that I was wrong.

B But look. The figures are right here in front of you.

A I demand a recount. you need to add them up again.

B I already have. You need to **face the facts.** You were wrong, and I was right.

A 아니. 난 내가 틀렸다고 인정하지 않겠어.

B 하지만 좀 봐. 이렇게 숫자가 네 앞에 있잖아.

A 다시 계산해 봐. 다시 한 번 합계를 내 보라고.

B 이미 해봤어. 사실을 받아들여. 네가 틀렸고 내가 맞았다니까.

숙어 78 cut a fine figure　두각을 나타내다

A You really **cut a fine figure** at my sister's wedding this weekend. I was really impressed.

B I always told you I looked good in a suit and tie.

A And now I believe you. Hey, Tom, how about we grab a cup of coffee this Saturday afternoon?

A 지난 주말, 내 여동생 결혼식 때 당신 정말 눈에 띄었어요. 정말 인상적이었다고요.

B 난 정장 차림에 넥타이를 매는 게 어울린다고 당신에게 늘 말했잖아요.

A 이제 당신 말 믿어요. 저기, 톰, 이번 토요일 오후에 커피 한잔 할래요?

숙어 79 take-home pay　(세금 등을 공제한)실수령 임금

A And after they take off taxes and union dues, there's barely anything left.

B I pay a ton into my pension. My **take-home pay** is basically nothing.

A The only good timing is we won't have to worry when we're older.

A 그리고 세금이랑 조합비 떼고 나면 남는 게 거의 없어요.

B 저는 연금에 돈이 꽤 많이 들어가요. 실제로 손에 쥐는 건 기본적으로 제로예요.

A 그나마 유일하게 좋은 점은 노후 걱정할 필요가 없다는 거네요.

숙어 80 entertain clients
고객을 접대하다

A I'm glad I caught you before you left. I need you to take those guys from Boston out.

B But you know I hate **entertaining clients**.

A I know, but how else can you get ahead in sales.

A 당신이 아직 안 가서 다행이에요. 보스턴에서 온 저분들 데리고 나가 접대 좀 하세요.

B 하지만 제가 고객 접대를 싫어한다는 거 아시잖아요.

A 알아요. 하지만 그거 말고 어떻게 당신이 영업에서 성공할 수 있겠어요?

숙어 81 push all one's buttons
누구를 화나게 하다

A Hey, don't let Gerg get you so angry.

B I can't help it. He knows how to **push all my buttons**.

A That's because it's easy to get you angry.

B But he needs to stop doing that.

A 야, 그레그가 너 화나게 만들도록 놔두지 마.

B 어쩔 수가 없어. 그 사람은 나를 화나게 하는 재주가 있다니깐.

A 그건 너를 화나게 만드는 게 쉽기 때문이야.

B 그래도 그는 이제 그런 짓 그만둬야 해.

숙어 82 wet blanket
흥을 깨는 사람

A And I think we should have the party at our place. We could have everyone over.

B Sure, but just think of all the cleaning up we'd have to do the next day.

A Come on. Don't be such a **wet blanket**. The party's going to be awesome.

A 그리고 우리 집에서 파티를 하는 게 좋을 것 같아요. 집으로 모두 초대할 수 있어요.

B 좋아요. 하지만 그 다음 날 청소해야 할 것들을 생각해 봐요.

A 그러지 말아요. 그렇게 분위기를 망치지 말아요. 파티는 정말 신날 거라고요.

숙어 83 tuition hike — 등록금 인상

A I can't believe this **tuition hike.** How do they expect us to pay this much more for our classes?

B I agree. It's insanity. By the time we graduate, we'll have tons of debt.

A Come on. Let's head down to the Student Union Building. I need th apply for every scholarship under the sun!

A 등록금이 인상됐다니 믿을 수가 없어. 수업료를 어떻게 이렇게나 더 많이 내라고 할 수 있어?

B 그러게. 정신 나갔어. 졸업할 때 되면 빚이 엄청날 거야.

A 기운 내. 우리 학생회관에 가보자. 난 이 세상 무슨 장학금이든 신청해야 돼!

숙어 84 crow's feet — 눈가의 잔주름

A The first thing I need to do is get rid of these **crow's feet**. It looks like there's cracked paint around my eyes.

B Oh, you're overreacting. It's not so bad. Besides, the bags under your eyes are the real problem.

A What? You know, you're not making me feel any better.

A 제일 먼저 눈가의 이 잔주름부터 없애야겠어요. 눈 주위에 페인트칠이 갈라진 것처럼 보여요.

B 민감하게 반응하는 거 같네요. 그렇게 심하지 않아요. 사실, 눈 밑의 처진 살이 정말 심각한 문제예요.

A 뭐라고요? 위로는커녕 악담을 하는군요.

숙어 85 lantern jaw — 주걱턱

A What's your ideal type, Jane? A guy who loo like Superman?

B With a **lantern jaw** and big muscles? No way! I prefer someone who more intellectual.

A Really? Well, in that case, would you like to come with me to the library this afternoon?

A 제인, 이상형이 어떻게 돼요? 수퍼맨처럼 생긴 남자요?

B 주걱턱에 근육질 몸매요? 말도 안 돼요! 전 지적인 사람이 좋아요.

A 정말이에요? 저, 그렇다면, 오늘 오후에 저랑 도서관에 같이 갈래요?

숙어 86 keep up one's end — 자기 몫을 다하다

A I ran into Jane at the store yesterday. It was a nightmare. That woman is as dumb as a post.

B I know exactly what you mean. She can't **keep up her end** of a simple conversation.

A Tell me about it. I tried to talk with her about the weather, but she had nothing to say. The weather!

A 어제 가게에서 제인을 우연히 만났는데, 악몽 같았어요.
그 여자는 정말 멍청해요.

B 무슨 말인지 잘 알아요. 간단한 대화도 안 되는 사람이잖아요.

A 내 말이요. 날씨 얘기를 하려고 했는데 아무 말도 못하더라고요. 날씨조차도요!

숙어 87 cold snap — 일시적 한파

A Don't forget to take your hat and gloves.
It's cold out today.

B But the weather's been getting warmer.
It was beautiful yesterday.

A Sure, but today's the start of a **cold snap**. Trust me.
It's freezing outside.

A 모자랑 장갑 가지고 가는 거 잊지 마.
오늘 날씨가 추워.

B 하지만 날씨가 점점 따뜻해지고 있잖아.
어제는 날이 정말 좋았다고.

A 그렇긴 한데 오늘부터 한파가 시작돼.
내 말 믿어.
밖이 무지 춥다니까.

숙어 88 be all skin and bones — 피골이 상접하다

A Just look at you! **You're all skin and bones.**

B I know, I know. It's my stomach. I can't seem to keep anything down. I've been in and out of the hospital for months.

A I am so sorry to hear that. I hope in the end it's nothing serious because you look just awful!

A 당신 얼굴 좀 봐요! 피골이 상접했어요.
무슨 일 있어요?
전엔 정말 건강했잖아요.

B 알아요, 안다고요. 위 때문에 그래요. 먹는 거마다 다 토해요. 몇 달 동안 병원을 들락거리고 있어요.

A 저런. 심각한 병은 아니면 좋겠네요. 당신 얼굴이 너무 아파 보이거든요!

숙어 89 shrimp | 키가 작은 사람

A Is this a picture of your new boyfriend?

B Yeah. So, what do you think of him?

A Well, he looks nice, but he's kind of a **shrimp**.

B Yeah, he isn't that tall, but he is still a nice guy.

A 이거 네 새 남자친구 사진이니?

B 응. 이 사람 어떤 것 같아?

A 글쎄, 괜찮아 보이는데, 키가 좀 작은 것 같네.

B 그래, 키는 그렇게 크지 않아도 괜찮은 사람이야.

숙어 90 cry a river | 눈물을 펑펑 쏟다

A What was wrong with Julie this afternoon?

B She heard some bad news from her family.

A Oh, my God, that's terrible.

B Yeah, nothing could stop her from **crying a river.**

A 오늘 오후에 줄리한테 무슨 일 있었어?

B 가족한테서 뭔가 안 좋은 소식을 들었나봐.

A 저런, 너무 안됐다.

B 그러게, 아무리 달래도 계속 엉엉 울기만 하더라.

숙어 91 have a heavy heart | 마음이 무겁다

A Are you sure that everything is okay these days?

B Oh, yeah, I'm handing the divorce alright.

A I don't know. It just looks like you **have a heavy heart**.

B I wouldn't say that, but there are some moments when I feel blue.

A 너 요즘 잘 지내고 있는 거 확실하니?

B 그래, 이혼이라는 거 잘 견디고 있어.

A 난 모르겠다. 내가 보기엔 네 마음에 슬픔이 가득한 것 같아.

B 그렇게까지 말할 수는 없지만, 때때로 기분이 우울해질 때가 있긴 해.

숙어 92 put one's foot in one's mouth | 입방정을 떨다

A I can't believe you asked her about her past troubles.

B Yeah, I guess I really **put my foot in my mouth**, didn't I?

A You can say that again.
Did you see the look on her face?

B I am so embarrassed. I don't think I can ever see her again.

A 걔 과거 문제에 대해 물어보다니 너 어떻게 그럴 수가 있니?

B 그러게 말이야. 나 정말 말실수한 것 같아, 그치?

A 두말하면 잔소리지.
걔 표정 봤어?

B 나도 어찌나 무안하던지. 다시는 걔 얼굴 못 볼 것 같아.

숙어 93 be red in the face
얼굴이 울그락불그락하다

A Did you take a look at Trevor?

B Yeah, he looked mad. What was wrong with him?

A I don't know, but he **was** really **red in the face.**

B He needs to calm down some.

A 트레버 얼굴 봤어?

B 응 무지 화난 것 같던데. 뭐가 문제야?

A 모르겠어. 하여튼 얼굴이 정말 벌개져 있던걸.

B 좀 진정해야겠더라.

숙어 94 fat chance
희박한 가능성

A I know I'm going to win the lottery tonight.

B There's a **fat chance** of that happening.

A Well, I can always hope for the best.

B But there is no way that you're going to win the lottery.

A 나 분명 오늘 밤에 복권에 당첨될 거야.

B 절대 그럴 리 없어.

A 뭐, 언제든 좋은 일이 일어날 거라고 바랄 수는 있잖아.

B 하지만 네가 복권에 당첨되는 일은 절대 없을 거다.

숙어 95 all worn out
기진맥진한

A How are you feeling today after yesterday's marathon?

B I must admit that I'm **all worn out.**

A You look pretty worn down.

B I think I need to take the day off and relax.

A 어제 마라톤을 했는데 오늘 기분이 어때?

B 고백하건대 나 완전히 기진맥진이야.

A 정말 지쳐 보인다.

B 나 오늘 휴가 내고 좀 쉬어야겠어.

숙어 96 boggle one's mind
너무 놀라서 심장이 뛰다

A This **boggle my mind**!

B What's does?

A I just can't believe all of these facts I'm reading in this book.

B Here, let me have a look at that.

A 이것 때문에 너무 놀랐지 뭐야.

B 뭔데?

A 지금 읽고 있는 책에 나와 있는 사실들 말이야, 도무지 믿을 수가 없어.

B 어디, 나도 한번 보자.

숙어 97 bug-eyed 눈이 휘둥그레진

A Did you know that we have to work this weekend?

B What? Are you kidding me?

A Don't get so **bug-eyed**. That's old news.

B It's the first I've heard of it.

A 우리 이번 주말에 일해야 된다는 것 알고 있었어?

B 뭐? 설마 농담이겠지.

A 그렇게 눈을 휘둥그렇게 뜰 것까진 없어. 다들 아는 거니깐.

B 난 지금 처음 듣는 말인데.

숙어 98 walk on eggs 살얼음판을 걷다

A You look like you're upset today.

B That's because my mother-in-law has just arrived.

A So, why should that make you upset?

B I feel like I'm **walking on eggs** when she's here. Everything has to be perfect.

A 너 오늘 기분이 안 좋아 보인다.

B 방금 장모님이 오셨기 때문이지.

A 그런데 왜 기분이 안 좋은 거지?

B 장모님이 여기 계시면 난 살얼음판 위를 걷는 기분이 들거든. 모든 게 완벽해야만 하니까.

숙어 99 yellow-bellied 겁이 많은

A I really believed that Trevor was braver than that.

B Yeah, he didn't even stand up to that guy who insulted him.

A I guess he is just **yellow-bellied** after all.

B Yup. He's all talk but no action.

A 난 정말이지 트레버가 그보다는 용감할 거라고 생각했어.

B 그래, 하지만 자기를 모욕하는 그 녀석 앞에서 당당히 맞서지도 못 했잖아.

A 걔는 결국 겁쟁이였던 거야.

B 맞아. 걔는 큰소리만 쳤지 행동으로 보여주지는 못해.

숙어 100 a piece of cake 누워서 떡먹기

A Do you think you can connect my computer?

B Don't worry. It's **a piece of cake.**

A Are you sure?It looks hard to me.

B I've been working on computers all my life. It's no sweat, really.

A 너 정말 내 컴퓨터 연결할 수 있겠어?

B 걱정 마. 식은 죽 먹기야.

A 정말이야? 나한테는 어려워 보이는데.

B 평생 컴퓨터 관련 일을 했는데 뭐. 그 정도는 정말 일도 아니야.

숙어 101 put someone to shame — 콧대를 납작하게 눌러버리다

A Who won the contest, Bill or Rick?

B Rick **put** Bill **to shame.** He did much better than Bill.

A Really? So the contest wasn't even close?

B No, Bill didn't perform very well.
He should be embarrassed.

A 그 시합에서 누가 이겼지? 빌이야, 아니면 릭이야?

B 릭이 빌을 눌러버렸지. 빌보다 훨씬 잘 하더라고.

A 정말? 그럼 시합이 막상막하였던 것도 아니네?

B 응, 빌이 잘 못했거든. 창피할 거야.

숙어 102 step on someone's toes — 난처하게 만들다

A I can't believe Steven said those things to our boss.

B He revealed some really embarrassing information about us.

A I guess he just doesn't care about **stepping on other people's toes.**

B Well, I'm sure he'll get what he deserves someday.

A 스티븐이 우리 부장님한테 그런 얘길 했다니 믿을 수가 없어.

B 정말이지 우릴 난처하게 만드는 얘길 했더군.

A 그 사람은 다른 사람이 난처해지든 말든 신경 안 쓰나 봐.

B 뭐, 그 사람 언젠가는 그 대가를 꼭 치르고 말 거야.

숙어 103 as white as a ghost — 유령처럼 창백한

A Are you okay? You look **as white as a ghost.**

B Yeah. I'm alright. I just need a minute to catch my breath.

A That was a close call you had back there.

B I know. I didn't think I was going to make it for a moment.

A 너 괜찮아? 얼굴이 하얗게 질렸어.

B 응. 괜찮아. 잠깐 숨 좀 돌릴게.

A 너 아까는 정말 아슬아슬했어.

B 그래. 잠깐 동안 내가 못 해낼 줄 알았지.

숙어 104 get cold feet — 겁이 나서 꽁무니를 빼다

A Are you sure you're going to go through with this?

B I'm not afraid to go bungee-jumping.

A It's okay if you **get cold feet**, you know.

B No, I'm going to conquer my fear and go ahead and do it.

A 너 정말 이거 할 수 있겠어?

B 번지 점프하러 가는 거 무섭지 않아.

A 있잖아, 못 하겠다고 해도 괜찮아.

B 아냐, 난 두려움과 맞서 이기고 나아가서 해내고 말거야.

숙어 105 catch some Zs — 꿈나라로 가다

A Where are you going right now?

B I'm tired. I'm going home to **catch some Zs.**

A What? It's only ten o'clock and all of your co-workers are here.

B Sorry, but I have got to get home and go to bed.

A 당신 지금 어디 가는 거예요?

B 피곤해서요. 집에 가서 잠을 좀 자려고요.

A 뭐라고요? 이제 10시밖에 안 된 데다가, 다른 직원들은 다 여기 있잖아요.

B 미안해요. 하지만 전 집에 가서 잠을 자야겠어요.

숙어 106 eat one's heart out — 약오르다

A Did you win yesterday's contest?

B No, I lost. And now, I'm really **eating mt heart out** because of it.

A Why is that? Was it that important for you to win?

B Yes, I prepared for the contest for the past 6 months.

A 어제 대회에서 이겼어?

B 아니, 졌어. 그래서 지금 그것 때문에 진짜 약올라 있어.

A 왜 그래? 거기서 이기는 게 그렇게 중요한 일이었어?

B 그럼, 난 지난 6개월 동안 그 대회를 준비했단 말이야.

숙어 107 have stickly fingers — 손버릇이 나쁘다

A What happened to your new employee?

B I had to fire him. He **had stickly fingers.**

A Are you serious? What did he steal from you?

B He stole some money and a few items from the store.

A 신입사원한테 무슨 문제가 있는 거죠?

B 해고시켜야겠어요. 손버릇이 나빠서요.

A 정말이에요? 당신한테서 뭘 훔쳤나요?

B 가게에서 돈하고 물건 몇 개를 훔쳐갔어요.

숙어 108 as sour as a lemon | 벌레 씹은 얼굴을 하고 있는

A Why is Linda so upset today?

B I'm not sure, but she looks **as sour as a lemon**.

A Why don't you go ask her what's wrong?

B What? Are you crazy? I'm not talking to her when she looks like that.

A 오늘 린다가 왜 저렇게 화가 나 있는 거지?

B 나도 잘 모르겠지만, 벌레 씹은 듯한 표정이네.

A 가서 뭐가 문제인지 한 번 물어보지 그래?

B 뭐라고? 미쳤어? 린다가 저러고 있을 땐 난 절대 말 안 걸어.

숙어 109 waffle | 결정을 못 짓고 꾸물거리다

A Have you made a decision yet?

B Well, I'm just not sure what to do.

A Will you stop **waffling** and just make up your mind?

B I'm sorry, but you have to give me some more time.

A 이제 결정을 내렸어?

B 글쎄, 어떻게 해야 될지 모르겠어.

A 이랬다저랬다 하지 말고 그냥 마음을 정하지 그래?

B 미안하지만, 시간을 좀더 줘야겠다.

숙어 110 forbidden fruit | 금단의 열매

A I'm going out on a date with Linda.

B You can't be serious. She's **forbidden fruit**!

A You mean that I shouldn't date her because she is the boss's daughter?

B That's exactly what I mean. She is off-limits.

A 나 린다랑 데이트할 거야.

B 말도 안 돼. 그녀는 넘봐선 안 될 존재야!

A 린다가 사장님 딸이라서 데이트하면 안 된다는 얘기야?

B 바로 그 말이지. 만나선 안 될 사람이라고.

숙어 111 go bananas | 미친 사람처럼 들뜨다

A Het, calm down!

B I can't help it. I'm just too happy.

A Yeah, but you're **going bananas**.

B Well, I just got the promotion I have been waiting for.

A 이봐, 진정해!

B 어쩔 수가 없어. 너무 기뻐서 그래.

A 그래, 그렇긴 한데 너무 흥분하고 있잖아.

B 글쎄, 내가 그렇게도 기다리던 승진을 했다는 거 아냐.

숙어 112 be nosy — 꼬치꼬치 캐묻다

A So, how much money do you make?

B I make enough to cover the bills.

A And, by the way, are you married?

B Why are you **being** so **nosy**? What's with the personal questions?

A 그래, 돈은 얼마나 벌어요?

B 뭐 그럭저럭 입에 풀칠할 정도는 벌죠.

A 그런데요, 결혼은 하셨어요?

B 왜 그렇게 꼬치꼬치 캐물으시죠? 그런 개인적인 질문은 왜 하시는 건데요?

숙어 113 in a nutshell — 한 마디로

A So, how did your date go last night?

B Well, it's a really long story.
Do you have time to hear it?

A Um, why don't you just give it to me **in a nutshell**?

B Okay. We had a great time, and I'll probably see her again.

A 그래, 어젯밤 데이트 어땠어?

B 글쎄, 얘기하자면 길어.
들을 시간 있어?

A 음, 그냥 짧게 요점만 말해 봐.

B 그래. 재미있었고, 아마 그 여자랑 또 만날 것 같아.

숙어 114 spill the beans — 비밀을 입 밖으로 흘리다

A If I tell you a secret, will you promise not to tell anyone?

B Of course. I won't **spill the beans** about whatever you tell me.

A I hope not, because if this ever gets back to me, it could ruin my reputation.

B Your secret is safe with me.

A 내가 비밀을 얘기해 주면 아무한테도 말하지 않겠다고 약속할 수 있어?

B 당연하지. 네가 무슨 말을 하든 절대로 발설하는 일 없을거야.

A 그러길 바래. 혹시라도 그 말이 내게 들리는 날엔, 내 평판은 끝장나는 거야.

B 네 비밀에 절대 안전을 보장하지.

숙어 115 On the job — 근무 중에

A Did you check out the bulletin board?

B No. Any news on it?

A Yes. Warren got a pink slip because he drank on the job.

B He did what? Oh my....

A Pretty shocking, huh? What kind of a person drinks **on the job**?

A 게시판 봤어?

B 아니. 뭐 새로운 소식이라도 붙었어?

A 응. 워렌이 업무 중에 술을 마셔서 해고됐대.

B 뭐라고? 세상에….

A 황당하지? 어떻게 근무 중에 술을 마시지?

숙어 116 To do something by the book — 원칙대로 처리하다

A Ben, you got a call from the president's office. He wants to see you right away. What's going on?

B Oh, no.

A Do you have an idea of what the call is about?

B I was only a couple of minutes late this morning and Mr. Kim reported me to the president.

A That's really bad. Mr. Kim always **does everything by the book**, you know.

A 벤, 사장실에서 전화 왔었어. 사장님이 지금 보자고 하신대. 무슨 일이야?

B 아, 큰일났다.

A 왜 전화가 온 건데?

B 오늘 아침 겨우 몇 분 늦었는데 김 부장님이 사장님께 보고했어.

A 안됐다. 김 부장님은 늘 원칙밖에 모르시잖아.

숙어 117 feel like a million dollars — 기분이 날아갈 것 같다

A How are you doing today?

B I couldn't be better. In fact, I **feel like a million dollars.**

A Why is that, Ed?

B I just got back from working out, and I feel great.

A 오늘 기분이 어때?

B 최고야. 사실, 날아갈 것처럼 기뻐.

A 왜 그런데, 에드?

B 방금 운동하고 왔거든. 그래서 기분이 좋아.

숙어 118 with regard to

~에 관해서(는)

A J Crew. Customer Service. May I help you?

B Yes. I'm calling **with regard to** an order I made a couple of days ago.

A Yes, ma'am. Is there something wrong?

B Yes, there is.

A 제이 크루 고객 서비스입니다. 무엇을 도와드릴까요?

B 네. 며칠 전에 한 주문 때문에 전화한 건데요.

A 네, 손님. 뭐가 잘못됐나요?

B 네.

숙어 119 on a roll

잘하고 있는, 잘나가는

A I've heard Mike is doing a very good job these days.

B You mean the new guy at the sales department? Yeah, he's **on a roll.**

A The other employees must envy him.

A 마이크가 요즘 일을 아주 잘한다고 들었어요.

B 영업부에 새로 온 직원 말하는 거예요? 그 친구 요즘 승승장구하고 있어요.

A 모든 직원들이 다 부러워하겠군요.

숙어 120 To knock on doors

일자리를 구하다

A I got a call from Sam yesterday.

B Yeah? How is he doing? He got a job?

A He's been **knocking on doors** since he quit this company but still can't find one.

B Gee.... He has a family to take care of.

A Sure. But it seems quite tough to get a job, you know.

A 어제 샘한테 전화 왔었어.

B 그래? 어떻게 지낸대? 취직은 했대?

A 여기를 그만둔 뒤 계속 이 자리를 찾고 있는데 아직 못 찾았대.

B 저런…. 부양할 가족도 있는데.

A 그럼. 그런데 알다시피 취직하기가 무척 어려운가봐.

숙어 121 To split hairs
사소한 일로 다투다

A Why are you wearing such a long face?

B I had a little argument with Henry this morning and it's been bothering me all day long.

A What did you guys have an argument about?

B Nothing serious. he made a mess in the bathroom and I was just freaked out.

A Why do all married couples always **split hairs**?

B I don't know. Do you think I owe him an apology?

A 왜 그렇게 우울해 보여?

B 아침에 헨리랑 좀 다퉜는데 하루 종일 신경이 쓰이네.

A 무슨 일로 다퉜는데?

B 별일도 아닌데. 목욕탕을 너무 어질러서 내가 또 화를 냈지.

A 왜 결혼한 사람들은 사소한 걸 가지고 항상 다투는 거야?

B 나도 몰라. 내가 먼저 사과해야 할까?

숙어 122 by that name
그런 이름의

A Hi. I was wondering if Mr. Park was in.

B I'm sorry, sir. Who did you say that was?

A Mr. Park. Mr. Jae Suk Park.

B There is no such person at this number.

A Isn't this 705-7867?

B Yes, it is. But there is no one **by that name** here.

A 안녕하세요. 박 이사님 계십니까?

B 죄송합니다만 누구라고 하셨죠?

A 박 이사님요. 박재석 이사님.

B 여기 그런 분 안 계시는데요.

A 705-7867 아닙니까?

B 번호는 맞는데, 여기에는 그런 분 안 계십니다.

숙어 123 To have get-up-and-go
활기차다

A Did you see Daniel today?

B Nope. Is he back from his vacation?

A Yes. He got very tan and seems to **have** a lot more **get-up-and-go**.

B Yeah? He must have had a really good time in California.

A Oh, I wish I went on a vacation too.

B Wouldn't we all?

A 오늘 대니얼 봤어?

B 아니. 휴가에서 돌아왔어?

A 응. 몸도 많이 탔고 훨씬 더 활기차 보이던데.

B 그래? 캘리포니아에서 아주 좋은 시간을 보냈나 보다.

A 아, 나도 휴가 가고 싶다.

B 누군들 안 그렇겠어?

숙어 124 mix-up | 혼란

A Is there a discrepancy between what you had ordered and what you have received?

B Yes, there is. They're the wrong color. My order was for three ivory all-season turtleneck shirts, not white.

A I'm sorry, ma'am. There must have been a **mix-up** in our dispatch.

A 주문하신 것과 받으신 물건에 문제가 있습니까?

B 네, 그래요. 색깔이 잘못됐네요. 제가 주문한 건 아이보리 색 터틀넥 셔츠 석 장이었는데요. 흰색이 아니고요.

A 죄송합니다, 손님. 발송에 혼동이 있었던 모양입니다.

숙어 125 boss around | 이래라 저래라 하다

A Have you called your mom? She'd really love to hear from you.

B I know. But she always **bosses** me **around** and tells me how to act.

A She's your mom. You know, it just means she loves you.

A 어머님께 전화하셨어요? 당신 소식을 몹시 듣고 싶어 하세요.

B 알아요. 근데 어머니는 항상 나한테 이래라 저래라 하고 행동 하나하나까지 다 간섭하셔요.

A 어머니이시니까요. 다 당신을 사랑하셔서 그러는 거예요.

숙어 126 keep in shape | 건강을 유지하다

A How often do you go to the gym?

B Usually five days a week. I really want to **keep in shape.**

A Me too. I should work out more often.

A 헬스클럽에 얼마나 자주 가세요?

B 보통 일주일에 5일이요. 정말 늘 건강하게 살고 싶거든요.

A 저도 그래요. 운동을 더욱 자주 해야겠어요.

숙어 127 bloodshot | (눈이) 충혈된

A This yellow dust is killing me. I can hardly breathe.

B Me, too. And my eyes are **bloodshot.**

A We need to stay inside and take some medicine.

A 황사 때문에 죽을 것 같아요. 숨을 못 쉬겠어요.

B 나도 그래요. 눈까지 충혈이 됐어요.

A 밖에 나가지 말고 약 좀 먹어야겠어요.

숙어 128 taste gross — 역겨운 맛이 나다

A Is there any milk left? I want to try out this new cereal, Cherry Big Pops.

B There should be some in the fridge, behind the fruit salad.

A Found it. Oh, it's past the expiration date. Blah! It **tastes gross**!

A 우유 남은 거 있어요? 새로 나온 이 '체리 빅 팝스' 시리얼을 한번 먹어 보고 싶어서요.

B 냉장고 안에 과일 샐러드 뒤에 보면 좀 있을 거예요.

A 찾았어요. 오, 유통기간이 지났네요. 윽! 맛이 갔어요!

숙어 129 off the record — 비공식적으로, 비공개를 전제로

A What else can you tell me about your company's plans for the future?

B Officially, nothing. But **off the record**, I can tell you that we're looking to corner the MP3 market.

A Really? That's very interesting.

A 당신 회사의 향후 계획에 대해 다른 할 말씀이 있으십니까?

B 공식적으로는 없습니다. 하지만 기사화하지 않는다는 전제하에 말씀드리자면, MP3 시장을 장악할 계획을 갖고 있습니다.

A 정말입니까? 그거 아주 흥미로운데요.

숙어 130 get to the bottom of — ~의 원인을 밝혀내다

A Could you delay the meeting until afternoon?

B We called this emergency meeting for a reason!

A You're right. Our top priority is **getting to the bottom of** these production delays.

A 회의를 오후로 좀 미룰 수 있을까요?

B 그럴 만한 이유가 있어서 이번 비상회의를 소집했잖아요!

A 맞아요. 최우선 사항은 생산 지연의 원인을 밝혀내는 거예요.

숙어 131 have a finger in every pie — 온갖 일에 참견하다

A The boss wants the company to get into electronics.

B What? But we're an insurance company.

A He said it's good to **have a finger in every pie.**

A 사장님은 우리 회사가 전자제품 사업에 진출하기를 바라고 있어요.

B 뭐라고요? 그렇지만 우리는 보험 회사잖아요.

A 우리가 사업을 다각화하는 것이 좋겠다고 말씀하셨어요.

숙어 132 key money — 전세 보증금

A I'm tired of paying rent.

B Well, we could always switch to **key money**, and then live rent-free.

A True, but we'll need a lot of money. I guess we'd have to get a bank loan.

A 집세 내는 거 정말 지긋지긋해요.

B 음, 우리는 언제든 전세로 바꿀 수 있어요. 그러면 집세를 안내도 돼요.

A 알아요, 하지만 목돈이 들잖아요. 아마 은행 대출을 받아야 할 거예요.

숙어 133 tell tall tales — 허풍을 떨다

A I see your husband got back from his fishing trip. Did he have a good time?

B Oh, it's impossible to know. You know how he is.

A He sure likes to **tell tall tales.**

A 남편이 낚시 갔다가 돌아왔다면서요. 재미있었대요?

B 아, 그거야 알 수 없죠. 우리 남편이 어떤 사람인지 잘 알잖아요.

A 그분이 허풍이 좀 세긴 해요.

숙어 134 raw deal — 부당한 대우

A I can't believe they fired him.

B He got a **raw deal.** All the employees are talking about it.

A He just made that one mistake and they let him go.

A 그들이 그를 해고했다니 못 믿겠어요.

B 그는 부당한 대우를 받았어요. 모든 직원들이 그 얘기를 하고 있어요.

A 그는 그 한 번의 실수로 해고당했어요.

숙어 135 from the horse's mouth — 믿을 만한 소식통으로부터

A Did you hear about Jim and Janice? Not only are they getting married, but she's pregnant.
B Get out! I can't believe it!
A It's true. I heard it straight **from the horse's mouth.** Janice told me.

A 짐이랑 재니스 소식 들었어요? 두 사람이 결혼한대요. 그뿐만 아니라 재니스가 임신을 했대요.
B 말도 안 돼! 못 믿겠어요.
A 사실이에요. 믿을 만한 소식통으로부터 들은 거예요.
재니스가 말했거든요.

숙어 136 go into labor — 산기가 있다, 진통이 시작되다

A It was really crazy. There we were, eating lunch in the restaurant, when all of a sudden this woman **goes into labor**.
B Are you for real? What did you do?
A We called 911 and then everyone begged her to hold on.

A 정말 말도 아니었어요. 우린 그 식당에서 점심을 먹고 있었는데 갑자기 이 여자가 진통을 하기 시작했어요.
B 정말이에요? 그래서 어떻게 했어요?
A 911에 전화를 건 다음, 모든 사람들이 그녀에게 조금만 참으라고 애원했죠.

숙어 137 under the weather — 몸이 좋지 않은, 아픈

A Are you okay? You look a little bit **under the weather**.
B I feel just awful. I haven't been this sick in years.
A I think you should go home and get some rest.

A 당신 괜찮아요? 좀 아파 보여요.
B 몸이 많이 안 좋아요. 이렇게 아픈 건 몇 년 만에 처음이에요.
A 집에 가서 좀 쉬는 게 좋겠어요.

숙어 138 not know beans — 쥐뿔도 모르다

A Can you help me with this problem?
B Maybe. What kind of help do you need?
A There is something wrong with my computer.
B Sorry, but I **don't know beans** about computers.

A 이것 좀 도와줄 수 있어?
B 아마도. 무슨 일이지?
A 내 컴퓨터가 뭔가 이상해.
B 미안하다. 난 컴퓨터에 대해서는 쥐뿔도 모르거든.

숙어 139 nasty weather | 궂은 날씨

A Don't forget to take your scarf. You'll catch a cold!

B It's not that cold out. I'll be fine with just my coat.

A Didn't you hear the forecast? They're expecting **nasty weather** this afternoon.

A 목도리 꼭 챙기렴. 감기 걸리겠다!

B 밖이 그렇게 춥진 않아요. 코트만 입어도 괜찮을 거예요.

A 일기예보 못 들었니? 오늘 오후에 날씨가 좋지 않다는구나.

숙어 140 be taken aback | ~에 깜짝 놀라다, ~에 충격을 받다

A Did you see Tom's new cell phone? It's awesome.

B Yeah, but it **was** really expensive. I was really **taken aback** when he told me the price.

A Well, I'm still going to get one. I need a smartphone.

A 톰이 새로 산 휴대전화 봤어요? 정말 멋져요.

B 네, 근데 정말 비싸더라고요. 톰이 가격을 말해줬을 때 깜짝 놀랐어요.

A 그래도 저는 하나 살 거예요. 스마트폰이 필요하거든요.

숙어 141 get a flu shot | 독감 예방 주사를 맞다

A I wonder if it's too late to **get a flu shot.**

B I think you still have time. Besides, it can't hurt, right?

A Right. I hate needles, but it's better safe than sorry.

A 독감 주사 맞기에 너무 늦은 게 아닌지 모르겠네요.

B 아직 맞을 수 있을 거예요. 그리고 아프지도 않잖아요, 그렇죠?

A 맞아요. 주사 맞는 건 싫지만 그래도 나중에 후회하는 것보다 미리 조심하는 편이 낫죠.

숙어 142 be all the rage | 큰 인기를 얻다, 대유행이다

A Check this out. Remember John from high school? Now he's married with three kids.

B Where did you get these pictures, though?

A From a social networking site. It's **all the rage** these days.

A 이것 좀 봐. 고등학교 때 존 기억해? 지금 결혼해서 애가 셋이래.

B 근데 이 사진 어디서 났어?

A 소셜 네트워킹 사이트에서. 요즘 이게 대유행이잖아요.

숙어 143 stink to high heaven — 지독한 냄새가 나다, 악취가 진동하다

A What's wrong with the bathroom?
It **stinks to high heaven.**

B I know. It looks like someone tried to flush some old food.

A I told you that Larry was going to be a terrible room-mate!

A 욕실에 무슨 문제가 있어요?
악취가 진동해요.

B 알아요. 누군가 오래된 음식물을 변기에 버리려고 했던 것 같아요.

A 래리는 못된 룸메이트일 거라고 내가 말했잖아요!

숙어 144 The apple of one's eye — 눈에 넣어도 아프지 않을 만큼 소중한 사람

A Did you hear what Sally did? She borrowed her father's car and wrecked it.

B I heard. It's a total write-off.
It's beyond repair.

A But we both know her father won't do anything to her.
She's **the apple of his eye.**

A 샐리 소식 들었어요? 아버지 차를 빌렸는데 망가뜨렸대요.

B 들었어요. 폐차하는 게 차라리 낫대요.
수리가 불가능한가 봐요.

A 하지만 우리 둘 다 알고 있듯이, 샐리 아버지는 그녀를 절대 나무라지 않으실 거예요. 그녀를 끔찍하게도 아끼시잖아요.

숙어 145 fresh-faced — 어리고 건강한, 동안의

A Wow, you look great. That new job must really agree with you.

B I know. I haven't felt this god in years. I finally have a job I like, and my life has totally changed.

A You look ten years younger. You're **fresh-faced** and smiling all the time.

A 와, 얼굴이 아주 좋아 보이는데요. 새로 시작한 일이 당신이랑 정말 잘 맞나 보네요.

B 맞아요. 이런 기분 느껴 본 게 몇 년 만이에요. 마침내 제가 원하는 일을 찾았어요. 그래서 인생이 완전히 달라졌어요.

A 10년은 어려 보여요. 동안에다 항상 웃고 있잖아요.

숙어 146 mutter under one's breath — 작은 소리로 불평하다

A I hate talking with Sean. Whenever I ask him to do something, I can hear him **muttering under his breath.**

B Really? That's so rude.

A Yeah, if he has something to tell me, he should come out and say it.

A 숀이랑 말하는 거 정말 싫어요. 그에게 뭔가 부탁을 할 때마다 들리지도 않는 소리로 투덜대거든요.

B 정말이에요? 아주 무례하네요.

A 맞아요. 나한테 할 말이 있으면 직접 말을 해야죠.

숙어 147 fringe benefits — 부가 혜택

A Here, try this one. Can you believe how good it is? Oh, try this sample, too.

B It melts in my mouth. It's so rich and sweet at the same time. Perfect!

A Working for the world's largest chocolate company sure has some great **fringe benefits.**

A 저기, 이거 한번 먹어봐요. 정말 맛있지 않아요?
아, 이 샘플도 맛봐요.

B 입 안에서 녹아요. 맛이 진하면서도 달콤해요.
정말 맛있어요!

A 세계 최대 초콜릿 회사에서 일하니깐 확실히 엄청난 부가 혜택이 있네요.

숙어 148 fair skin — 흰 살결, 흰 피부

A Where are you going without your hat?
You know how quickly you can burn.

B But it's cloudy out. Look at how overcast it is.
There's no sun!

A With your **fair skin**, you can never be too careful.
Now, here's your hat.

A 모자도 안 쓰고 어디 가는 거예요?
햇볕에 금장 탄다는 거 알잖아요.

B 하지만 밖이 흐려요. 구름으로 뒤덮인 것 좀 봐요.
해가 없다고요!

A 당신같이 흰 피부는 아무리 조심해도 부족하다고요.
자, 여기 당신 모자 있어요.

숙어 149 hard feelings 적의, 나쁜 감정

A I'm so sorry about what I said.
Can you ever forgive me?
B I don't know. What you said really hurt. You know
I'm sensitive about my clothes.
A Come on, no **hard feelings**, huh?

A 내가 했던 말에 대해 정말 미안해요. 용서해 줄래요?
B 모르겠어요. 당신 말에 정말 상처 받았어요. 내가 옷에 민감하잖아요.
A 그러지 마요. 언짢게 생각하지 말아요. 네?

숙어 150 stiff shoulder 경직된 어깨

A I don't think I should have tried yoga yesterday. Now I've got a **stiff shoulder**.
B From yoga? I'm sure it's just because it was your first time. You need to keep going.
A Maybe you're right. I'll give it one more try.

A 어제 요가를 하지 말았어야 했나 봐요. 어깨가 뻐근해요.
B 요가 때문에요? 요가를 처음 해서 그런 게 분명해요.
꾸준히 계속해야 돼요.
A 당신 말이 맞을지도 모르겠네요. 한 번 더 해봐야겠어요.

숙어 151 wisdom tooth 사랑니

A Hey, with your cheeks all swollen like that, you look like a chipmunk.
B Hey, don't make me laugh. It hurts when I laugh.
I just got my **wisdom teeth** pulled.
A I had the same thing done last year.
It was really painful.

A 저기, 양 볼이 그렇게 부어 있으니 꼭 얼룩 다람쥐 같아요.
B 웃기지 좀 말아요. 웃으면 아프단 말이에요. 방금 사랑니를 뽑았거든요.
A 저도 작년에 사랑니 뽑았어요. 정말 아팠죠.

숙어 152 hard to put into words — 말로 표현하기 어려운

A What is it about the report that you are unhappy with, Ted?

B It's **hard to put into words**. But, overall, it's just not what I wanted.

A I can try to fix it, but you have to help me. You have to make specific recommendations.

A 테드, 보고서의 어떤 부분이 마음에 안 드는 거예요?

B 말로 표현하기는 어려워요. 하지만 전반적으로 내가 원했던 게 아니에요.

A 수정은 해보겠지만 도와주셔야 해요. 구체적으로 제안을 해주셔야 해요.

숙어 153 nip in the air — 매서운 추위

A There sure was a **nip in the air** this morning.

B Me, too. I almost froze to death waiting for the bus coming to work.

A It's not just the temperature, you know. It's the wind that makes it so cold.

A 오늘 아침에 정말 추웠어요. 모자를 쓰고 와서 정말 다행이었어요.

B 저두요. 회사 오는 버스 기다리다 얼어 죽을 뻔했어요.

A 기온 때문만은 아닌 것 같아요. 바람까지 불어서 너무 추워요.

숙어 154 playing favorites — 편애하다

A Gina told me she got this Friday off. That's not fair!

B Why are you so angry? Do you think she doesn't deserve it?

A No. It's just the boss **playing favorites** again.

A 지나가 이번 주 금요일에 휴가를 냈대요. 불공평해요!

B 왜 그렇게 흥분하는 거에요? 지나가 그럴 만한 자격이 없다고 생각하세요?

A 아뇨. 상사가 또 다시 편애를 하니까 그렇죠.

숙어 155 go for　~을 택하다

A Have you had a chance to look over the menu?

B Yes, but I still don't know what to get. Is the chicken any good?

A It's very good, sir, but I would **go for** the fish. It's the chef's specialty.

A 메뉴 살펴보셨어요?

B 예, 하지만 아직도 뭘 먹어야 할지 모르겠어요. 치킨 괜찮나요?

A 매우 좋습니다, 고객님. 하지만 저라면 생선으로 하겠어요. 주방장 특선 요리거든요.

숙어 156 squeeze A in　A를 위해 짬을 내다

A I want to stay fit. but I', too busy to exercise at the health club.

B Then try doing short workouts whenever you get the chance.

A Good idea. I can **squeeze some exercise in** during lunch break.

A 건강을 유지하고 싶은데 너무 바빠서 헬스 클럽에서 운동할 수가 없어요.

B 그러면 기회가 있을 때마다 간단한 운동이라도 하세요.

A 그게 좋겠네요. 점심 시간에 짬을 내서 운동을 해도 되겠어요.

숙어 157 pay through the nose　엄청난 돈을 치르다, 바가지 쓰다

A I can't believe our team won the National Cup soccer championship.

B Yeah, we saw the final game live at the stadium. We had front-row seats!

A Wow! I guess you had to **pay though the nose** for your rickets.

A 우리 팀이 내셔널컵 축구 챔피언십에서 우승했다는 사실이 믿기지 않아요.

B 네, 우린 경기장에서 경기를 관람했어요. 좌석도 앞줄이었어요!

A 와! 입장권에 엄청난 돈을 치르셨겠어요.

숙어 158 go easy on ~을 너무 많이 사용하지 않다

A I'd like to get an iced tea, but it seems a bit expensive. Is it bottomless?

B No, but I'd be happy to give you one free refill.

A In that case, I'll have the iced tea and a ham and mustard. **Go easy on** the mustard, please.

A 아이스티를 마시고 싶은데, 좀 비싼 것 같아요.
리필 가능한가요?

B 아니오. 하지만 무료로 한 번 리필해 드릴게요.

A 그렇다면 아이스티와 겨자소스 뿌린 햄 주세요.
겨자소스는 조금만 넣으시고요.

숙어 159 a blast from the past 옛 추억을 떠올리게 하는 사람[물건]

A Mary, is that you? I can't believe it. It is you.

B Bill? Bill Johnson! Long time no see.
What **a blast from the past**!

A Seeing you brings back a lot of good memories.

A 메리? 너 맞니? 정말 믿기지 않아. 너 맞구나.

B 빌? 빌 존슨! 오랜만이야. 옛 추억이 확 밀려오네!

A 너 보니까 좋은 추억이 많이 생각나네.

숙어 160 down in the dumps 우울한, 의기소침한

A What's wrong, Tom? You look so sad.

B I've been **down in the dumps** recently.
My business is not making money.

A Don't worrym everything will be OK.

A 톰, 무슨 일 있어요? 얼굴이 안 좋아 보여요.

B 요즘 몹시 우울해요.
장사가 잘 안 되거든요.

A 너무 걱정하지 마세요. 다 잘될 거에요.

숙어 161 make headway 진척을 보이다, 전진하다

A It looks like we're going to be here all night.

B Well, I think we're **making** some real **headway**.

A Sure, but It's still going to be tomorrow morning by the time we finish.

A 밤새 여기에 있을 것 같아요.

B 그래도 어느 정도 실질적인 진척을 보이고 있잖아요.

A 맞아요, 하지만 다 끝내려면 내일 아침이나 되어야 할 거에요.

숙어 162 jump at ~을 흔쾌히 받아들이다

A What would you say if I offer you a job right now?

B I would **jump at** the chance to work here.
Are you offering me a job?

A Yes, actually. You're the most qualified candidate for this job.

A 지금 당장 제가 일자리를 드리겠다고 하면 뭐라고 말씀하시겠어요?

B 여기서 일할 기회를 두 말 않고 받아들이겠습니다.
제게 자리를 주시는 건가요?

A 네, 그래요. 이 업무에 가장 적합한 자격을 갖춘 지원자이시거든요.

숙어 163 give ~ a break on... ~에게 …을 깎아주다

A I just don't think this product is exactly what I need.
Can I get a refund?

B Would you be interested in keeping the product if the price were a bit lower?

A Sure, I think about keeping it if you **gave me a break on the price**.

A 이 제품은 제게 꼭 필요한 게 아니에요.
환불 받을 수 있을까요?

B 가격을 할인해 드리면 그 제품을 그대로 쓰시겠어요?

A 물론이죠. 할인해 주시면 그대로 쓸지 생각해볼게요.

숙어 164 across the board 전반적으로

A It looks like the entire schedule for the conference has been changed.

B How can they do that at the last minute? How's this going to affect us?

A We'll have to change our plans **across the board**.
What a hassle!

A 컨퍼런스 전체 일정이 바뀐 것 같아요.

B 그 사람들은 어떻게 마지막에 임박해서 그러지요? 이게 우리한테 어떤 영향을 미칠까요?

A 우리 계획들을 전반적으로 바꿔야 할 거에요.
골치가 아프네요!

숙어 165 sweater weather — 쌀쌀한 날씨

A We'd better wear our jackets at tonight's outdoor concert. I heard the temperature would drop below freezing.

B No, it won't get that cold. It'll be around 10 degrees Celsius all evening.

A Ahm then, that's just **sweater weather**.

A 오늘밤 야외 공연장에서 재킷을 입는 게 좋을 거에요.
기온이 영하로 떨어진대요.

B 아뇨, 그렇게 춥지는 않을 거에요.

A 아, 약간 쌀쌀한 날씨겠군요.

숙어 166 be pressed for — 쪼들리다

A Is there going to be enough time at the meeting for my presentation?

B I don't know. We **are** really **pressed for** time.
Everyone wants to be out of there by five.

A I see. In that case, I'll wait until the next weekly meeting before I present my ideas to the board.

A 회의에서 내가 프레젠테이션을 할 시간이 충분할까요?

B 글쎄요, 우리가 정말 시간에 쫓기고 있기는 해요. 모두들
5시까지는 끝내고 싶어하고요.

A 알겠어요. 그렇다면 다음 주간 회의 때까지 기다렸다가 이사회에 내 아이디어를 제출해야겠네요.

숙어 167 talk down — 폄하하다, 하찮게 여기다

A Have you heard anything good about this delivery company?

B No. Actually, I've heard Tom **talking down** about it before.

A Really? In that case, let's try to find another company to use. I don't want any hassles.

A 이 배송업체에 대해 좋은 얘기 들은 적 있어요?

B 아뇨. 실은 톰이 전에 그 회사에 대해 부정적으로 말하는 걸 들은 적이 있어요.

A 정말이에요? 그렇다면 다른 업체를 찾아서 이용해 봅시다. 골칫거리를 만들고 싶지는 않아요.

숙어 168 step on one's toes | ~의 감정을 상하게 하다

A What happened at the meeting? You let Tom **step on your toes.**

B Tom disareed with me, but I was able to get my points across.

A No one knew what you were talking about.

A 회의 때 무슨 일이 있었던 거에요? 톰 때문에 당신 기분이 몹시 상했다면서요.

B 톰은 저와 의견이 달랐지만, 저는 요지를 납득시킬 수 있었어요.

A 당신이 무슨 말을 하고 있었는지 아무도 몰랐어요.

숙어 169 rain check | 구입 우선권, 우천 순연권

A Hi, I'm looking for Healthy World green tea.
It's on sale, right?

B Yes. we're out of it now. Would you like a **rain check**?

A OK. I'll come back next week then.

A 안녕하세요. 헬시월드 녹차를 찾고 있어요.
할인 중인 거 맞죠?

B 네. 다 떨어졌는데 구입 우선권이라도 드릴까요?

A 좋아요. 그럼 다음 주에 올게요.

숙어 170 be on speaking terms | 친한 사이이다

A Why don't you and Jane come out for moviegoing with us this Friday?

B Well, is it ok if I come alone? Jane and I **aren't really on speaking terms** these days.

A Seriously? But I thought things were going really well with you guys.

A 이번 금요일에 우리 영화 보러 가는데 제인이랑 같이 올래?

B 음, 나 혼자 가도 돼? 나 요즘 제인이랑 말도 잘 안 하고 지내거든.

A 정말? 난 너희 둘이 사이 좋게 지내는 줄 알았는데.

숙어 171 ease up on — ~을 적게 하다, ~의 횟수를 줄이다

A I don't think our team can attend the conference in New York.

B Really? As far as I know, your team goes every year.

A Right. But our supervisor wants to **ease up on** business travel this year.

A 우리 팀은 뉴욕에서 열리는 회의에 참석 못할 것 같아요.

B 정말이에요? 제가 알기로는 당신 팀은 매년 가는 것 같던데요.

A 맞아요. 하지만 상사가 올해 출장 횟수를 줄이고 싶어하세요.

숙어 172 get on with — ~을 계속하다, 처리하다

A I've heard that we'll be working together on this project. I'm Tom.

B Sorry to say this, Tom. But we've got no time to waste. Let's start going through this report.

A Sure. I'll **get on with** it right away.

A 우리가 이 프로젝트를 함께 할 거라고 들었어요. 저는 톰입니다.

B 톰, 이렇게 말해서 미안한데요. 시간을 낭비해서는 안 돼요. 이 보고서부터 검토합시다.

A 그러죠. 지금 바로 처리하겠습니다.

숙어 173 a fish out of water — 물 떠난 물고기

A Hey, Sing a song for us.

B No thanks. I really don't like singing.

A Come on. Give it a try.

B Sorry, but I feel like **a fish out of water** when I try to sing.

A 야, 노래 하나 불러봐.

B 사양하겠어. 난 노래하는 거 정말 안 좋아해.

A 그러지 말고. 한번 해봐.

B 미안하지만 난 노래만 하려면 너무 어색해서 말이야.

숙어 174 bull's-eye — 정통으로 맞힌 것

A So, do you know the answer to the problem?

B Yes, but why don't you try to solve it instead?

A Is the answer forty two?

B **Bull's-eye**! You hit the nail right on the head.

A 그래, 넌 이 문제의 답을 알고 있니?

B 그럼. 그래도 네가 대신 한번 풀어 봐.

A 답이 42야?

B 정답이야! 바로 맞혔어.

숙어 175 a bull in a china shop — 난장판을 만드는 사람

A What happened in this room? Everything is a mess!

B Tom brought his two children over, and they destroyed everything.

A It looks like there was **a bull in a china shop** here.

B I know. We should never let them come back here again.

A 이 방에 무슨 일 있었어? 엉망진창이네!

B 톰이 자기 애 둘을 데리고 왔는데 걔들이 다 엉망으로 해놨지 뭐야.

A 완전히 난장판을 만들어 놓고 간 것 같네.

B 맞아. 다시는 걔들 여기에 못 오게 해야겠어.

숙어 176 rest on one's laurels — 과거의 영광에 안주하다

A Is Sandy going to compete in the science fair this year?

B No, I don't think so.

A But she won the contest last year. She should compete again.

B So she's going to **rest on her laurels**. She doesn't need to prove anything.

A 올해 과학 박람회에 샌디도 나가나?

B 아니. 아닐 것 같은데.

A 하지만 작년 대회에서 그녀가 우승했잖아. 다시 한 번 겨뤄야지.

B 이제 안주해 버리는 거지. 더 이상 증명해 보일 게 없잖아.

숙어 177 take a catnap — 잠깐 눈을 붙이다

A You looked tired. Why don't you get some sleep?

B I'd love to, but I have too many things to do.

A Well, you should at least **take a catnap**.

B That's a good idea. Can you wake me up in half an hour?

A 피곤해 보이네. 잠 좀 자는 게 어때?

B 나도 그러고 싶은데 할 일이 너무 많아서.

A 그럼 잠깐 눈이라도 좀 붙여.

B 그게 좋겠다. 30분 있다가 나 좀 깨워 줄래?

숙어 178 a fly in the ointment — 흥을 깨는 사람

A Hey, I didn't get enough food on my plate!

B Well, you can always go back and get seconds.

A That's not fair! You have more than I do!

B don't be **a fly in the ointment**. You're going to ruin the party for everyone.

A 야, 내 접시에는 음식이 별로 없잖아!

B 음, 다시 가서 한 접시 더 가져오면 돼.

A 불공평해! 네가 나보다 더 많잖아!

B 분위기 좀 깨지마. 모두를 위한 파티인데 네가 망치려고 하잖아.

숙어 179 have a big mouth — 떠벌리고 다니다

A Why did you tell everyone about our problems?

B I don't know. It just slipped out.

A You **have** such **a big mouth**. Why can't you keep it closed sometimes?

B I'm sorry. I guess that I just talk before I think.

A 왜 우리 문제를 모든 사람들한테 말해 버린 거니?

B 모르겠어. 얼떨결에 말이 나와버렸어.

A 너 정말 입 가볍다. 가끔은 입 좀 다물고 있을 수 없니?

B 미안해. 난 생각보다 말이 앞서나 봐.

숙어 180 step into the ring — 시도하다

A So, what do you think I should do?

B **Step into the ring**. It doesn't hurt to try.

A That's good advice.

B Of course it is. Just try it at least once.

A 그래 내가 어떻게 했으면 좋겠어?

B 한번 해봐. 뭐 밑질 거 없잖아.

A 맞는 말이다.

B 당연하지. 한 번 정도는 시도해 보는 거야.

숙어 181 putt one's chest out — 의기양양하다

A I guess that Max must have gotten promoted.

B What makes you say that?

A Look at him. He is really **puffing his chest out**.

B Oh, right. How could I not have noticed?

A 맥스가 승진을 한 게 분명해.

B 왜 그렇게 말하는데?

A 저 친구 좀 봐. 저렇게 어깨에 힘을 주고 있잖아.

B 정말 그러네. 난 왜 눈치를 못 챘지?

숙어 182 let the cat out of the bag — 비밀을 발설하다

A Did you tell Larry about my secret?
B I promise I didn't tell anyone.
A I wonder who **let the cat out of the bag** then.
B I don't know, but it wasn't me.

A 래리한테 내 비밀 얘기했어?
B 절대 아무한테도 얘기 안 했어.
A 그렇다면 누가 소문을 퍼뜨렸는지 모르겠네.
B 잘 모르겠지만 난 아니야.

숙어 183 carry the ball — 임무를 맡다

A Jack, I'd like you to **carry the ball** this time.
B But I don't know what to do, Mr. Burton.
A It's time that you learned some leadership skills.
B In that case, I'll do my best.

A 잭, 이번엔 당신이 일을 맡아줘야겠어.
B 하지만 전 뭘 해야 할지 잘 모르겠어요, 버튼 씨.
A 리더십 기술을 좀 익혀둬야 할 때야.
B 그렇다면 최선을 다하겠습니다.

숙어 184 cut the mustard — 기대에 부응하다

A I heard that Ben dropped out of school.
B He just wasn't able to **cut the mustard**.
A Maybe he should have studied more often instead of drinking everyday.
B Yeah, that probably would have helped him out a lot.

A 벤이 학교를 중퇴했다고 들었는데.
B 생각대로 잘 안 됐나 봐.
A 매일 술이나 마실 게 아니라 공부를 더 했어야지.
B 그래, 그랬으면 도움이 많이 됐을 텐데.

숙어 185 check someone — ~을 저지하다

A We're losing business because of the upstart company.
B We must find a way to **check them** so we don't lose all of our customers.
A Well, you're the boss. You figure out what to do.
B Give me some time to think about it.

A 새로 생긴 회사 때문에 장사가 안 되고 있어요.
B 우리 고객들을 다 잃지 않도록 그들을 막을 방법을 찾아야 합니다.
A 사장님이시니 방법을 생각해 주세요.
B 생각할 시간을 좀 줘요.

숙어 186 To bring home the bacon　생계를 책임지다

A Do you know when Kent is going to be back to work?

B The day after tomorrow. I think.

A Okay. I hope he's doing well.

B Yeah, I hope he pulls himself together A.S.A.P. too.

A He will. He has to be the person who **brings home the bacon** now since his father passed away.

A 언제부터 켄트가 다시 출근하는지 혹시 알아?

B 내일 모레부터일걸.

A 그렇구나. 잘 지내고 있는지 모르겠다.

B 그래. 빨리 기운을 차려야 할 텐데 말이야.

A 아마 그럴 거야. 아빠가 돌아가셨으니 이제 집안의 생계를 책임져야 하잖아.

숙어 187 slim to none　(가능성 등이) 희박하다

A How will this affect the long term market?

B It won't. The short term market, yes, but the long term market-no. Not a bit.

A How can you be so sure?

B In my opinion, the investors overreacted to one new figure and the chances of the Federal Reserve heightening interest rates are **slim to none.**

A 장기적으로 시장에 어떤 영향을 미칠 것 같습니까?

B 없습니다. 단기적으로는 몰라도 장기적으로는 아무런 영향을 미치지 못할 겁니다. 전혀요.

A 어떻게 그렇게 확신 할 수 있죠?

B 제 의견으로는, 투자자들이 한 개의 통계에 과잉반응을 보였다고 생각하고 연방 준비 은행이 금리를 높일 가능성은 희박하다고 봅니다.

숙어 188 To spread like wildfire　순식간에 번지다

A Kelly, did you tell anybody that I'm going out with Peter?

B Oh, I'm sorry. I didn't mean to. It was a slip of the tongue.

A How could you do that? I asked you to keep it to yourself.

B I'm terribly sorry. But I only told Susie, no one else.

A It makes no difference. Don't you know that kind of news **spreads like wildfire**?

A 켈리, 너 내가 피터랑 사귄다는 거 다른 사람에게 얘기했지?

B 미안해. 그러려고 했던 건 아닌데, 그냥 입에서 튀어나와 버렸어.

A 어떻게 그럴 수가 있어? 내가 너만 알고 있으라고 했잖아.

B 정말 미안해. 하지만 난 정말 수지한테밖에 얘기 안했어.

A 그게 무슨 상관이야. 이런 말은 순식간에 퍼진다는 거 몰라?

숙어 189 To pump out — 뽑어내다

A Oh, my god! Close the window right now.

B What's that dirty gas that car is pumping out.

A We'd better change lanes too. The wind shield is getting filthy.

B Okay. Isn't here any law to regulate those cars **pumping out** fumes?

A There might be one. But nobody follows the rule on the street, you know.

A 맙소사! 창문 닫아, 빨리.

B 저 차 왜 저렇게 공해를 뿜어내는 거야?

A 차선도 바꾸는 게 낫겠다. 차 앞유리도 더러워지겠어.

B 그래. 저렇게 공해를 뿜어내는 차를 규제하는 법은 없나?

A 있겠지. 하지만 알다시피 길에선 아무도 법을 안 지키잖아.

숙어 190 To go/sell like hot cakes — 날개 돋친 듯 팔리다

A What a headache! We're in a big trouble now.

B What's going on?

A You know the newly launched pocket computer of our competitor? It's **going like hot cakes** now.

B Does the newspaper say so?

A Yes. We'd better come up with something before Mr. Lee shows up.

B Gee.... How come those guys are always a step ahead of us?

A 아이구 머리야! 우리 큰일났다.

B 무슨 일이야?

A 우리 경쟁사가 새로 출시한 포켓 컴퓨터 알지? 날개 돋친 듯 팔린대.

B 신문에 그렇게 났어?

A 응. 부장님 오시기 전에 뭔가 묘안을 짜내야겠는걸.

B 이런. 어떻게 매번 상대방이 우리보다 한 수 위일 수 있지?

숙어 191 wine and dine someone — 비즈니스 접대를 하다

A Are you coming home for dinner tonight?

B Sorry, but I have to **wine and dine** Mr. Taylor tonight.

A Are you trying to do business with him?

B Yes, so I need to take him out to dinner and talk about my proposal.

A 오늘 밤에 저녁 먹으러 집에 올거지?

B 미안해, 오늘 밤 테일러 씨랑 접대 약속이 있어.

A 그 사람하고 거래하려고?

B 응, 그래서 밖에서 같이 저녁 식사하면서 내 제안에 관해 얘기해야 해.

숙어 192 be really pissed off — 정말 화내다

A He **was really pissed off** yesterday. I've never seen him that angry.

B I couldn't imagine how he could treat you like that. He is usually a calm person. I don't know what got into him.

A He might feel overwhelmed right now. I'd better not beat myself up over him.

B Right, Don't be upset at him.

A 그는 어제 정말 화가 났었어. 전에는 그렇게 화낸 모습을 본적이 없어.

B 그가 널 그렇게 대하다니 상상할 수 없다. 그는 평상시엔 침착한 사람이야. 그가 무엇 때문에 그랬는지 모르겠다.

A 지금쯤은 아마 그도 당황하고 있을지 몰라. 나도 그 일에 대해 너무 고민하지 않으려 해.

B 그래, 맞아. 그에게 너무 화내지 마.

숙어 193 graveyard shift — 야간 근무

A Where were you last night?

B I was working the **graveyard shift.**

A Wasn't Sean supposed to do that shift yesterday?

B He was, but he had a family emergency.

A Did someone die on him again?

B Hope not.

A 어젯밤에 어디 있었어?

B 야간 근무하고 있었어.

A 어제 근무는 숀이 하기로 돼 있지 않았었나?

B 그러기로 돼 있었는데 집에 급한 일이 생겨서.

A 주변에서 또 누가 죽었대?

B 아니길 바라야지.

숙어 194 take some time apart — 떨어져 있는 시간(냉각기)을 가지다

A You don't seem yourself recently, is there anything wrong?

B Eric and I decided to **take some time apart**. We might get divorced.

A How come? I thought of you two as a perfect couple.

B I don't think we are meant to be together, but there has to be someone out there just perfect for me.

A 요즘 평소 같지 않은데, 무슨 안 좋은 일 있어요?

B 에릭과 저는 당분간 떨어져 있는 시간을 좀 갖기로 했어요. 우리 아마 이혼할 것 같아요.

A 무엇 때문에요? 나는 두 사람이 완벽한 부부 사이인 줄 알았어요.

B 아마도 우린 천생연분이 아닌 것 같아요. 나에게 완벽하게 맞는 사람이 따로 있을 것 같아요.

숙어 195 be fed up with~ | ~에 질리다

A I got stuck working late. **I'm fed up with** working at this firm. I can't keep my eyes open any longer.

B Did you stay up last night? Take a nap!

A I can't. I've got to get this done within 3days and attend the conference meeting.

B Don't stress out. I can handle your work if you want me to fill in for you.

A 밤늦게까지 일을 했어. 이 회사에서 일하는 것에 질렸어.
더 이상 눈을 뜰 수가 없군.

B 어제 밤샘했어? 잠시 눈 좀 붙이지 그래!

A 안 돼. 3일 이내로 이 일을 끝내야 해. 게다가 회의에 참석해야 해.

B 너무 스트레스 받지 마. 원한다면 내가 대신해서 네 일을 처리해 줄게.

숙어 196 Up in the air | 아직 미정이다

A I hear that Kenny will be transferred to America soon. Is that true?

B It's **up in the air.**

A I see. In case Kenny is reassigned to America, who's going to succeed him as the branch manager?

B It's up for grabs.

A Kenny really has good connections in the company.

A 케니가 미국으로 전근 간다고 하던데, 사실이니?

B 아직 확실하지 않아.

A 알겠어. 케니가 미국으로 발령받으면 후임 지점장은 누가 될까?

B 그것도 확실치 않아.

A 케니는 회사 내에 연줄이 있나봐.

숙어 197 be in traffic | 교통 체증에 걸리다

A Where are you heading to?

B Metropolitan Art Museum, please. How long does it take to get there?

A I bet approximately 1 hour.

B Really? You mean we **are in traffic**?

A We are stuck in a traffic jam. Traffic is murder at this time of day.

A 어디로 갈까요?

B 메트로폴리탄 예술 박물관으로 가요. 얼마나 걸릴까요?

A 대략 한 시간쯤 걸릴지 모릅니다.

B 정말이에요? 교통 때문에 그런가요?

A 교통 체증에 걸린 거죠. 이 시간대의 교통이 하루 중에 가장 끔찍합니다.

숙어 198 quote a price — 시세를 부르다

A Overseas Sales Department. Sarah Conners speaking.

B Hi! I'm interested in your HDTVs. Do you have a sales office in Korea?

A Yes, we do. In fact, we can arrange a sales visit for you today. Where are you located?

B Uh... That won't be necessary. Could you just **quote** me **a price** for the 29" one?

A 해외 판매 부서 세라 코너스입니다.

B 안녕하세요. 귀사의 HDTV에 관심이 있는데요. 한국에 판매대리점이 있나요?

A 예, 있습니다. 오늘 중으로 방문판매를 주선할 수 있습니다. 어디에 계시죠?

B 어…, 그럴 필요 없어요. 그냥 29인치의 시세만 알려주시겠어요?

숙어 199 share one's optimism — 낙관론에 동의하다

A I'm afraid I don't **share your optimism**.

B Why not?

A I don't think things will turn around so soon.

B Reason?

A The union's taken the hard line.

A 난 너의 낙관론에 동의하지 않아.

B 왜?

A 경기가 그렇게 빨리 호전되진 않을 것 같아.

B 이유는?

A 노조가 강경한 자세를 취하고 있거든.

숙어 200 run the risk — 모험하다

A We can't **run the risk** of provoking a strike.

B Who said anything about a strike?

A The press.

B You can't always trust the press.

A But this time it's different.

A 파업을 초래하는 위험을 무릅쓸 수는 없어.

B 파업이라니, 누가 그래?

A 언론.

B 언론을 항상 믿을 수는 없어.

A 하지만 이번엔 달라.

숙어 201 have no option

선택의 여지가 없다

A As far as I'm concerned, we **have no option.**

B What do you mean?

A We have to trim our work force.

B I beg to differ on that point.

A How will we manage the situation then?

A 내가 아는 한 우리에겐 선택의 여지가 없어.

B 무슨 뜻이지?

A 인력을 감원해야만 해.

B 그 의견에 난 동의할 수 없어.

A 그럼 이 상황을 어떻게 처리할 거야?

숙어 202 lay off

해고하다

A How do we go about it then?

B As far as I know, **laying off** personnel isn't the answer.

A What do you suggest we do at this point in time then?

B I believe these setbacks are only temporary.

A So you're saying things will turn around soon.

A 그럼 이 일을 어떻게 진행하지?

B 내가 아는 한 직원들을 해고하는 건 답이 아니야.

A 그럼 이 시점에서 우리가 뭘 해야 한다고 제안하는 거야?

B 내 생각에 지금의 불경기는 일시적인 것에 불과해.

A 그래서 네가 하는 얘긴 경기가 곧 회복될 거라는 말이야?

숙어 203 Lock, stock, and barrel

모든 것

A I've been trying to talk to Leo since last week. He doesn't answer my call.

B Did he owe you something?

A Not exactly. He borrowed one of my books and I just wanna get it back.

B A book? That doesn't sound too bad. Don't be shocked. Leo sold everything and moved to Texas.

A What?

B Yeah, I mean everything-**lock, stock and barrel**-and nobody can reach him now.

A 지난주부터 계속 리오에게 전화하고 있는데 도무지 받지 않네.

B 혹시 너 걔한테 돈 빌려줬어?

A 그건 아닌데. 내 책 한 권을 빌려갔는데 돌려받고 싶어서.

B 책 한 권? 그건 괜찮을 것 같네. 놀라지 마. 리오가 모든 걸 처분하고 텍사스로 가버렸대.

A 뭐?

B 응, 완전히 하나도 남김없이 모든 걸 다 처분하고 지금은 누구와도 연락이 안 돼.

숙어 204 To bite the dust | 죽다

A Did you watch the TV series '24' last night?

B You bet. You know I love that show.

A I worked all night and forgot to set my VCR. What happened?

B Jack Bauer finally got the chip in his hand but the chip was seriously-damaged.

A Yeah? Did the Iraqi agent do something to help Jack?

B Sure. He did a great job and **bit the dust** at the end of the show.

A 어제 TV 시리즈 '24' 봤어?

B 당연하지. 내가 좋아하는 거 알잖아.

A 난 어제 늦게까지 일했는데 녹화하는 걸 깜빡했어. 어떻게 됐어?

B 잭 바우어가 결국엔 칩을 손에 넣었는데 그 칩이 몹시 손상돼버렸어.

A 그래? 그 이라크 요원은 그 과정에서 뭔가 해냈어?

B 물론. 큰 역할을 하고는 끝날 때쯤 죽었어.

숙어 205 Hang by a hair | 매우 위태롭다

A You look so serious reading the newspaper. What's in it?

B Another local computer tycoon failed, it says.

A I heard that. It's getting worse and worse.

B Local computer market seems to **hang by a hair**, according to the report.

A 신문에 뭐가 났기에 그렇게 표정이 심각해?

B 국내 굴지의 컴퓨터 회사가 또 망했대.

A 나도 들었어. 상황이 점점 나빠지고 있어.

B 기사를 보면 국내 컴퓨터 시장이 매우 위태로운 것 같은데.

숙어 206 Go under | 파산하다, 망하다

A Gang-Nam was hard hit by the depression.

B Yeah, I know at least ten companies that have **gone under**.

A Everybody's had to try to reduce their overheads to remain competitive.

B We've cut ours by 60%.

A 이번 불황으로 강남도 심한 타격을 받았습니다.

B 그래요. 제가 알기로도 적어도 10개 회사는 파산했습니다.

A 모두가 경상비를 줄여 경쟁력을 유지하도록 노력해야 했습니다.

B 우리 회사는 경상비를 60%나 삭감한 걸요.

숙어 207 Make myself clear — 확실히 이해시키다

A Our prices are the lowest in the entire industry. I thought I **made myself clear.**

B I know that, but your offering is not enough.

A We could give you more products in each box for just a fraction of the price more. What do you think?

B That's fine. I accept your offer.

A 업계에서 저희 가격이 가장 저렴합니다. 제가 분명히 말씀 드린 것 같은데요.

B 알고 있습니다만 제시한 조건이 만족스럽지 않습니다.

A 가격을 조금만 올리면 각 상자에 상품 몇 개씩을 더 넣어 드릴 수 있습니다. 어떻게 생각하세요?

B 좋습니다. 제의를 받아들이지요.

숙어 208 Much and then some — 추가로

A The price of this computer is 150 dollars, isn't it?

B It costs that **much and then some.**

A Do you mean this computer costs more?

B You're right if you include the price of RAM and VRAM.

A 이 컴퓨터 가격이 150달러 맞습니까?

B 그렇습니다만 조금 추가될 수 있습니다.

A 가격이 더 비싸다는 건가요?

B 만약 RAM과 VRAM의 가격을 포함하면 그렇습니다.

숙어 209 to shape up — 만족스럽게 발전하다

A The manager told them they'd better **shape up** or they'll get a pink slip.

B I knew he'd get around to it.

A I'm glad he clamped down on them.

A 만족스러운 결과를 못 낸다면 해고될 거라고 경영인이 그들에게 말했답니다.

B 난 그가 적절한 조치를 취할 거란 걸 알았어요.

A 저는 그가 엄격한 조치를 취했다는 게 반갑네요.

숙어 210 Know it inside out — 샅샅이 알다

A Is your factory near here?

B Yes, it is within walking distance. Let me show you.

A You seem to **know this** place **inside out.**

B Yes I do. If you have any technical questions, please ask me.

A 공장이 여기서 가까운가요?

B 예, 걸어갈 수 있는 거리입니다. 제가 안내해 드릴게요.

A 이곳 지리를 꿰뚫고 계시나 봐요.

B 네, 그렇습니다. 기술상의 의문점도 저에게 물어보세요.

숙어 211 Not in the same league

같은 수준이 아닌, 격이 다른

A What company is your main competitor?

B I'm tempted to say The King Company but they're so strong that we're **not even in the same league** as them. They're the best in the world.

A Do you mean that two companies can't be compared on the same scale?

B Yes. But we serve niche markets they don't cover.

A 강력한 경쟁사는 어디인가요?

B 킹 회사라고 말하고 싶습니다만, 거긴 너무 강해서 우리와는 격이 다릅니다. 그들은 세계 최고니까요.

A 두 회사가 규모 면에서 비교가 되지 않는다는 말씀인가요?

B 예, 하지만 저희는 그들이 커버하지 않는 틈새 시장을 공략하고 있습니다.

숙어 212 Ball park figure

대략의 수치

A Are you all set for the presentation this afternoon?

B Pretty much. Oh, I'm so nervous.

A You'll get used to it.

B I have a question. Do I have to memorize every number on the document?

A Not necessarily. But you'd better know some important figures. At least, you know, a **ball park figure**.

B Got it. Thanks.

A 오늘 오후에 있을 발표 준비는 다 했어?

B 거의. 진짜 떨린다.

A 곧 익숙해질 거야.

B 질문이 있는데 보고서에 있는 수치들을 다 외워야 하나?

A 꼭 그럴 필요는 없지만 중요한 수치는 아는 게 좋지.
적어도 대략 얼마쯤 되는지 정도는.

B 알았어. 고마워.

숙어 213 the name of the game

핵심, 중요한 것, 요점

A Downsizing and layoffs are **the name of the game** now. Everybody is farming out as much work as they can.

B There's a limit to how far we can go with that.

A Yes, our unions are really getting uptight about it.

A 조직 감축과 정리 해고가 중요한 시점이에요. 모두가 가능한 한 많은 일을 외부에 위탁하고 있죠.

B 그래도 그런 식으로는 한계가 있어요.

A 맞아요. 우리 노조도 점점 강경한 태도를 보이고 있죠.

숙어 214 At the outside
기껏해야, 겨우, 고작해야

A What are our chances of landing the contract to build a bridge?

B Not too good, I'm afraid.

A What would you say the odds are?

B Well. It'll be ten percent **at the** very **outside**.

A 그 교량 건설 계약을 따낼 가능성은 얼마쯤 되지?

B 별로 좋지 않을 것 같아 걱정이야.

A 그럼 가능성이 도대체 어느 정도라는 거야?

B 글쎄. 기껏해야 10% 정도일 거야.

숙어 215 To pound / hit the pavement
직장을 구하려고 노력하다

A Jobs are hard to come by these days.

B I hear John's been **pounding the pavement** for a long time.

A Has nothing suitable come along for him?

B I wonder how he makes ends meet.

A 요즘에는 일자리를 얻기가 힘들어요.

B 내가 듣기로는 존이 오랫동안 직장을 구하려 애쓰고 있대요.

A 맞는 직장이 없어서?

B 생활은 어떻게 하는지 궁금하네.

숙어 216 To gain ground on
더 가까이 가다, 세력을 넓히다

A Sales are up!

B That means we're definitely **gaining ground on** our competitors.

A They'll soon be trying to take us over!

B We need a more aggressive marketing strategy if we want to capture a bigger share of the market.

A 판매량이 증가하고 있습니다!

B 그 말은 우리가 경쟁사들에 비해 세력이 확장되었단 뜻입니다.

A 그들은 곧 우리를 앞서려고 할 것입니다.

B 우리가 보다 큰 시장점유율을 차지하려면 더 적극적인 마케팅 전략이 필요합니다.

숙어 217 Pow-wow 회의

A Did you read the newspaper today?

B Only the front page. Something on it?

A The newly launched product of B&B got an excellent review.

B Oh, those guys seem pretty good at public relation.

A I think we need to have a **pow-wow** in my office right away.

B Okay. I'll be right there.

A 오늘 신문 봤어?

B 1면만 봤는데. 무슨 뉴스라도 있어?

A B&B의 새로 출시된 상품이 아주 좋은 평을 받았어.

B 그 회사는 홍보를 꽤 잘하는 것 같아.

A 당장 내 사무실에서 회의를 좀 했으면 하는데.

B 알았어. 바로 갈게.

숙어 218 To put one's nose to the grindstone 매우 열심히 일하다

A What's going on? It's so unusually quiet this morning.

B Shh. Ranold just got reprimanded by Mr. Alcott.

A For what? He got caught chatting on the computer again?

B Yeah. Mr. Alcott got furious this time.

A That's why everyone is **putting their nose to the grindstone** this morning.

A 무슨 일이야? 왜 이렇게 사무실이 조용해?

B 쉿. 레이놀드가 방금 알코트씨에게 몹시 혼났어.

A 또 근무 중에 컴퓨터 채팅하다 걸렸어?

B 응. 알코트씨가 이번엔 진짜 화났어.

A 그래서 오늘 아침 다들 이렇게 열심히 일하는구먼.

숙어 219 Hang out one's shingle 개업하다

A Excuse me. I'm looking for Mr. Shepherd.

B I'm sorry but he's not working here any more.

A Really? Then do you know what company he's working for now?

B Mr. Shepherd is going to **hang out his shingle** this coming June.

A Okay. Do you have his phone number, by any chance?

A 실례지만 셰퍼드씨를 찾는데요.

B 죄송합니다만 회사를 그만두셨습니다.

A 그래요? 그럼 지금 어디서 일하는지 알 수 있을까요?

B 셰퍼드씨는 오는 6월에 자신의 사무실을 열 예정입니다.

A 알겠습니다. 혹시 셰퍼드씨의 전화번호를 알 수 있을까요?

숙어 220 To take early retirement

조기 퇴직하다

A Jane **took early retirement**.

B No kidding. I thought she'd die on the job.

A The reward for her retirement was a golden handshake of several years' pay.

B She got herself a really sweet deal.

A 제인이 조기 퇴직을 했대.

B 정말? 제인은 죽을 때까지 일할 것 같았는데.

A 퇴직에 대한 보상으로 몇 년의 연봉에 상당하는 특별 퇴직금을 받는다는군.

B 상당히 좋은 조건이군.

숙어 221 On the road.

외근 중이다

A Don't send me any email this week. Call me on my cell phone instead.

B Okay. Why is that?

A I'm going to be **on the road** on business most of the week.

A 이번 주에는 나한테 e메일 보내지 말고 휴대전화로 연락해.

B 알았어. 그런데 왜?

A 이번 주는 업무 때문에 대부분 외근 중일 거야.

숙어 222 To twiddle one's thumbs

빈둥거리다

A Come in. Sit down, make yourself at home.

B Thanks. I need a rest. I've been on my feet all day.

A How was your first day at work?

B Really boring. I had nothing to do. I just sat at my desk **twiddling my thumbs.**

A 들어와. 앉아서 편히 쉬어.

B 고마워. 난 휴식이 필요해. 하루 종일 서있었어.

A 첫 출근인데 어땠니?

B 정말로 따분했지. 나는 할 일이 없더라. 단지 책상에 앉아 기다리는 것밖에는 할 일이 없었어.

숙어 223 shake like a leaf

사시나무처럼 떨다

A Hey, what's wrong with you.

B What are you talking about?

A You're **shaking like a leaf**.

B It's just that strong noise startled me for a second.

A 야, 무슨 일 있어?

B 무슨 말 하는 거야?

A 너 지금 사시나무 떨듯이 떨고 있잖아.

B 이상한 소리에 잠시 놀란 것 뿐야.

숙어 224 Gravy Train — 쉽고 편한 일

A What do you do for a living these days?

B I'm working as a secretary at an attorney's office Monday to Friday. And I'm also moonlighting at a few places.

A Isn't it too much for you to moonlight?

B Not really. I usually baby-sit a girl next door and she's always asleep even before I get there. It's a sort of a **gravy train.**

A 요즘 무슨 일 해?

B 주중에는 변호사 사무실에서 비서로 일해. 아르바이트도 좀 하고 있어.

A 아르바이트까지 하는 건 너무 벅차지 않아?

B 그렇지도 않아. 주로 옆집 아기를 돌보는데 내가 가기도 전에 늘 잠들거든. 그 정도면 쉬운 일이지 뭐.

숙어 225 To set an example — 모범을 보이다

A My supervisor always works late. I think she wants **to set an example.**

B My boss is rarely afraid to take risks. I really want to follow his example.

A What do you think is needed to succeed as a manager?

B I suppose a manager needs to be able to adapt to a changing environment, having a sense of proportion.

A 우리 상사는 항상 늦게까지 일해. 내 생각엔 모범을 보이려고 그러시는 것 같아.

B 우리 상사는 모험을 두려워하지 않지. 난 정말 본받고 싶어.

A 관리자로서 성공하기 위해서는 무엇이 필요하다고 생각해?

B 관리자는 변화하는 환경에 적응할 수 있는 능력과 균형 감각이 필요할 것 같아.

숙어 226 Labor of love — 자원봉사

A Did you have a nice weekend? You look a little exhausted.

B I do? Yeah, I feel a little tired but a **labor of love** always makes me happy.

A Oh, was it yesterday you guys were supposed to pay a visit to the orphanage?

B Yes. I had a great time with kids.

A 주말 잘 보냈어? 좀 피곤해 보이네.

B 그래? 사실 좀 피곤하긴 한데 자원봉사를 해서 기분은 좋아.

A 아, 보육원에 가기로 한 날이 어제였어?

B 응. 애들이랑 좋은 시간 보냈어.

숙어 227 Out of the loop — 일에서 손 뗀

A I have a couple of questions about last quarter's budget. Do you know who I should talk to?

B It's definitely Jason. He was in charge of the budget for more than three years.

A But isn't he **out of the loop**? He's in the HR division.

B It doesn't mean that he can't help you. Actually, he has an obligation to help you because he used to do the same job as you.

A 지난 분기 예산에 대해 궁금한 것이 있는데 누구에게 물어봐야 하죠?

B 제이슨이요. 그가 3년 이상 예산 업무를 담당했으니까요.

A 그런데 이젠 이 일과 무관하지 않나요? 인사팀에 있잖아요.

B 그래도 도와줄 순 있죠. 그가 전임자니까 도와줄 의무가 있다고 생각하는데요.

숙어 228 Give Notice — 통지하다

A You missed work today. What happened?

B I wasn't feeling well so I visited my physician this afternoon.

A You should **give notice** even in an emergency.

B I'm so sorry about that. Next time I will call and let you know in advance.

A 오늘 회사에 안 나왔던데 무슨 일이죠?

B 몸이 안 좋아서 병원에 갔었어요.

A 급한 상황이라도 사전에 미리 연락 주셔야 합니다.

B 정말 죄송합니다. 다음엔 미리 전화해서 알려 드리겠습니다.

숙어 229 to give someone credit for — …를 칭찬하거나 존경하다

A You did a great job, Mr. Long.

B I can't take all the credit, Ms. King. I had a lot of help from everyone here.

A That's great. I like it when everyone works well together.

B **The credit for our success** goes to everyone in this department.

A Mr. Long, 아주 잘하셨습니다.

B Ms. King, 저 혼자 한 일이 아닙니다. 여기 있는 모든 분들이 도와주셨어요.

A 아주 좋아요. 저는 모두가 협력해서 일하는 것을 좋아합니다.

B 공은 이 부서의 모든 사람들에게 돌아가야 합니다.

숙어 230 Blow your own horn. 자화자찬하다

A Please tell us about an achievement of which you are particularly proud.

B Well, I'm not really one to **blow my own horn**, but I do have one achievement I'm proud of: I was the top regional salesman at my previous company for seven years!

A 특별히 자랑할 만한 성과가 없다면 말해 주세요.

B 그다지 자화자찬하는 성격은 아니지만 자랑스럽게 여기는 성과가 하나 있습니다. 전 직장에서 칠 년 동안 그 지역 최우수 판매 사원이었습니다!

숙어 231 have sweaty palms 손에 식은땀이 나다

A I thought John was a little nervous tonight.

B Why do you say that ?

A I shook hands with him before the show, and he **had sweaty palms**.

B Well, he seemed to handle himself well in front of the audience.

A 오늘밤에 존이 좀 긴장했던 것 같아.

B 왜 그렇게 생각해?

A 쇼가 시작되기 전에 악수를 했는데, 손바닥이 땀으로 젖었더라구.

B 글쎄, 청중들 앞에서는 잘 해내는 것 같았는데.

숙어 232 Starting a family. 첫 아이를 갖다

A You've been married for five years. When do you think you will **start a family**?

B My wife and I are trying to save a little bit more money before we start having kids.

A That sounds like a smart plan.

A 네가 결혼한 지 5년이 됐네. 첫 아이는 언제 가질 생각이야?

B 아이를 갖기 전에 돈을 좀 더 모으려고 하고 있어.

A 현명한 생각이네.

숙어 233 The in-laws. 시댁(또는 처가)

A So how is married life treating you?

B It's fantastic. It's exciting starting a life with my husband.

A That sounds great. What about **the in-laws?**

B Well, I think I need some time to work on that

A 그래, 결혼생활은 어때?

B 환상적이야. 남편과 시작하는 삶이 너무 신나.

A 그거 잘됐네. 시댁이랑은 어때?

B 글쎄, 그건 조금 더 시간이 필요할 것 같아.

숙어 234 Match made in heaven. 천생연분

A How long have you been married?

B Our tenth anniversary is in August, but it feels like we were married just yesterday.

A Wow. Sounds like a **match made in heaven.**

A 결혼한 지 얼마나 됐어?

B 8월이면 결혼 10주년인데도 어제 결혼한 것처럼 느껴져.

A 와, 천생연분인가보다.

숙어 235 One's hair stands on end. 머리카락이 쭈뼛 서다

A That horror film really scared me.

B Yeah, **my hair was standing on end** the whole time.

A Especially at the end of the movie.

B Yeah, it sure was quite a shocker.

A 그 공포 영화 정말 무서웠어.

B 그래, 영화 보는 내내 무서워서 머리털이 다 서 있었다니까.

A 특히 마지막 장면에서 그랬지.

B 맞아, 정말 충격적인 장면이었어.

숙어 236 have a broken heart 사랑의 상처를 안고 있다

A How are you handling your breakup with Doug?

B Not too well. He **broke my heart.**

A Don't worry. Time heals all wounds.

B Thanks for trying to cheer me up.

A 너 더그랑 헤어지고 나서 어떻게 잘 지내고 있니?

B 별로, 마음에 상처를 받았어.

A 걱정하지 마. 시간이 지나면 다 괜찮아질 거야.

B 나 기운 나게 해주려고 애쓰는 거 고마워.

숙어 237 one's cup of tea — 취향에 딱 맞는 일

A Do you know how to crate computer graphics?

B Sure I do. It's **my cup of tea**.

A Oh, that's right. You used to work for a computer company.

B Yeah, that's where I learned how to make graphics.

A 너 컴퓨터 그래픽 만들 줄 알아?

B 알고말고, 내 주특기인걸.

A 아, 맞다. 너 전에 컴퓨터 회사에서 일했었지.

B 응. 거기서 그래픽 제작하는 법을 배웠지.

숙어 238 scared stiff — 몸이 얼어붙은

A Why don't you get out oif the way of that car ?

B When I saw it coming, I got **scared stiff**.

A It's a good thing that the car swerved out of the way at the last moment.

B Yeah, or else I might not even be here.

A 너 왜 차가 올 때 비켜서지 않았니?

B 차가 오는 걸 보고는 너무 놀라서 몸이 굳어버렸어.

A 마지막 순간에 자동차가 비켜 가서 천만다행이야.

B 그래, 안 그랬으면 난 이 자리에 없을지도 몰라.

숙어 239 Stuck in Traffic — 도로가 막히다

A I don't understand why we are **stuck in traffic**, but the other direction is clear.

B Maybe there's an accident ahead.

A I bet it's all the rubberneckers trying to get a look at the accident scene.

A 반대방향은 잘 가는데 왜 우리 도로만 막히는지 모르겠어.

B 아마 앞에 사고가 났나 봐.

A 장담하는데 사고 구경하려는 사람들 때문일 거야.

숙어 240 big cheese — 거물

A Who is that person over there?

B That's my boss, Ms. Kelly.

A So, she's the **big cheese** around here.

B Yeah, she runs this entire department.

A 저기 저 사람 누구야?

B 우리 부서장인 켈리 씨야?

A 그러니까 저 사람이 여기서 우두머리네.

B 그렇지, 이 부서 전체를 관리하거든.

숙어 241 eat one's words. 실언을 했다고 인정하다

A I said the most foolish things at the party tonight.

B You sure did. What were you thinking?

A I'll have to go apologize and **eat my words.**

B That's pretty manly of you. I hope those words don't taste too bad.

A 나 오늘밤 파티에서 정말 멍청한 말을 해버렸어.

B 너 진짜 그랬어. 도대체 무슨 생각으로 그런 거야?

A 가서 사과하고, 창피하지만 내가 말실수 한 걸 인정해야겠어.

B 꽤 남자답구나. 그렇다고 너무 창피해 하진 마.

숙어 242 a tough nut to crack 속을 알 수 없는 사람

A I don't understand Stacy at all.

B She can be mysterious some of the time.

A No kidding. She's a **tough nut to crack.**

B May be she is just a private person and doesn't like to talk about herself.

A 난 스테이시가 도무지 이해가 안 돼.

B 한동안은 그 속을 알 수 없을 수도 있지.

A 농담이 아니야. 걘 도통 속을 알 수가 없다고.

B 그냥 내성적인 아이라 자기 얘기 하는 걸 좋아하지 않는 걸 거야.

숙어 243 water under the bridge. 이미 지나가버린 일

A I'm surprised to see you working with Marty.

B Why?

Do you mean because of our problems in the past ?

A That's exactly what I'm talking about.

B We've forgotten about our problems.

It's all **water under the bridge.**

A 네가 마티와 함께 일하는 걸 보고 깜짝 놀랐어.

B 왜?

옛날에 우리 사이에 있었던 문제 때문에?

A 내가 말하려던 게 바로 그거야.

B 그 문제에 대해선 잊어버렸어.

이미 지나간 일이잖아.

숙어 244 all tuckered out — 몹시 지친

A I think I'm going to go to bed now.

B But it's only nine o'clock!

Why are you going to sleep so early?

A I'm **all tuckered out**. I've been up since six-thirty.

B Oh, in that case, you'd better get some sleep now.

A 나 이제 자야겠어.

B 이제 9시밖에 안 됐잖아!
왜 이렇게 일찍 자려고 하는데?

A 너무 지쳤어. 6시 30분에 일어났단 말이야.

B 아, 그렇다면 지금 좀 자야겠다.

숙어 245 gravy train — 놀고먹는 일

A You know, you must have the best job in the world.

B Yeah, it is pretty good now that I think about it.

A Pretty good? Your job is an absolute **gravy train**.

B Well, it's good, but I don't know if I would go that far.

A 야, 넌 세상에서 제일 좋은 직업을 갖고 있는 거야.

B 그래, 이제 생각해 보니 꽤 괜찮은 것 같다.

A 꽤 괜찮아? 이봐, 네 일은 완전히 놀고 먹는 거라니까.

B 글쎄, 좋긴 한데, 그 정도로 좋은 건지는 잘 모르겠는데.

숙어 246 cry over split milk — 엎질러진 물 때문에 슬퍼하다

A I can't believe how many bad things have happened today. Today has been a disaster.

B Hey, there is no use in **crying over spilt milk**.

A What do you suggest that I do?

B Why don't you just grin and bear it?

A 오늘 나쁜 일들이 얼마나 많았는지 몰라. 정말 끔찍한 하루였어.

B 야, 이미 엎질러진 물인데 울어봐야 소용 없잖아.

A 내가 어떻게 했으면 좋겠니?

B 그냥 씩 웃고 견뎌내는 거지 뭐.

숙어 247 erupt like a volcano — 분노가 폭발하다

A Wow! Can you believe that staff meeting we just had?

B Mr. Mitchell totally **erupted like a volcano** in there.

A What was his problem anyway?

B I guess he couldn't keep his anger bottled up any longer.

A 와, 방금 있었던 직원회의 말이야, 대단하지 않았어?

B 미첼 씨 완전히 화산처럼 폭발하더군.

A 그런데 그 사람 왜 그런 거야?

B 화가 치밀어 오르는 걸 더 이상 참을 수가 없었나봐.

숙어 248 have a ball — 신나게 놀다

A This party is not too boring, is it?

B No way. I'm **having a ball** here.

A Do you really think so?

B Yeah, it's easily the best party of the year.

A 이 파티 그렇게 지루하지는 않다, 그치?

B 지루하다니, 난 엄청 신나는걸.

A 정말 그렇게 생각해?

B 그래, 이 파티는 단연코 올해 최고의 파티야.

숙어 249 blow one's top — 뚜껑이 열리다

A You know, you really need to control your anger.

B Why do you say that?

A Because you look like you're going to **blow your top**.

B Well, I just can't take it anymore.
I'm going to explode.

A 있잖아, 넌 정말이지 화가 나더라도 좀 참을 필요가 있어.

B 왜 그런 말을 하는 건데?

A 네가 당장이라도 뚜껑이 열릴 것 같아 보여서 말야.

B 그래, 이제 더 이상은 못 참겠어. 폭발해 버릴 것 같아.

숙어 250 run out of breath — 숨이 차다

A Stop. Stop. I'm **running out of breath.**

B Come on. We've only run 5miles so far.

A Can't I just catch my breath for a minute?

B Okay. One minute, and then we start jogging again.

A 그만. 그만 하자. 숨이 너무 차.

B 힘내. 우리 지금까지 5마일밖에 안 뛰었어.

A 잠깐 숨 좀 돌릴 수 없을까?

B 좋아. 1분만이야. 그리고 다시 뛰기 시작하는 거다.

숙어 251 as happy as a clam — 싱글벙글한

A You know, you've had a smile on your face all day long.

B I can't help it. I'm **as happy as a clam.**

A I wish I were as happy as you.

I could really use some cheering up.

B Don't worry so much, and then you might be as happy as me.

A 있잖아, 너 하루 종일 얼굴에 웃음이 떠나질 않는 것 같다.

B 어쩔 수가 없어. 입이 자꾸 벌어져서 말이야.

A 나도 너처럼 행복했으면 좋겠다. 정말이지 기분 좋아지게 하는 게 있었으면 좋겠어.

B 그렇게 걱정하지 마. 그러면 너도 나처럼 행복해질 거야.

숙어 252 as quiet as a lamb — 말수가 적고 얌전한

A Steve hasn't said anything during the meeting.

B He's just sitting there **as quiet as a lamb.**

A Why doesn't he ever speak up?

B He's too shy. Plus he's a follower, not a leader.

A 스티브 말이야, 회의 시간에 도통 말이 없더군.

B 그 사람은 그저 조용히 앉아 있기만 하지.

A 그 친구 도대체 왜 말을 안 할까?

B 무척 수줍어하잖아. 게다가 지지자 타입이지 지도자 타입이 아니거든.

숙어 253 shy away from — 부끄러워서 못하다

A Did Eric talk to Kris last night?

B No, I don't think that he did.

A Really? He told me that he was going to introduce himself to her.

B He was planning to, but he **shied away from** doing it at the last moment.

A 어젯밤에 에릭이 크리스한테 말을 걸었어?

B 아니, 그런 것 같지 않던데.

A 정말? 나한테는 그녀에게 자길 소개하겠다고 했는데.

B 그럴 생각이었는데 마지막 순간에 부끄러워서 꽁무니를 뺀 거지.

숙어 254 be down in the dumps — 기분이 영 말이 아니다

A Sally looks like **she's down in the dumps** these days.

B I know. Doesn't she look terrible?

A Take it easy on her.

She's going through some tough time.

B Hey, why don't we try to lift her spirits and brighten her day?

A 샐리가 요즘 기분이 말이 아닌 것 같아.

B 알아. 걔 정말 힘들어 보이는 것 같지 않니?

A 편안하게 대해 줘. 지금 힘든 시기를 겪고 있으니까.

B 이봐, 우리가 기분 좀 좋아지게 기운을 북돋아주는 건 어떨까?

숙어 255 chicken out — 겁이 나서 물러나다

A Did Gunther go ahead and back up his promise?

B No, he talked a lot about it but **chickened out** at the last moment.

A I thought he was really going to try scuba diving.

B Nope. I guess he is just a chicken at heart.

A 건서 말이야, 그 일을 해서 자기가 한 약속을 지켰어?

B 아니, 말은 잘도 하더니 마지막 순간에는 꽁무니를 빼버리는 거 있지?

A 난 그 사람이 정말 스쿠버 다이빙을 하려는 줄 알았어.

B 아니야, 속으로는 겁쟁이인 것 같아.

숙어 256 get toasted. — 묵사발이 되다

A Now, be sure to play as hard as you can today.

B Okay, I'll do my best.

A And try not to **get toasted** like last week.

B Yes, sir. I'll try not to mess up like I did last time.

A 자, 오늘 최선을 다해 열심히 경기에 임하도록.

B 네, 최선을 다하겠습니다.

A 그리고 지난주처럼 완패당하지 않게 잘 해.

B 알겠습니다. 지난번처럼 엉망으로 만드는 일 없도록 노력할게요.

숙어 257 bored stiff | 좀이 쑤신

A Why don't we leave the house and watch a movie?

B Good idea. I'm **bored stiff** just sitting here.

A Yeah.

We should do something since it's Friday night.

B Okay, so let's go to the theater and catch a movie.

A 밖에 나가서 영화 한 편 보는 게 어때?

B 좋은 생각이다. 여기 앉아만 있자니 좀이 쑤신다.

A 그러게. 금요일 밤이니까 뭐든 해야지.

B 좋아. 극장에 가서 영화 한 편 때리는 거야.

숙어 258 bread and butter | 먹고 살기 위한 일

A Do you now how to operate this machine?

B Are you kidding? Of course I do.

A Oh, I didn't know that.

B Yeah, it's my **bread and butter**. I've been working with machines since I was young.

A 이 기계 어떻게 작동시키는지 알아?

B 농담하니? 당연히 알지.

A 그래? 아는 줄 몰랐어.

B 내가 그걸로 먹고 살잖아. 어릴 때부터 기계 다루는 일을 했거든.

숙어 259 lose face | 체면이 구겨지다

A Are you just going to stand there and say nothing?

B She can spread all the false rumors about me she wants. I don't care.

A But if people believe her, it might cause you to **lose face**.

B That's okay. It won't cause me any embarrassment if it's not true.

A 그렇게 아무 말도 안 하고 수수방관하고 있을 거야?

B 그녀가 나에 대한 거짓말을 마음대로 퍼뜨리고 다니든 말든 난 상관 안 해.

A 하지만 사람들이 그녀가 한 말을 믿으면, 네 체면이 말이 아닐 텐데.

B 그러라지. 그게 사실이 아닌 이상 내가 부끄러운 일은 없을 거야.

숙어 260 have egg on ones' face — 우스운 꼴이 되다

A You know, you just told your boss something incorrect.

B That's okay. He'll never find out the truth.

A I wouldn't be so sure. If he does learn the truth, you will **have egg on your face.**

B I'm not worried. He's not going to check up on me

A 있잖아, 방금 너 부장님한테 뭔가 잘못 말했어.

B 괜찮아, 부장님은 뭐가 맞는 건지 절대로 모르실 거야.

A 그렇지 않을 텐데. 만약에 부장님이 사실을 알게 되면 넌 그야말로 개망신당할 거야.

B 난 걱정 안 해, 부장님은 내 말을 확인할 사람이 아냐.

숙어 261 kick oneself — 자책하다

A Did you really get up and sing in front of everyone?

B Yes. I could **kick myself** for doing that.

A But you're the worst singer in the world.

B I know. That's why I'm so embarrassed.

A 너 정말 일어서서 모두들 앞에서 노래 불렀니?

B 응. 그런 짓을 하다니 미쳤지.

A 하지만 너 노래 진짜 못 하잖아.

B 알아. 그러니까 그렇게 창피하단 얘기지.

숙어 262 be in seventh heaven — 천국이 따로 없다

A Do you know whether you got accepted into the program?

B No, I haven't heard anything yet.

A Good luck. I know how eager you are to get in.

B Yeah, if I get in, I'll **be in seventh heaven.**

A 너 그 과정에 합격됐는지 알고 있니?

B 아니, 아직 연락 못 받았는데.

A 행운을 빈다. 난 네가 얼마나 들어가고 싶어하는지 알아.

B 그래, 만약 붙으면 천국에 있는 기분일 거야.

숙어 263 To get into the swing of things — 새로운 환경에 적응하다

B Caroline Finkbeiner. You can call me Carol.

A Right. How are you?

B Pretty good. But I'm still a complete rookie here, you know.

A That's exactly what I came through when I got here from Houston.

B Yeah? How long did it take you **to get into the swing of things** here?

B 캐롤라인 핑크바이너에요. 그냥 캐롤이라고 불러주세요.

A 맞다. 어떻게 지내세요?

B 좋아요. 하지만 아시다시피 전 여기선 아직 새파란 신참이라서요.

A 나도 휴스턴에서 처음 왔을 때 똑같은 경험을 했었거든요.

B 그래요? 여기서 적응하는 데 얼마나 걸리셨어요?

숙어 264 And then Some — ~에다 더하여

A You got a new computer!

B Yes. There was a bog sale at Best Buy last weekend.

A I'd guess it cost about $1,500.

B It cost that much and then some be-cause I also bought extra VRAM.

A 새 컴퓨터를 구입하셨네요!

B 네. 지난 주말 베스트바이에서 세일을 했어요.

A 제 생각엔 1500달러 정도 하겠는데요.

B VRAM과 함께 샀기 때문에 그보단 좀 더 들었어요.

숙어 265 If you haven't been there — 그 입장에 처해 보지 않으면

A Is Raymond not coming today?

B No. He doesn't seem to ready to work.

A He's been away for more than a week.
Isn't it too long?

B Look, he's just lost his mother. Can't you have a heart?

A I may sound harsh, but what happened is what happened.

B **If you haven't been there**, you don't know exactly what it's like.

A 레이먼드는 오늘도 결근인가?

B 응. 아직 일할 준비가 안 된 것 같아.

A 일주일 이상 결근인데 너무 긴 거 아니야?

B 이봐, 그는 막 어머니를 여의었는데.
좀 이해할 순 없어?

A 냉정하게 들릴지 모르지만, 이미 벌어진 일은 어쩔 수 없잖아.

B 그 입장에 처해 보지 않고서 그 심정을 어떻게 알겠어.

숙어 266 To each his own. 개인취향이지

A I visited the Museum of Modern Art when I was in New York.

B I don't understand modern art.

I'm never sure what the artist is trying to say.

A Personally, I loved it! **To each his own,** I suppose.

A 뉴욕에 갔을 때 현대미술관에 갔었어.

B 난 현대미술은 잘 모르겠더라.

작가가 무슨 말을 하려는 건지 모르겠어.

A 난 개인적으로 너무 좋던데! 뭐, 개인취향이겠지.

숙어 267 top up 가득 채우다, 보충하다

A Would you like to order some copy toner as well? It's on sale.

B I have some already, but I guess I could **top up** my supply. Give me three.

A Perfect. All together your order comes to 110 dollars.

A 복사기 토너도 같이 주문하시겠어요? 지금 할인 중이거든요.

B 토너가 있긴 한데 소모품을 좀 더 사놓아도 될 것 같아요. 세 개 주세요.

A 좋습니다. 다 합쳐서 주문 금액은 100 달러입니다.

숙어 268 make all the right noises 듣고 싶어하는 말을 하다

A I guess all your complaining finally paid off.

B Complaining? I just explained to management how much we're worth.

A Sure. I guess you just **made all the right noises.**

A 당신이 그렇게 불평하더니 마침내 성과를 거두신 것 같군요.

B 불평이라뇨? 저는 그저 우리가 얼마나 유능한 인재인지 경영진에게 설명했을 뿐이에요.

A 네. 적절하게 말을 잘 하신 것 같아요.

숙어 269 not bother with ~에 신경 쓰지 않다

A What are your New Year's resolutions?

B Actually, I **don't bother with** those.

They're always short-lived promises.

A Yeah, every year I pay a lot of money for a gym membership but never go!

A 새해 결심이 뭐에요?

B 실은 전 그런 거 신경 안 써요.

늘 작심삼일이니까요.

A 맞아요. 전 해마다 비싼 돈 주고 헬스 클럽 회원권 끊어 놓고는 한 번도 안 가요!

숙어 270 Dean's list — 우등생 명단

A Check it out! I made the **Dean's list.**
Wait until my father hears about this!

B Wow. Congrats.
I guess all that hard work really paid off in the end.

A It sure did. This is the sort of thing that looks great on a resume.

A 이거 좀 봐! 내가 우등생 명단에 올랐어. 아빠가 이 소식을 들으면 놀라실 거야!

B 와 축하한다. 그렇게 열심히 공부하더니 결국 보람이 있었구나.

A 맞아. 이력서에 한 줄 적으면 있어 보이잖아.

숙어 271 by a whisker — 간발의 차이로

A Have you heard the news?
Ban-Ki moon got re-elected.

B I heard that he won **by a whisker.**

A What are you talking about?
He actually won unanimously.

A 소식 들었어요?
반기문 총장이 재선됐대요.

B 가까스로 당선됐다고 들었어요.

A 무슨 소리 하는 거예요?
만장일치로 당선됐는데요.

숙어 272 A cross word — 어떤 사람과 논쟁을 갖는 것

A How long have your grandparents been married?

B They'll b celebrating their golden wedding in two months' time.

A Fifty years! Goodness, that's a really long time.

B Yes, they were actually childhood sweethearts.

A And they still seem a very happy couple.

B Oh they are. My grandmother always says that there has never been **a cross word** between them.

A They've never had a cross word? That must be some kind of record.

A 너의 조부모님이 결혼하신 지 얼마나 되셨어?

B 2달 후면 금혼식을 올리실 거야.

A 50년! 이런 정말 오래 되셨구나.

B 그래. 그들은 어린 시절부터 애인이셨어.

A 아직도 아주 행복한 커플이신 것 같던데.

B 오 그래, 할머니께서는 항상 할아버지와 한 번도 논쟁을 가져 본 적이 없다고 하셨어.

A 논쟁 한 번 없었다고? 기록에 남을 만하군.

숙어 273 Keep my nose clean — 나쁜 일에 휘말리지 않는다

A Have you heard about Linda's husband?

B No, and I don't

A He's having an ....

B Before you cut me off, I was going to say I didn't want to hear it. Gossiping isn't my thing.

A But, it's my thing. Lunch just isn't fun without a bit of gossip.

B Well, I just want to **keep my nose clean**.

A Oh, well. Suit yourself

A 너 Linda 남편에 관한 얘기 들었니?

B 아니 난 못 들었어.

A 그가….

B 네가 내 말을 끊기 전에 내가 그 얘기를 듣고 싶어 하지 않았다고 말하려고 했었어. 수다는 싫어!

A 하지만 그건 내 취향이야. 수다 없인 점심이 신날 수 없지.

B 글쎄, 난 휘말리고 싶지 않은데

A 음 마음대로 해.

숙어 274 Veg out — 집에서 마냥 늘어진 채로 시체놀이를 하다

A Hi John. It's been a long time. What have you been up to?

B Nothing much. I'm just working a lot of overtime. What about you?

A Same. It seems as if I spend day and night at the office.

B This weekend I'm planning on just relaxing/

A What are you going to do?

B I'm just going to rent a couple of movies and just **veg out** all weekend.

A Now, that sounds like the perfect way to relax

A 안녕 존, 오랜만이야. 어떻게 지냈니?

B 별 일 없었어. 일만 열심히 했지 넌?

A 마찬가지야 사무실에서 밤낮으로 시간을 보낸 것 같아.

B 난 이번 주말에 휴식만 취하려고

A 너는 뭐 할 거니?

B 몇 편의 영화를 빌려와서 주말 내내 아무것도 하지 않고 쉬려고.

A 휴식을 취하기에 완벽한 방법이겠는걸.

숙어 275 Pitch in ~에 협조하다

A Turn off that TV, now!
B What? I can't hear you. The TV is too loud.
A I said turn off that TV!
B But Mom! my favorite show is on.
A I don't care what is on. I need you to **pitch in** and do some housework.
B but, mom....
A go do the dishes first.

A 당장 TV 끄거라.
B 뭐라구요? 티비 소리가 너무 커서 잘 안 들려요.
A TV 끄라고 말했어!
B 하지만, 엄마. 제가 제일 좋아하는 프로그램 한단 말이에요.
A 뭐가 하든 상관없어. 난 네가 협조해서 집안일을 해줬으면 한단다.
B 하지만, 엄마.
A 설거지부터 해라.

숙어 276 over the counter 처방전 없이 살 수 있는

A My allergies are killing me.
B Have you tried seeing a doctor?
He could give you something for your itchy eyes.
A Right. This **over-the-counter** medication is worthless.

A 알레르기 때문에 죽겠어요.
B 병원 가봤어요?
의사 선생님이 눈 가려운 데 먹는 약을 처방해 주실 거예요.
A 맞아요. 처방전이 필요 없는 이런 약들은 별 효과가 없어요.

숙어 277 On cloud nine 더할 나위 없이 행복한

A You're looking happy today.
B I am. i've never been happier.
A Did you win the lottery or something?
B No. Last night Dan proposed to me.
He finally popped the question.
A That's great!
B It sure is. I've been **on cloud nine** all day long.
A Well. you'd better come down.
There's work right here on Earth for you to do.

A 너 오늘 기분 좋아 보이는구나.
B 그래 어느 때보다 행복해.
A 너 복권이라도 당첨됐니?
B 아니, 지난밤 Dan이 내게 프로포즈를 했어.
그가 드디어 프로포즈를 했다니까!
A 오!
B 하루 종일 더할 나위 없이 행복했었어.
A 좀 진정하는 게 좋겠어.
너가 지금 해야 할 일이 있잖아.

숙어 278 Carry the can — 결과에 책임을 지다

A Our new marketing manager is absolutely hopeless.

B I'm not surprised. I've been hearing from other people that he's pretty incompetent.

A Yes and it's not only his ideas that are no good. but the ways he tries to get us to put them into practice. They just don't work.

B That must make life very difficult. It does, but it's even worse. He tries to put the blame for failure on us, but we're determined not to **carry the can** for his mistakes.

A Why should you? It's his responsibility.

A 우리의 새 마케팅 매니저가 정말 절망적이야.

B 나는 놀랍지 않아. 그가 매우 무능력하단 소리를 다른 사람으로부터 들었거든.

A 그의 아이디어는 물론이고 우리가 아이디어를 실행하게 하는 방법도 엉망이야. 그것이 생활을 힘들게 만들지.

B 훨씬 더 나빠. 그는 실패에 대한 책임을 우리에게 지우려해. 그러나 우리는 그의 실수에 대한 책임을 지지 않기로 결심했어.

A 네가 왜 그래야 되지? 그건 그의 책임이잖아?

숙어 279 Pain in the neck — 성가신 사람

A Watch your language!

B Sorry. but I can't help it. It's so frustrating.

A Is there something the matter sith your laptop?

B Something the matter!

It's **an absolute pain in the neck**. Every time I try to log on to read my e-mail, it loses the connection, It's happened about ten times so far.

A It may not be the laptop. It could be that the wireless connection is unreliable here.

B I suppose you could be right. I'll try to find somewhere where the connection is more stable.

A 말조심해!

B 미안하지만 어쩔 수 없어. 정말 화가 나서 말이야.

A 노트북에 뭐 문제 있어?

B 문제가 좀 있지! 정말 골칫거리야. 내가 이메일을 보려고 로그인을 하기만 하면 접속이 끊어져. 지금까지 10번이나 그랬어.

A 노트북 문제가 아닐지도 몰라. 여기서 무선 인터넷 접속은 믿을 수가 없거든.

B 네가 맞는것 같아. 무선접속이 안정적인 곳 좀 찾아볼게.

숙어 280 Break it to someone ~에게 안 좋은 소식을 알리다

A So, do you think I'll get the job? I'm really hoping I do.

B I hate to **break it to you**, but you're not going to get it. You're just not qualified.

A I see. Well, maybe next time.

A 그래서 당신 생각에는 내가 거기 취직할 거 같아요? 난 정말 그러길 바라고 있어요.

B 이런 말은 하고 싶지 않지만 거기 안 될 거예요. 당신은 그만한 자격이 안 되잖아요.

A 알았어요. 음, 아마 다음번에는 되겠죠.

숙어 281 Cut me dead 못 본 체 하다

A Well I just couldn't believe it.

B You don't look best pleased. What happened?

A I bumped into Dana in the street just now and started to talk to her but she just **cut me dead**.

B Well, she can be moody at the best of times.

A That's true but I've still been trying hard to think if there's anything I've said or done recently to make her behave like that.

B I wouldn't worry if I were you. She'll be in a better mood tomorrow. I'm sure.

A 정말 믿을 수가 없어!

B 너 좋아보이지 않구나. 무슨 일 있니?

A 내가 방금 길에서 Dana를 만났는데 그녀가 날 외면했어.

B 글쎄. 그녀는 순조로울 때라도 언짢을 때가 있어.

A 맞아. 근데 난 그녀를 이처럼 행동하게 만든 말이나 행동이 최근에 있었는지 생각을 계속 하고 있었어.

B 내가 너라면 걱정하지 않을 텐데. 그녀는 내일이면 기분이 좋아질거야. 확실해.

숙어 282 Wrap up negotiations 협상을 마무리하다

A There are only a few minor things to hammer out. Soon, we can sign the contract.

B I agree. We're almost ready to **wrap up negotiations**.

A But first, we need to finally agree on a price. I still think you're asking too much.

A 이제 몇 가지 사소한 사항만 타결하면 돼요. 곧 계약에 서명할 수 있어요.

B 맞아요. 협상을 마무리할 준비가 거의 다 됐어요.

A 하지만 우선, 가격에 대해 최종적으로 합의해야 돼요. 제 생각에는 여전히 가격이 너무 높은 것 같아요.

숙어 283 Catch you later. 나중에 봐요

A Bill, it's Jane over in Accounting. I need to go over some of these numbers with you. They don't add up.

B Sorry, but I'm about to step into a meeting. I'll have to **catch you later.**

A Sure, but just make sure that you do. I really need you to explain some of these payments, OK?

A 빌, 경리부 제인이에요. 이 수치들을 당신이랑 검토해 봐야겠어요. 앞뒤가 안 맞아요.

B 미안하지만 지금 회의 들어가야 해요. 나중에 연락할게요.

A 알았어요. 꼭 연락 주세요. 이 지불 금액 일부에 대한 설명이 꼭 필요해요.

숙어 284 Go belly up 도산하다, 파산하다

A It's final.

B What?

A I couldn't get the loan.

B Really?

A My uncle's afraid that our company is going to **go belly up.**

B Come on, Jeff. Don't let it get you down too much. There's still hope.

A It would take a miracle at this point.

B I'll keep my fingers crossed.

A 끝이야.

B 왜?

A 이제 대출을 받을 수가 없어.

B 정말?

A 삼촌이 우리 회사가 파산 할 거라고 해.

B 힘내, 제프. 너무 낙담하지는 마. 희망이 있을거야.

A 지금의 상황에서도 기적은 있겠지.

B 행운을 빌게.

숙어 285 Hit it off 죽이 맞다, 사이좋게 지내다

A I noticed you and Tom really **hit it off** at the party this past Saturday.

B Yeah, We have a lot in common. And, he's really cute, too. I hope he asks me out.

A I'm so happy to hear you say that, because Tom's been asking me about you.

A 지난 토요일 파티 때 보니까 당신이랑 톰이 정말로 죽이 잘 맞던데요.

B 네, 우린 공통점이 많아요. 게다가 그는 정말 귀여워요. 그가 나한테 데이트 신청해주면 좋겠어요.

A 그렇게 말하니 정말 기쁘네요. 톰이 당신에 대해 나한테 이것저것 물어봤거든요.

숙어 286 To a T

정확히, 꼭 들어맞게

A I've been doing really well on my diet.

B How much have you lost in total?

A Last week I lost five punds, but this week I gained tow. I don't know what's wrong.

B Are you following the diet plan I gave you?

A I'm following it **to a T**. I haven't had one slip.

B Are you drinking enough water?

A I drink at least eight glasses of water each day.

B Just give it more time. This happens sometimes. You'll soon be back on track. You have my word on it.

A 내가 다이어트에 정말 최선을 다했어.

B 체중이 전부 얼마나 줄었어?

A 지난주에 5파운드가 빠졌는데, 이번 주에 2파운드가 쪘어. 왜 그런지 모르겠어.

B 내가 너에게 준 다이어트 계획을 지켰니?

A 정확히 지켰지. 어떤 실수도 없었어.

B 물도 충분히 마셨어?

A 하루에 물을 적어도 8잔은 마셨어.

B 시간을 좀 더 가져봐. 가끔 그럴 수 있어. 다시 원래대로 돌아갈 거야. 내가 한 말 명심해.

숙어 287 Double up

둘이서 함께 쓰다

A It looks like there was a mistake with our reservation, so they're asking us to **double up**.

B What are you talking about? Sharing the same room? Well, I guess there's no other choice.

A Yeah. Look, it'll be fine. There're separate beds, and we'll be at the conference most of the day anyway.

A 우리 예약이 잘못됐는지 우리더러 방을 함께 쓰라고 요청하네요.

B 무슨 소리하는 거예요? 같은 방을 쓰라뇨? 하기야 다른 선택의 여지는 없을 것 같네요.

A 네, 보세요, 괜찮을 거예요. 침대가 따로따로 있고, 어쨌든 우린 거의 하루 종일 회의장에 있을 거잖아요.

숙어 288 Close call

위기일발, 아찔한 상황

A Watch out! You almost hit that bus. Didn't you see it coming up behind you?

B Sure. But I figured there was enough room. Oh, well.

A Oh, well? That was a very **close call**. You need to be more careful. Next time, I'm driving.

A 조심해요! 저 버스랑 부딪칠 뻔했잖아요. 버스가 뒤따라오는 거 못 봤어요?

B 봤어요. 근데 충분한 공간이 있다고 생각했어요. 그럴 수도 있죠, 뭐.

A 그럴 수도 있다고요? 하마터면 정말 큰 일 날 뻔했다고요. 좀 더 조심해야 돼요. 다음에는 내가 운전할게요.

숙어 289 A piece of my mind — 솔직한 의견, 비난

A Hello, Mr Willis. What seems to be the problem?

B I want to give you **a piece of my mind.** Do you know what your secretary said to me yesterday.

A What's that?

B She told me you weren't in the office and I'd just have to wait to talk to you. A secretary told me to wait.

A I apologize. I will speak to her about the tone she uses with customers.

B You had better, Otherwise, I might take my business elsewhere.

A 안녕, Willis, 뭐 문제 있니?

B 내가 너에게 따끔히 한 마디 해야겠어. 어제 너의 비서가 내게 했던 말 아니?

A 뭔데?

B 그녀가 내게 네가 사무실에 없다며 얘기를 하려면 기다려야 한다고 하지 뭐야! 나보고 기다리라고 하다니.

A 사과할게! 내가 그녀에게 손님에게 쓰는 말투에 대해 말해야겠는걸!

B 그러는게 좋을거야. 그렇지 않으면 내 일을 다른 곳에서 해야 할 지도 몰라.

숙어 290 Monkey business — 속임수, 바보 같은 짓

A What are you doing, Kenny? You're supposed to be helping me clean.

B I'm tired of cleaning the house, Mom. I want to have some fun.

A After you finish your chores, you can go outside and play.

B Why can't I go play now?
It's such a nice day outside.

A I've had enough of your **monkey business**. get back to work.

B OK, Mom. I'll finish cleaning.
But afterwards, I'm going outside.

A 너 뭐하는 거야, Kenny? 엄마 청소하는 거 도와주기로 했잖아.

B 엄마! 집 청소는 지겨워요. 재미있는 거 하고 싶어요.

A 집안일 끝나고 밖에 나가 놀렴.

B 지금 가면 안 될까요?
밖에 날씨 참 좋은데.

A 네 헛소리 들을 만큼 들었어. 얼른 일해.

B 예, 엄마, 청소할게요.
청소 다하면 저 나갈거에요.

숙어 291 Dog-eat-dog. 치열한, 인정사정없는

A Hey, let that car in. Come on.
Slow down and let him in.

B No one yielded for us. It's a **dog-eat-dog**, world, Mike.
Nobody helps me, and I don't help anybody.

A Well, could you try to be just a little bit nicer?

A 이봐요, 저 차 끼어 줘요. 그러지 말고요. 속도 줄여서 저 차 먼저 가게 해요.

B 우리한테는 아무도 양보를 안 했다고요. 마이크, 세상은 냉정해요. 누구도 나를 도와주지 않아요. 나도 도움 줄 필요 없고요.

A 흠, 조금만 마음을 곱게 쓸 수 없어요?

숙어 292 A can of worms 될 수 있으면 건들고 싶지 않은 귀찮은 문제

A How's it going, Carol?

B Not bad. But I had a weird conversation with Paul this morning.

A What happened?

B We were just talking nicely, but then I asked him about his wife.

A Oh, no. You shouldn't have opened **a can of worms.**

B Yeah, I know. He spent abot half an hour telling me about it.

A What did he say?

B Well. I guess she's hanging out with some rock stars in town.

A 어떻게 지내니, 캐롤?

B 나쁘지 않아. 근데 오늘 아침 폴과 섬뜩한 대화를 나눴어.

A 무슨?

B 우리가 좋게 얘기를 하다가 내가 그의 아내에 대해 물었었거든.

A 오. 이런 네가 해서는 안 될 일을 벌였군.

B 맞아. 나도 알아. 그러자 그가 아내에 대해 30분 동안이나 얘기를 하지 뭐야.

A 그가 뭐라고 했는데?

B 아내가 시내에서 록 스타들과 돌아다녔다고 하더라고.

숙어 293 Toe the line

규칙을 따라야한다

A Now that we're roommates, we're going to have to do things differently.

B What do you mean?

A We're going to have to split all the bills down the-middle.

B Sure. No problem!

A You say that now, but make sure you **toe the line.**

B Don't worry, Robin. Have I ever let you down?

A Do you want me to honestly answer that?

A 우리가 한 방을 쓰게 되었으니 뭔가 다르게 해야겠어.

B 무슨 말이야?

A 모든 청구서를 반으로 나눠서 내야겠어.

B 물론이지.

A 네가 지금은 그렇게 말하지만 규칙을 지켜 줘야 해.

B 걱정 마! Robin 내가 언제 실망시킨 적 있었니?

A 넌 내가 사실대로 답하길 원하니?

숙어 294 Loud and clear

아주 이해하기 쉽게

A And if your work's not done by three, you're out of here! you get me?

B Yes, boss. I hear you **loud and clear**.

A Good, because I've had enough of your laziness. This is your last chance!

A 그리고 세 시까지 일을 못 끝내면 해고예요! 알아들었어요?

B 네, 사장님. 잘 알겠습니다.

A 좋아요. 이제 게으름 좀 그만 피워요. 이번이 마지막 기회예요!

숙어 295 Show one's true colors

본색을 드러내다

A I guess Jill **showed her true colors** at the meeting yesterday.

B I was really disappointed in her.
She blamed everyone for the project's failure but herself.

A Well, what can you expect?
She's the boss's daughter. She's never going to admit making a mistake.

A 질이 어제 회의 때 본색을 드러낸 것 같아요.

B 그녀한테 정말 실망했어요. 그 프로젝트가 실패한 탓을 자신이 아니라 다른 모든 사람들한테 돌렸잖아요.

A 뭘 기대하겠어요? 사장님 딸인데, 자신의 실수를 결코 인정하지 않을 거라고요.

숙어 296 Look like death warmed over — 곧 죽을 것 같다

A Good morning! you're looking better. Jeez, yesterday evening you **looked like death warmed over.**

B Tell me about it. But I am feeling better.
My fever broke late last night.

A Good to hear. let me see.... bend down so I can feel your forehead. Yup, the fever's nearly gone.

A 좋은 아침! 훨씬 좋아 보이네요. 세상에, 어제 저녁에는 다 죽어가더니만.

B 그러게요. 하지만 이제 괜찮아졌어요. 지난 밤 늦게 열이 내리기 시작했어요.

A 잘됐네요. 어디보자…. 이마 좀 만져보게 숙여 봐요. 네, 열이 거의 내렸네요.

숙어 297 Feel like jelly. — 떨리다

A I heard you ran into Jane at the shopping center. Did you actually talk with her?

B I couldn't even walk over to say hi. My legs **felt like jelly**, and I thought I was going to puke.

A I know the feeling. I always feel terrible whenver I run into my ex-boyfriend, too.

A 쇼핑센터에서 제인을 우연히 만났다고 들었어요. 제인이랑 말도 했어요?

B 다가가서 인사조차 할 수 없었어요. 다리가 후들후들 거리고 토할 것 같았어요.

A 어떤 기분인지 알아요. 나도 옛 남자친구와 우연히 만날 때마다 소름이 늘 끼쳐요.

숙어 298 Play it by car. — 상황을 봐서 결정하다

A What are your plans for this weekend?
I hear a lot of new movies are opening.

B Yeah, I'm not sure what I'm going to do.
I'm meeting Tim Saturday morning. We'll just **play it by car.**

A Okay. But if you think of something cool to do, call me.

A 이번 주말 계획 있어요?
새 영화가 대거 개봉한다고 들었어요.

B 맞아요, 뭘 할지는 잘 모르겠어요. 토요일 아침에 팀을 만날 건데, 그때 상황 봐서 정하려고요.

A 좋아요. 하지만 뭐 신나는 일 생각나면 나한테도 전화 줘요.

숙어 299 Cash on the barrelhead　현금으로

A The guy wanted ten thousand for the car, but I offered him nine thousand dollars, **cash on the barrelhead.**

B Did he go for it?

A Sure. As soon as he saw I had the cash right there with me, it was a done deal.

A 그 남자가 차 값으로 만 달러를 불렀지만, 현금으로 9천 달러를 제가 제의했어요.

B 그가 받아들였나요?

A 네. 제가 현금을 갖고 있다는 걸 안 순간 거래는 이미 끝났죠.

숙어 300 Couch potato　소파에 앉아 하루 종일 TV만 보는 사람

A I'm worried about you, Jane. Is everything alright at home?

B I guess. I'm just sort of feeling down these days. You know that Tom broke up with me, right?

A Yeah, but that's no reason to be a **couch potato**. you need to get out and have some fun.

A 제인, 당신이 걱정스러워요. 집에서 잘 지내고 있는 거죠?

B 네. 요즘 좀 우울할 뿐이에요. 톰이랑 헤어진 건 알고 있죠?

A 네, 하지만 그렇다고 집에서 하루 종일 TV나 보고 있을 이유는 없어요. 나가서 신나게 놀아야 돼요.

숙어 301 Be a match for ~　~의 맞수가 되다

A I heard Jimmy is going to play Mike after work. Doesn't he know Mike was a great tennis player back in high school?

B He'll **be** no **match for Mike**. I think Jimmy just started learning to play.

A Well, I'm sure Mike will go easy on him.

A 지미가 퇴근 후에 마이크와 테니스를 칠거라고 들었어요. 마이크가 고등학교 때 뛰어난 테니스 선수였다는 걸 지미는 몰라요?

B 그는 절대 마이크 상대가 안 될 거예요. 지미는 이제 막 테니스를 배우기 시작한 걸로 알고 있어요.

A 글쎄요, 마이크가 분명 그를 살살 다룰 거에요.

숙어 302 Be crushed 충격을 받다, 낙심하다

A I heard that you and Tom broke up. How are you doing?

B I'm so sad, mike. I'**m crushed.** I can't understand why he did it.

A Well, just remember that time heals all wounds. You're hurting now, but you'll get through this.

A 톰이랑 헤어졌다면서요. 잘 지내고 있어요?

B 너무 슬퍼요, 마이크. 정말 마음이 아파요. 그가 왜 그랬는지 이해가 안 돼요.

A 음, 시간이 약이라는 말을 잊지 말아요. 지금은 아프지만 곧 이겨낼 거에요.

숙어 303 Pull one's leg 놀리다, 농담하다

A And then I told him that the party was at Jane's apartment, but really it was over at Mike's.

B You're **pulling my leg**. I don't believe you. There's no way you were brave enough to do that.

A Are you sure? Ask Tom for yourself, then. He'll tell you what happened.

A 그래서 그에게 제인의 아파트에서 파티를 했다고 말했지만 실은 마이크의 집에서 끝났어요.

B 농담하는 거죠? 안 믿어요. 당신은 그런 거짓말을 할 만한 용기가 있는 사람이 절대 아니에요.

A 정말 그렇게 생각해요? 그럼 톰에게 직접 물어봐요. 무슨 일이 있었는지 그가 이야기 해 줄 거예요.

숙어 304 On the go 끊임없이 활동하여, 정신없이 바쁜

A I heard you just got back from a big conference. How was it?

B The meetings were good, but we didn't have a chance to see any of the sites. I was in Paris, but didn't visit one museum!

A Well, that's the price you pay for a life **on the go**.

A 중요한 학회에 참석했다가 막 돌아왔다고 들었어요. 학회는 어땠어요?

B 회의는 유익했는데, 유적지를 한 곳도 볼 기회가 없었어요. 파리에 있었는데도 박물관은 한 군데도 못 갔어요!

A 글쎄요, 그거야 당신이 정신없이 바쁘게 사는 대가죠.

숙어 305 Touch on ~을 간단히 언급하다

A Dave, why didn't you come to the seminar this morning?

B Sorry, Tina. I slept in and didn't get to the office until after ten.

A You missed some great presentations. One of the speakers **touched on** time management

A 데이브, 오늘 오전에 세미나에 왜 참석하지 않았어요?

B 미안해요, 티나. 늦잠을 자서 사무실에 도착하니 10시가 넘었어요.

A 유익한 발표였는데 놓치셨네요. 연사 중 한 명이 시간 관리에 대해 간단히 언급했거든요.

숙어 306 Out of sorts 몸이 불편한, 기분이 언짢은

A You've been **out of sorts** these last few days.

B Not really. My dad is really sick. In fact, we had to take him to the hospital las night.

A I'm so sorry to hear that. I hope everything turns out OK.

A 지난 며칠 동안 기분이 좀 안 좋아 보이네요.

B 꼭 그렇지만은 않아요. 아버지가 많이 편찮으세요. 실은 간밤에도 아버지를 병원에 모시고 가야 했어요.

A 그 소식을 들으니 안됐군요. 모든 일이 다 잘되기를 바랄게요.

숙어 307 Have a sharp tongue. 독설을 퍼붓다

A You really need to watch what you say around customers, John. That guy was pretty upset with you.

B It wasn't my fault. he said I was bad at my job, and all I did was defend myself.

A Sure, but did you need to make fun of his accent, too? you shouldn't **have** such **a sharp tongue**.

A 존, 고객들 있는 데서는 정말 말조심해야 돼요. 저 사람이 당신에게 화가 아주 많이 나 있었어요.

B 그건 제 잘못이 아니었어요. 저더러 일하는 게 형편없다고 말해서 제 자신을 변호한 것뿐이라고요.

A 그건 그렇지만 그의 말투까지 조롱할 필요가 있었어요? 그렇게 함부로 말하면 안돼요.

숙어 308 Can't take a hint — 눈치를 못 채다

A Can you believe Mike's still asking to be sent on the business trip?

B **Can't** he **take a hint**? The boss doesn't want to send him after the disaster in Chicago.

A Sure, but mike thinks that one wasn't his fault. Man, that guy is really thick.

A 마이크가 출장 보내 달라고 아직도 요청하고 있다는데 믿어져요?

B 눈치도 없대요? 시카고에서 대형사고 친 후로 사장님이 그를 보내고 싶어 하지 않잖아요.

A 맞아요. 근데 마이크는 그게 자기 책임이 아니라고 생각해요. 아, 그 사람 정말 둔해요.

숙어 309 Shape up or ship out — 열심히 하지 않으려면 나가라

A I've been going over your performance reviews, and they're frankly not very good.

B I know. I have been really struggling with this new job. I think I need help with some of these projects.

A Actually, you really need to **shape up or ship out**. Either you get better or I'll have to seriously think about firing you.

A 당신 고과를 검토하고 있는데, 별로 좋지 않아요.

B 네. 이번에 새로 맡은 일 때문에 정말 애를 먹고 있어요. 이 프로젝트에서 일부는 도움이 필요한 것 같아요.

A 제대로 안 할 거면 회사 그만둬요. 개선되지 않으면 당신을 해고 하는 걸 진지하게 고민해 봐야 할 거예요.

숙어 310 Two cents — 의견, 견해

A This whole project is a complete disaster.

B I think it's not that terrible.
But that's just my **two cents.**

A Well, I appreciate your opinion. But, I think we need to start all over again. Call James.

A 이 전체 프로젝트는 완전 실패작이에요.

B 그렇게 엉망인 것 같지는 않은데요.
제 짧은 소견이지만요.

A 글쎄요, 의견은 감사해요. 하지만 우린 처음부터 다시 시작해야 할 것 같아요. 제임스에게 전화하세요.

숙어 311 job opening — 빈자리, 공석

A I heard there's a **job opening** in the marketing department.

B Really? Where did you hear that?
Are they going to bring in someone new?

A No. Actually, I think they're trying to find someone in the company who will transfer in.

A 마케팅 부서에 결원이 생겼다고 들었어요.

B 정말이에요? 어디서 들었어요?
사람을 새로 채용한대요?

A 아니요. 실은 직원들 중에서 전직 (부서) 이동을 희망하는 사람을 찾고 있다는 것 같아요.

숙어 312 Keep one's (your) shirt on. — 진정해

A Have you been following the market today?
We're heading for a crash!

B **Keep your shirt on**. Things will rebound soon.

A What? The prics are going to continue to fall.
Sell! Sell! Sell!

A 오늘 주식 시장 지켜봤어요?
이러다 폭락하겠어요!

B 진정해요. 곧 반등할 거에요.

A 뭐라고요? 주가가 계속해서 떨어질 거라고요.
팔아요! 팔아! 매도해요!

숙어 313 Read my lips — 내 말을 잘 들으세요

A Are you sure the company is going to be giving out any raises this year?

B **Read my lips**. No new raises. There's no money for it.

A I get it. But it's juse not fair. There was enough money to redecorate the executive bathroom, wasn't there?

A 회사에서 올해 임금 인상을 하지 않는다는 게 확실해요?

B 내 말 잘 들어요. 올해는 인상 없어요. 그럴 돈이 없다고요.

A 알았어요. 하지만 공평하지 않은 것 같아요. 간부들 화장실을 리모델링 할 돈은 있었잖아요, 안 그래요?

숙어 314 look like hell
안색이 좋지 않다

A You **look like hell** warmed over.

B I'm just a little under the wather, that's all.

A Nope. You **look like hell** I've seen healthier corpses. Frank, you look terrible!

A 안색이 너무 안 좋아 보이네요.

B 그냥 몸이 좀 안 좋아서 그래요. 다른 건 없어요.

A 아니요. 몰골이 말이 아니에요. 죽은 사람도 당신보다는 나을거에요. 프랭크, 정말 끔찍해 보인다고요!

숙어 315 point-blank
단도직입적으로

A So, then I asked him **point-blank** if he had taken my stapler.

B And, what did he say?
Did he finally admit he's taken it?

A Nope. He acted dumb, like he had no idea what I was talking about.

A 그래서 내 스테이플러를 가져갔는지 그에게 단도직입적으로 물었어요.

B 그랬더니 그가 뭐래요?
자기가 가져갔다고 결국 시인했어요?

A 아니요. 마치 벙어리처럼 내가 무슨 말을 하는지 모르겠다는 표정을 짓더라고요.

숙어 316 line of credit
대출 한도, 마이너스 통장

A The guy down at the bank said he'd give me a **line of credit**.

B Cool. It's like being approved for a loan instantly.
Hey, can I get one, too?

A I'm not sure about you.
You've got bad credit, don't you?

A 은행 남자 직원이 나한테 마이너스 통장을 만들어 주겠대요.

B 잘됐네요. 대출을 즉시 받을 수 있는 거니까요.
저기, 저도 하나 만들 수 있을까요?

A 당신은 잘 모르겠어요.
당신은 신용이 나쁘지 않나요?

숙어 317 get itchy feet　역마살이 끼다

A You actually requested to get transferred to Minnesota? Why?

B I've already lived here in Texas for five years.

I'm starting to **get itchy feet.**

A I know the feeling, but Minnesota? Really?

You know it's winter there six months a year, right?

A 정말 미네소타로 전근을 요청했어요? 왜요?

B 여기 텍사스에서 벌써 5년 살았어요.

몸이 근질거리기 시작해요.

A 그 기분은 알겠지만, 미네소타라고요? 정말이에요?

거긴 일 년에 6개월이 겨울인 건 알고 있죠?

숙어 318 lose track of time　시간 가는 줄 모르다

A John, it's Betty. Where are you? I've been sitting at the coffee shop waiting for twenty minutes.

B Betty! Oh, no. I completely **lost track of time.**

I'm still at home! I'll leave right now.

A Don't bother, John.

This is the last time you come late for a date. Good-bye, John.

A 존, 베티에요. 지금 어디에요? 커피숍에 앉아 20분 째 기다리고 있다고요.

B 베티! 이런, 시간이 이렇게 되는 줄 정말 몰랐어요.

아직 집에 있어요! 지금 바로 나갈게요.

A 그럴 필요 없어요, 존.

데이트에 늦는 건 이번에 마지막이에요.

잘 있어요, 존.

숙어 319 get under one's skin　짜증나게 하다

A Can you believe Mike wants to change the company pension plan? Again?

B That sort of thing really **gets under my skin.**

I hate it.

A I know. The plan is fine the way it is.

He's making changes for no good reason.

A 마이크가 회사 연금 제도를 바꾸려고 한다는 게 믿어져요? 또 바꾼대요!

B 그런 일은 정말 짜증나요.

마음에 안 든다고요.

A 맞아요. 연금 제도는 지금 이대로도 괜찮은데.

그는 이렇다 할 이유도 없이 바꾸고 있어요.

숙어 320 blow one's own horn
자화자찬하다, 자기 자랑을 늘어놓다

A Hey, Jane. I heard about your promotion. Congratulations. Must have been because of the Miller account.

B Well.... I don't like to **blow my own horn**....

A Come on!
Everyone knows how you saved the company millons.

A 이봐요, 제인. 당신 승진 소식 들었어요. 축하해요. 밀러 고객건 때문이군요.

B 글쎄…. 자화자찬을 하고 싶지는 않지만….

A 아니에요!
당신이 어떻게 해서 회사가 수백만 달러를 절감하게 했는지 모두들 알고 있다고요.

숙어 321 have zero[no] chemistry
공감대가 전혀 없다

A It was a good movie, but the acting was terrible.

B Yeah, the stars just **had zero** onscreen **chemistry**.

A I think it was the age difference. He was just too old to play her boyfriend. He looks like her dad!

A 영화는 좋았는데 연기는 형편없었어요.

B 네, 배우들이 영화에서 서로 공감대가 전혀 형성되지 않았어요.

A 나이 차이 때문에 그런 것 같아요. 남자 배우가 여자 배우의 남자 친구 역을 하기에는 너무 늙었잖아요. 꼭 여자의 아빠를 보는 것 같다고요!

숙어 322 tie up loose ends
결말을 짓다, 마무리하다

A I heard you've run into some trouble with the Peterson account. Need any help?

B No, we're actually ahead of schedule.
Just need a day or so to **tie up loose ends.**

A I see. Well, if you need me, I'm just a phone call away.

A 피터슨 고객사와 문제가 있다고 들었어요. 도움이 필요해요?

B 아뇨, 사실 일정보다 빨리 진행되고 있어요.
마무리하는 데 하루 정도 필요한 것 뿐이에요.

A 알았어요. 음, 내 도움이 필요하면 바로 전화해요.

숙어 323 work for peanuts | 쥐꼬리만한 월급을 받고 일하다

A You're still here?
I can't believe how many hours you work in a day.

B I know, but I really want to get that promotion.
I need the extra cash.

A Tell me about it.
We're **working for peanuts**!

A 아직도 여기 있어요?
도대체 하루에 몇 시간이나 일하는 거에요?

B 알아요. 하지만 꼭 승진하고 싶어요.
여유 자금이 필요하거든요.

A 무슨 말인지 알아요.
우린 쥐꼬리만한 한 월급을 받으면서 일하고 있잖아요!

숙어 324 pig out | 과식하다, 게걸스럽게 먹다

A I'm so hungry I could eat a horse.
Let's order two of everything!

B Cool. Let's **pig out**. I'll start my diet tomorrow!

A Right. So, should we get vanilla shakes or chocolate shakes? Or, how about both?

A 너무 배고파 죽을 지경이에요.
뭐든 두 개 주문해요!

B 좋아요. 우리 돼지처럼 먹어 봐요. 다이어트는 내일부터 할 거에요!

A 그래요. 그럼 바닐라 쉐이크나 초콜릿 쉐이크 먹을까요? 아니면 둘 다는 어때요?

숙어 325 take one's breath away | 숨이 멎을 듯이 아름답다, 깜짝 놀라서 숨이 막히다

A I'm so happy we decided to have our honeymoon at Niagara Falls.

B Me, too. Just look at it!
It really **takes your breath away.**

A Oh, you mean the waterfall? Yeah, it's nice. But I was talking about the hotel. You know this is where they filmed Superman II, right?

A 신혼여행을 나이아가라 폭포로 가기로 결정해서 정말 기뻐요.

B 나도 그래요. 이것 좀 봐요!
정말 숨이 멎을 것 같아요.

A 아, 그 폭포 말하는 거예요? 네, 정말 멋져요. 근데 난 호텔 얘기하는 거였어요. 이 호텔이 〈슈퍼맨Ⅱ〉 촬영한 곳 맞죠?

숙어 326 where do you get off~? 어디서 감히 ~하는가?

A **Where do you get off** telling me I'm wrong?
B But, sir, you're wrong.
We need to invest in that stock.
A I don't care what you think.
I'm in charge around here.

A 어디서 감히 내가 틀렸다고 말을 하는 건가? 난 자네 상사라네!
B 하지만 부장님 판단이 잘못됐습니다.
저희는 그 주식에 투자를 해야 합니다.
A 자네가 어떻게 생각하든 그건 내가 알 바가 아니네.
여기 책임자는 나니까.

숙어 327 stay over 하룻밤 자다

A The company will arrrange for a hotel.
We'll get you one close to the convention hall.
B Oh, that won't be necessary.
I have an old army buddy who lives in San Diego. I'll **stay over** at his place.
A Great. But make sure to keep your receipts for any meals. The company will cover them.

A 회사에서 호텔을 잡아줄 거예요.
컨벤션홀에 가까운 곳으로 잡아드릴게요.
B 아, 그럴 필요 없어요.
샌디에이고에 사는 군대 친구가 있어요.
거기서 잘 거예요.
A 잘됐네요. 하지만 식사 영수증은 꼭 챙겨두세요.
회사에서 지불할 거예요.

숙어 328 in the hot seat 곤경에 처한, 매우 어려운 입장에 놓여 있는

A I heard you were dragged into the boss's office yesterday. What was that all about?
B He had a bunch of questions about the quarterly report. He sort of put me **in the hot seat.**
A Well, I'm sure you were able to give good answers. You're always on top of your work.

A 어제 사장실에 불려갔다면서요. 무슨 일 때문이었어요?
B 분기 보고서에 관해 사장님이 질문을 퍼부으셨는데 제가 쩔쩔맸어요.
A 음, 분명 대답을 잘하셨을 거에요. 당신은 일 처리가 늘 완벽하잖아요.

숙어 329 be on pins and needles — 초조하다, 안절부절못하다

A Have you heard back from you boss yet?
Is he sending you on that business trip to Paris or what?

B I still don't know, and it's killing me. I can't sleep at night and even the thought of food turns my stomach.

A I'**m on pins and needles**, too. Wait! What was that? Did you hear that? It's your phone! Answer it!

A 사장님한테 다시 연락이 왔었어요? 파리인가 어딘가로 당신을 출장 보내신대요?

B 아직 잘 모르겠는데 죽을 맛이에요. 밤에 잠도 안 오고 음식 생각하면 속이 메스꺼워요.

A 저도 초조해죽겠어요. 잠깐만요! 뭐였죠? 들었어요? 당신 전화예요! 어서 받아봐요!

숙어 330 drive a hard bargain — (흥정 등에서) 세게 밀어붙이다

A I really want to make this deal happen.
Bill, but the terms aren't right for me.

B I could come down in price a bit, but you'd have to buy more units.

A Fine. You **drive a hard bargain**!

A 빌, 이 거래를 꼭 성사시키고 싶지만 조건이 안 맞아요.

B 가격을 조금 더 깎아드릴 수는 있지만 그럴 경우 물건을 더 구입하셔야 돼요.

A 그렇게 하죠. 흥정을 참 잘하시네요!

숙어 331 slip out — 무심코 튀어나오다

A So, you actually told the boss what you thought about his ties?

B I know, I know. But, it just sort of **slipped out.**
Now he's super angry.

A I would imagine so. His son buys him those ties.
You better find some way to make it up to him.

A 그래서 넥타이에 대해 어떻게 생각하는지 사장님께 사실대로 말씀 드렸다고요?

B 네, 맞아요. 하지만 나도 모르게 말이 나와버렸어요.
지금 몹시 화가 나 있으세요.

A 그럴 거 같아요. 그 넥타이 아드님이 사준 거라는데.
그걸 만회할 방법을 찾는 게 좋겠어요.

숙어 332 talk in one's sleep 잠꼬대하다

A So, who's Mike, Betty? Some new friend of yours?

B What are you talking about? Mike?

I don't know anyone named Mike.

A Really? Then, how com e kept saying his name, over and over again? you were **talking in your sleep**!

A 그래서 마이크가 누구예요, 베티? 새로 사귄 친구예요?

B 무슨 소리 하는 거예요? 마이크라뇨? 마이크라는 사람은 알지도 못해요.

A 정말이에요? 그런데 왜 그의 이름을 계속해서 말했어요? 당신이 잠꼬대를 했다고요!

숙어 333 be rained out 우천으로 취소되다

A Can you believe our bad luck?

We finally get a chance to see an MLB game and it'**s rained out.**

B It's killing me! We waited so long for this chance.

At least we'll get our money back on the tickets, right?

A Who cares? Our plane leaves tomorrow.

We'll never get to see a pro baseball game.

A 정말 운이 없네요. 드디어 메이저리그 야구 경기를 볼 기회가 왔는데, 우천으로 취소됐대요.

B 미치겠네! 이 기회를 얼마나 오랫동안 기다려 왔는데.

그래도 티켓은 환불받을 수 있는 거 맞죠?

A 알 게 뭐에요? 우리 비행기는 내일 출발하는데.

앞으로 프로야구 경기 볼 기회는 절대 없을 거라고요.

숙어 334 blow hot and cold 이랬다 저랬다 하다, 변덕이 심하다

A Did you finally ask the boss for a raise?

B I tried, but he keeps **blowing hot and cold.**

He can't decide.

A Well, go into his office and demand a raise.

That's the only way to get one!

A 사장님한테 급여 올려달라고 요구했어요? 척, 당신은 요구할 자격 있어요.

B 얘기는 해봤는데, 계속 이랬다저랬다 하시기만 하고 결정을 못하시네요.

A 그럼 사무실로 가서 인상을 요구해요. 그 방법밖엔 없어요!

숙어 335 cut corners — 경비를 절감하다, 대강 하다

A The costs are through the roof.
You bought new smartphones for everyone on staff?

B Sure. We needed them, and you can't **cut corners** when it comes to new technology.

A I just hope you know what you're doing.
Those phones cost us an arm and a leg each!

A 경비가 급증하고 있어요.
전 직원에게 신형 스마트폰을 사줬다면서요?

B 네, 스마트폰이 필요했어요. 그리고 신기술에 관한 한 경비를 아끼면 안 돼요.

A 당신이 지금 무슨 짓을 하고 있는 건지 알고 있으면 좋겠네요. 이 전화기들 한 대 값이 어마어마하다고요!

숙어 336 Go easy on me — 잘 좀 봐줘

A Now, **go easy on me**. This is my first time on skis. I'm a bit nervous.

B Don't worry. This is the bunny hill, so it's got a nice, gentle slope.

A Well, I think I'm ready. So, what should I do first?

B You need to put your skis on properly....
You've got them on backwards!

A 자, 잘 좀 봐줘. 스키는 처음이야.
좀 떨려.

B 걱정 마. 여기는 초보자 코스라서 경사가 가파르지 않아.

A 준비 됐어. 그럼 뭐부터 해야 하지?

B 스키를 제대로 신어야 해….
너 거꾸로 신었잖아!

숙어 337 get away with — ~하고도 처벌을 받지 않다

A I'm calling about an order I placed two weeks ago. The name is Johnson.

B Let me see.... I have no record of any order under that name.

A What? But I already sent you a check. You won't **get away with** this.

A 2주 전에 한 주문에 관해 전화 드리는데요.
제 이름은 존슨입니다.

B 확인해보죠. 그런 이름으로는 주문 기록이 전혀 없는데요.

A 뭐라고요? 하지만 이미 수표를 보냈는데요. 이번 일은 무사히 넘어가지 못할 거예요.

숙어 338 be in the air
~의 기운이 감돌다

A Spring **is in the air**!
B We'll be able to plant our garden and paint the house.
A Jeez. Now that I think of it, winter is not so cad after all.

A 봄기운이 감돌아요!
B 정원에 꽃도 심고 페인트칠도 좀 해야겠어요.
A 맙소사. 지금 생각해보니 겨울도 괜찮네요.

숙어 339 clear one's throat
헛기침하다

A No matter what I did, I couldn't get his attention.
B I guess he wasn't picking up on your signals.
A I don't think so. I **cleared my throat** about ten times right beside him.

A 내가 뭘 해도 그 사람이 나에게 관심을 보이지 않았어요.
B 당신이 보낸 신호를 알아차리지 못했나 보네요.
A 그건 아닌 것 같아요. 그 사람 바로 옆에서 헛기침을 한 열 번은 했거든요.

숙어 340 loom large
(위기나 문제 등이) 부각되다 현실로 다가오다

A I heard that MM Motors lost one-billion dollars last quarter.
B Yes, bankruptcy may be **looming large** for that company.
A We need to make a greater effort not to make the same mistake.

A MM 모터스가 지난 분기에 10억 달러의 손실을 입었대요.
B 예, 그 회사는 파산 가능성이 부각되고 있어요.
A 우리도 같은 실수를 하지 않으려면 더욱 노력해야 해요.

숙어 341 be fed up with
~에 싫증나다, ~에 진저리나다

A **I'm fed up with** all your complaining. If you don't like my cooking, you can make yourself dinner.
B But it's your job to cook
A What? It's your job to fix things around the house, but you never do!

A 당신 불평하는 거 정말 지긋지긋해요. 내가 해준 음식이 마음에 안 들면 당신이 직접 저녁을 차려 먹으면 되잖아요.
B 하지만 요리는 당신이 할 일이에요.
A 뭐라고요? 고장난 집안 물건 수리는 당신 일인데도, 당신은 절대 안 하잖아요!

숙어 342 fit in 적응하다, 어울리다

A I hear you're new here. So, how do you like it so far?

B It's somewhat worrisome, but I really like working in marketing. I love being creative.

A Well, I think you'll **fit** right **in**.

A 새로 입사하셨다고 들었는데요. 지금까지 어떠세요?

B 좀 걱정되기는 하지만 마케팅 업무는 정말 마음에 들어요. 전 창의적인 일을 좋아하거든요.

A 네. 곧 적응하실 거예요.

숙어 343 in one's good graces. ~의 호감을 사는

A I can'ts believe how terrible this report is.
It's filled with spelling mistakes.

B Well, there's nothing we can do about it.
The manager won't say anything to Tom.

A I guess that's th advantage of being **in someone's good graces**.

A 이 보고서 완전히 엉망이네요.
오타 투성이에요.

B 음, 그건 우리가 어떻게 할 수 없어요.
과장님은 톰에게 아무 말씀도 안 하실 걸요.

A 그게 누군가의 총애를 받는 사람의 특권인 것 같군요.

숙어 344 be irritated with. ~에게 짜증이 나다

A Did you see Jay's face at the tenants' meeting?
He looked like he wanted to kill Betsy.

B You're exaggerating.
But he **was** really **irritated with** her.

A I'll say.
She's got to be the worst neighbor in the world.

A 세입자 회의 때 제이 얼굴 봤어요?
벳시를 죽이기라도 할 것처럼 보였어요.

B 그건 과장인 것 같고요,
근데 벳시에게 화가 나 있긴 했었어요.

A 맞아요.
벳시가 세상에서 제일 못된 이웃인 건 틀림없어요.

숙어 345 black ice. 빙판

A Did you see that?
The car in front of us just slid right through the intersection.

B Yikes. I think there's a patch of **black ice** by the traffic lights. Hold on!

A Pump the brakes! Pump the brakes! Wow.
I thought we were going to rear-end that car.

A 저거 봤어요?
앞차가 방금 교차로를 지나가다 미끄러졌어요.

B 이런. 신호등 옆에 빙판이 있는 것 같아요. 꽉 잡아요!

A 속도를 줄여요! 브레이크를 계속 밟으라고요! 와.
저 차를 들이박을 뻔했어요.

숙어 346 be sidelined. (경기에) 출전을 못하다, 일을 못하다

A Do you have that report I asked for?
It's already three.

B Sorry. I'm running a bit late.
I **got sidelined** by something else.

A Fair enough. But I need that report on my desk by the end of the day.

A 내가 요청한 그 보고서 다 준비됐어요?
벌써 세 시에요.

B 죄송해요. 좀 늦어지고 있어요.
다른 일 때문에 못했어요.

A 알았어요. 하지만 퇴근 전까지는 내 책상 위에 보고서를 올려놓으세요.

숙어 347 pass out. 의식을 잃다, 기절하다

A Are you okay?
You look like you're about to **pass out**.

B I feel really dizzy.
And the room looks like it's spinning around me.

A Here, sit down. I'll go and call you and ambulance. It might be serious

A 괜찮아요?
곧 쓰러질 것 같아 보여요.

B 많이 어지러워요.
방이 빙빙 도는 것 같아요.

A 여기 좀 앉아요. 가서 구급차 불러올게요. 심각한 병일지도 몰라요.

숙어 348 on edge. 초조하여, 불안하여

A Did you feel that? I think I just felt the floor move.

B Relax, You're just being overly sensitive.

We don't get big earthquakes here.

A I know, I know. But after what I saw happen in Japan, I'm feeling **on edge**.

A 그거 느꼈어요? 방금 바닥이 흔들린 것 같아요.

B 침착해요. 지금 너무 예민한 것 같아요. 이곳은 큰 지진이 일어나지 않아요.

A 나도 알아요. 하지만 일본에서 일어난 일을 보고 나니까 불안하다고요.

숙어 349 be on crutches. 목발을 짚고 다니다

A I guess I can't play soccer for a while, doc.

B That's right. You're going to **be on crutches** for at least a few weeks.

A What will the other players on the team think?

They were counting on me.

A 의사 선생님, 한동안 저는 축구를 하지 못하겠네요.

B 맞아요. 적어도 2, 3주는 목발을 하고 있어야 할 거예요.

A 같은 팀 선수들이 어떻게 생각할까요? 저를 믿고 있었는데 말이죠.

숙어 350 get down to 본격적으로 ~을 시작하다

A We've covered a lot of the small stuff.

Now, let's **get down to** the nitty-gritty.

B The first thing we need to do is decide on pay raises this year. How much can we offer?

A Profits have been up and our employees have worked hard. I think eight percent is fair.

A 소소한 사항들을 많이 다뤘습니다. 이제는 본론으로 들어가죠.

B 첫 번째 논의사항은 올해의 임금 인상 결정입니다. 우리가 얼마나 제안할 수 있을까요?

A 수익이 올랐고 직원들도 열심히 일했으니 8%가 괜찮은 것 같습니다.

숙어 351 make it up to

보상(배상)을 하다

A Jane, where are you? I've been waiting at the restaurant for you for twenty minutes!

B Tom? Oh, no. It totally slipped my mind.
I'm so sorry. How can I **make this up to** you?

A Well, I guess you can buy me lunch tomorrow.

A 제인, 어디예요? 레스토랑에서 20분간 기다리고 있어요.

B 톰? 오, 이런. 까마득히 잊고 있었어요. 죄송해요. 아휴, 이걸 어떻게 하죠?

A 글쎄요, 내일 점심을 사면 될 것 같아요.

숙어 352 take down

적다, 기록하다

A Who's going to **take down** the minutes of the meeting? Does anyone want to volunteer?

B I did it last time, so it's someone else's turn this time.

A OK, Jane. You're off the hook. How about you Tom? Today is your lucky day!

A 누가 의사록을 작성할 건가요? 지원자 있습니까?

B 제가 지난번에 했으니 이번에는 다른 사람이 할 차례입니다.

A 알았어요, 제인. 당신은 제외시켜 줄게요. 톰 당신은 어때요? 오늘 운이 좋네요!

숙어 353 pick up the tab

지불하다

A Well, I guess that's it for today.

B It's just about dinner time. Would you like to grab a bite to eat? I can put it on my expense account.

A Great. And since your company is **picking up the tab,** let's go to that nice new French place that just opened downtown.

A 그럼 오늘은 이만 마치겠습니다.

B 저녁 식사 시간이 거의 다 됐네요. 뭐 좀 간단히 드시겠어요? 제 경비로 처리할게요.

A 좋아요. 귀사에서 지불을 할 테니 그럼 시내에 막 오픈한 괜찮은 프랑스 레스토랑으로 가보죠.

숙어 354 Hold your horses! 서두르지 마!

A We're finally ready to go. Now, step on it.
I don't want to be late for work.

B **Hold your horses**! There's something wrong with the battery. See? No lights.

A Are you trying to tell me the battery is dead?
Seriously?

B Looks like it. Don't worry.
We just need some-one to give us a boost.

A 이제 출발할 준비가 됐으니 속력을 내자.
회사에 늦으면 안 돼.

B 서두르지 마! 배터리가 뭔가 이상해. 보여? 불이 안 들어와.

A 배터리가 나갔다는 말이야?
정말이니?

B 그런 것 같아. 걱정 마.
우리 차에 배터리를 연결해 줄 사람만 있으면 돼.

숙어 355 window dressing 겉치레

A Why don't we print these charts up in color?

B I don't think we need to do that.

A Why not?
The boss will think we're doing a good job.

B But all that is just **window dressing**.

A 우리 이 도표를 컬러로 프린트하는 게 어떨까?

B 그럴 필요는 없을 것 같은데.

A 왜?
사장님이 우리가 일을 잘한다고 생각하실 텐데.

B 하지만 그런 건 다 겉치레에 불과하잖아.

숙어 356 hit below the belt 야비한 공격을 하다

A Mark told the boss some lies about you.

B What? What did he say?

A He said that you were late to work and were calling him names.

B That's **hitting below the belt**! Why would he say that?

A 마크가 사장한테 너에 대해서 몇 가지 거짓 보고를 했어.

B 뭐? 뭐라고 했는데?

A 출근도 늦고 사장님 흉을 보고 다닌다고 말야.

B 그건 야비한 짓이잖아! 왜 그렇게 말한 거지?

숙어 357 get sacked — 해고되다

A I heard that the company is having lots of problems.

B You're right about that.

Karen just **got sacked** this morning.

A That's terrible. Is your job in any danger?

B I don't think I'm going to get fired, but it might happen.

A 그 회사 문제가 많다고 들었어.

B 네 말이 맞아.

카렌이 오늘 아침에 잘렸어.

A 끔찍하군. 네 자리는 괜찮니?

B 나는 해고될 것 같진 않지만 가능한 일이지.

숙어 358 eat humble pie — 잘못을 인정하다

A You know that I'm right and you're wrong.

B There is no way that you're right.

A Look, Here's the proof. What do you think now?

B Well, it looks like I'm going to have to **eat humble pie** tonight.

A 내 말이 맞고 네가 틀렸다는 거 너도 알잖아.

B 네 말이 맞을 리가 없어.

A 봐, 여기 증거가 있잖아. 이제 어떻게 생각해?

B 글쎄, 내키진 않지만 오늘 밤은 내가 틀렸다는 걸 받아들여야겠군.

숙어 359 mover and shaker — 거물급 인사

A Are you still having problems finding a job?

B Yeah, and I just don't know what I should do.

A Why don't you talk to Trevor?

He's a real **mover and shaker**.

B Do you really think he could help me find a job then?

A 너 아직도 직장 구하기가 힘든가봐?

B 응, 이제 정말 어떻게 해야 될지 모르겠어.

A 트레버한테 한 번 얘기해 보는 게 어때? 진짜 힘 좀 쓰는 친구거든.

B 그 사람이 정말 내가 취직하도록 도와줄 수 있을까?

숙어 360 spoon-feed 숟가락으로 떠먹여주다

A This homework is too hard. Can you give me some help?

B I've already shown you how to do it twice.

A Yeah, but can you show me just one more time, please?

B If I help you any more, I might as well just **spoon-feed** you the answers.

A 이 숙제는 너무 어려워. 나 좀 도와줄래?

B 어떻게 하는 건지 벌써 두 번이나 가르쳐줬잖아.

A 그래도 한 번만 더 가르쳐주면 안 되겠니?

B 더 도와주려면, 차라리 아예 답을 가르쳐주는 게 낫겠다.

숙어 361 score a touchdown 한 건 크게 올리다

A We really need to **score a touchdown** in today's meeting.

B That's the truth. We have to do well.

A If we don't sell our product, our jobs might be in jeopardy.

B Okay, let's just do a good job today.

A 오늘 회의에서는 정말 크게 한 건 올려야 하는데.

B 맞아. 우리 정말 잘 해야 돼.

A 물건을 팔지 못하면 우리 자리가 위태로워질지도 몰라.

B 좋아, 오늘은 잘 좀 해보자!

숙어 362 face off 대결하다

A Who is participating in the finals??

B John will be **facing off** against Marty.

A Which one of them is favored to win?

B John is a small favorite right now.

A 결승에 누가 올라가지?

B 존이 마티와 대결을 벌이게 될 거야.

A 누가 이길 거 같아?

B 지금은 존이 조금 더 기대를 모으고 있지.

숙어 363 bottle up

화를 꾹 참다

A Can you believe how Mr. Mitchell didn't even get angry back there?

B I thought he would explode.

A He did a good job of keeping his feelings **bottled up**.

B But I'm sure he'll let them out later.

A 아까 미첼 씨 말이야. 화도 안 냈다는 게 믿어지니?

B 나는 그 사람 폭발할 줄 알았는데.

A 정말 화를 꾹꾹 잘 참고 있더라.

B 하지만 나중에는 터질 거라고 봐.

숙어 364 tongue-tied

말문이 막힌

A Come on. What's the answer?

B Um.... er.... well....

A What's the matter?
Why are you so **tongued-tied** all of a sudden?

B Uh.... well, it's on the tip of my tongue.

A 그래. 답이 뭐지?

B 저…. 그게….

A 무슨 일이야?
갑자기 왜 말문이 막힌 거지?

B 어…. 글쎄, 혀끝에서 뱅뱅 도는데 잘 생각이 안 나네요.

숙어 365 have a sore throat

목이 아프다

A Are you going to go to the party tonight?

B I think I'm going to take a pass on it.

A Come on. You need to have some fun.

B I **have a sore throat** and don't think I should go out tonight.

A 오늘밤 파티에 갈거니?

B 난 안 가려고.

A 그러지 말고, 넌 좀 즐겨야 돼.

B 목이 좀 따끔거리고 아픈 거 같아서 오늘밤에는 안 나가는 게 좋을 거 같아.

숙어 366 below par

수준 이하의

A What did you think of my performance today?

B It wasn't so good. In fact, it was **below par**.

A I know that I wasn't my best, but I tried hard.

B I think you need to practice more.

A 오늘 내 공연 어땠어?

B 그리 좋진 않았어. 사실은 기대 이하야.

A 최선을 다하진 못했지만 그래도 열심히 했는데.

B 더 연습을 해야 할 것 같다.

숙어 367 strike out — 실패하다

A So, did you go up to Susie and ask her out?

B Yeah, I asked her to see a movie with me tonight.

A And, what did she say?

B She said no. I really **struck out.**

A 그래서 너 수지한테 가서 데이트 신청했어?

B 응, 오늘밤 나랑 영화 보자고 했지.

A 그러니까 뭐래?

B 싫대. 완전히 실패했지.

숙어 368 horse around — 장난을 치다

A What on earth are you two doing?

B We're just trying to have some fun.

A Well, stop **horsing around**, and get down from the tree.

B Okay, Mom. We're coming down right now.

A 너희 둘 도대체 뭐 하는 거니?

B 그냥 놀아요.

A 자, 장난 그만 치고 나무에서 내려와.

B 네, 엄마. 지금 바로 내려갈게요.

숙어 369 in the doghouse — 잘못해서 근신 중인

A What are you doing this weekend?

B I'm probably just going to hang out at home.

A Aren't you going to go out with your girlfriend?

B I can't. We had a big fight yesterday, so I'm **in the doghouse** now.

A 이번 주말에 뭐 할 거니?

B 그냥 집에서 시간을 보낼 것 같아.

A 여자 친구랑 데이트 안 할 거야?

B 못 해. 어제 심하게 싸워서 나 지금 근신하는 중이거든.

숙어 370 elbow room — 여유 공간

A This room is really cramped right now.

B It's so stuffy that I can hardly even breathe.

A We need some **elbow room.**

B Let's go outside and go a breath of fresh air.

A 이 방 말이야. 지금 너무 비좁은 거 같아.

B 너무 답답해서 숨쉬기조차 힘들어.

A 여유 공간이 좀 필요한데 말이야.

B 우리 밖에 나가서 신선한 공기나 좀 마시자.

숙어 371 have someone's ear — 주의를 끌다

A Why didn't John do what I told him he should?

B Because Mike told him to do something different.

A Yeah, but his advice was totally wrong.

B But Mike **has John's ear**, so John always does what he says.

A 왜 존은 내가 하라는 대로 하지 않은 거지?

B 마이크가 존한테 다르게 하라고 얘길 해줬거든.

A 알아. 하지만 걔가 해준 충고는 완전히 틀린 거잖아.

B 하지만 존은 마이크가 하는 말을 잘 들으니까 항상 걔가 말하는 대로 하는 거지.

숙어 372 face the music — 사태에 용감하게 대처하다

A Why do you look so down today?

B I had a traffic accident yesterday driving my dad's car. It's got a big dent.

A Really What are you going to do now?

B I'm going to **face the music** and tell him about it.

A 너 오늘 왜 그렇게 우울해 보이니?

B 어제 아빠 차를 몰다가 자동차 사고가 났는데, 차가 많이 찌그러졌어.

A 정말이야? 너 이제 어떻게 할 거야?

B 내가 한 일에 책임을 지고 아버지께 말씀드려야지 뭐.

숙어 373 can't stomach something — 참고 견딜 수가 없다

A You look really upset today.

B That's because my boss was hitting on me all day.

A That's terrible. I can't believe he did that.

B I know. I **can't stomach harassment**, especially by a person who should know better than that.

A 너 오늘 굉장히 화나 보인다.

B 우리 부장이 하루 종일 날 희롱하더라고.

A 세상에. 그 사람이 그랬다니 믿을 수가 없어.

B 그러게. 나 희롱당하는 거 더는 못 참겠어. 특히 그러지 말아야 한다는 것 정도는 알아야 하는 사람한테 말이야.

숙어 374 ace something — ~을 완벽하게 해내다

A Hi, Mary. Why do you look so happy?

B I just **aced my history exam**!

A That's great.
You were really worried about that, weren't you?

B Yeah, but I wound up getting a perfect grade!

A 안녕, 메리. 왜 그렇게 즐거운 표정이야?

B 역사 시험 끝내주게 잘 봤거든!

A 잘 됐네.
많이 걱정했잖아!

B 응, 그런데 결국 만점을 받았지 뭐야!

숙어 375 catch one's eye — 눈길을 끌다

A Did you manage to get Alicia's attention?

B No. I tried to **catch her eye**, but she didn't notice me.

A Well, you can always talk to her after lunch.

B Yeah, I guess I'll just have to try the direct appraoch with her.

A 그래 너 앨리시어의 관심은 좀 끌었어?

B 아니, 걔 눈길을 끌려고 해봤는데 아는 척도 안하더라고.

A 글쎄, 점심시간 후에는 언제든지 걔한테 말을 걸 수 있을 텐데.

B 그래, 그냥 직접 접근하는 쪽으로 시도해 봐야겠어.

숙어 376 dorp one's gloves — 결연히 맞서다

A We can't let Fumford beat us again.

B You're right. So what should we do?

A It's time to **drop our gloves** and get serious.

B Okay! Let's come up with a plan to win next time.

A 럼퍼드에게 다시 패해서는 안 돼.

B 네 말이 맞아. 그럼 어떻게 해야 하지?

A 이제 확실하게 대응할 준비를 하고 진지하게 생각해 봐야지.

B 좋았어! 다음 경기에서 이길 수 있는 방법을 생각해 보자고.

숙어 377 keep a straight face — 표정 관리를 하다

A Did you see Larry fall down the stairs?

B Yes, I did. I really wanted to laugh.

A You didn't laugh, did you?

B NO, I **kept a straight face**. But I felt like laughing.

A 래리가 계단에서 구른 거 봤어?

B 응, 봤어. 진짜 웃고 싶더라.

A 안 웃었지?

B 그럼, 표정 관리 했지. 하지만 웃고 싶었어.

숙어 378 twist someone's arm ~을 협박하다

A Why is Sally at this party? She hates parties.

B I **twisted her arm** and got her to come.

A What did you do to convince her?

B I told her she couldn't borrow my car unless she came to the party.

A 샐리가 이 파티에 웬일이지? 걔 파티 싫어하잖아.

B 내가 협박해서 오게 했지.

A 어떻게 했는데 넘어왔어?

B 파티에 오지 않으면 내 차를 빌릴 수 없을 거라고 했어.

숙어 379 put my foot down 분명히 말하다

A You need to stop watching TV and do your homework!

B But Mom, this is my favorite program.

A I'm **putting my foot down**. Do your homework now!

B Okay, I'll go to my room and do it.

B 하지만 엄마, 이건 제가 제일 좋아하는 프로란 말이에요.

A 분명히 말하는데, 지금 숙제해!

B 알았어요, 방에 가서 숙제할게요.

숙어 380 eat like a horse 엄청 많이 먹다

A What are we having for dinner tonight?

B I thought I'd cook some steak and potatoes.

A Be sure to make a lot.

I'm so hungry I could **eat like a horse.**

B Don't worry.

I'm sure there will be more than enough for you.

A 오늘 저녁 메뉴가 뭐지?

B 스테이크하고 감자 요리를 할까 생각해 봤어.

A 많이 해놔.

나 지금 배가 너무 고파서 엄청 많이 먹을 수 있거든.

B 걱정 마. 충분히 먹고도 남을 만큼 할 테니까.

숙어 381 to make (both) ends meet 수입 한도 안에서 지출하다

A I hear Mark is between jobs.

B Oh, he's been out of work for a long time now.

A I wonder how he **makes ends meet.**

A 내가 듣기론 마크는 지금 충전기간이래.

B 그래. 그는 오랫동안 실직상태에 있었지.

A 난 그가 어떻게 생계를 꾸리는지 궁금해.

숙어 382 carry the torch | 이끌다

A What are you going to be doing tonight?

B I have to attend a charity event.

A Oh, right. I heard that you are **carrying the torch** for that organization.

B Yeah, somebody has to lead them, you know.

A 너 오늘 저녁에 뭐하니?

B 자선 행사에 참가해야 돼.

A 아, 맞다. 네가 그 단체 대표라고 들었는데.

B 그래, 누군가는 책임지고 이끌어야 하잖아.

숙어 383 A May-December marriage. | 나이 차이가 많이 나는 결혼

A I heard you father remarried. He must be happy.

B He sure is.
Especially because his wife is 20 years younger!

A Well, **May-December weddings** are all the rage these days.

A 네 아버지 재혼하셨다는 얘기 들었어. 행복하시겠다.

B 당연하지.
새어머니가 20살이나 어려서 특히 더 좋으신 것 같아.

A 나이 차이가 많이 나는 결혼은 요즘 모두들 원하는 거잖아.

숙어 384 Save one's breath | 잠자코 있다

A Mr. Bartlett has been looking all over for you.

B I know. I'm trying to avoid him.

A Did you do something wrong to him?

B Nope. I'm sure he wants to ask me about Randy and I won't say anything.

A Oh, I get it.
Yeah, you'd better **save your breath** about Randy.

B Absolutely. I don't want to end up miserably in the middle of their fight.

A 바틀렛씨가 계속 너를 찾던데.

B 알아. 일부러 피해 다니는 중이야.

A 뭐 잘못했어?

B 아니. 그가 랜디에 대해 물어보려는 게 분명한데 난 아무말도 안 할 거니까.

A 아, 알았다.
그럼, 랜디에 관해서라면 잠자코 있는 게 낫지.

B 물론이지. 그 둘 싸움에 끼어서 나만 곤란해지는 건 싫으니까.

■ 어떤 말이든 해봤자 아무 소용도 없음이 분명할 때 그냥 조용히 잠자코 있는 것을 가리키는 표현입니다.

숙어 385 Bad Eggs — 말썽을 일으키는 사람들

A Susan in the accounting department is thinking of quitting.

B Why is that?

A It seems some of her coworkers in the office are giving her a hard time.

B We have to get rid of the **bad eggs** in that department.

A 경리부 수전이 회사를 그만둘 생각이라는 군.

B 무슨 일인데요?

A 사무실 안의 몇몇 동료가 수전을 힘들게 하는 모양이야.

B 그 부서에서 문제를 일으키는 사람들을 내보내야 하겠네요.

숙어 386 A matter of life and death — 매우 중요한 문제

A What on earth is going on with my computer?

B There is goes again.

A I'm at a dead end.

I've gotta finish this work today no matter what happens.

B Didn't you get your computer checked just last week?

A Yes, I did. Gosh....This work is **a matter of life and death** to me. What should I do?

B Just be cool and give a call to a computer guy.

A 도대체 내 컴퓨터가 왜 이러는 거지?

B 컴퓨터가 또 말썽이군.

A 큰일이네. 무슨 일이 있어도 오늘 안에 이 일을 끝내야 하는데.

B 바로 지난주에 컴퓨터 점검받지 않았어?

A 그랬지. 맙소사…. 이 일은 나에겐 생사가 걸린 일인데. 어떡하면 좋아?

B 침착하고 컴퓨터 수리 기사에게 전화를 해봐.

숙어 387 on cloud nine — 아주 행복한, 하늘이라도 오를 것 같은 기분인

A What's gotten into the entry-level employee?

B What do you mean?

A She's been **on cloud nine** since the last week.

B Oh, didn't you hear? She was promoted to manager last month.

A 그 신입사원 어떻게 된 거야?

B 무슨 뜻이야?

A 지난주부터 계속 들떠 보여서.

B 아. 못 들었어? 지난달에 매니저로 승진했잖아.

숙어 388 hold back 숨기다, 감추다, 보류하다

A What's new?

B Nothing good, I'm afraid.

They're **holding back** on their investment for the time being.

A I suppose they want to see how things develop a little more.

A 무슨 새로운 소식 있어?

B 별로 좋은 건 없어. 그들이 투자를 얼마 동안은 보류하고 있을 테니까.

A 내 생각엔 그들이 상황의 추이를 좀 더 지켜보려는 것 같아.

숙어 389 Challenging Work 보람 있는 일, 매력적인 일

A I want to recommend Lee as manager for that assignment.

B Yeah, but can he hack it?

A Well, he's been asking for more **challenging work.**

B OK. Then let's see what he can do with it.

A 난 그 일의 관리자로 Lee를 추천하고 싶어.

B 그래. 하지만 그가 해낼 수 있을까?

A 그는 좀 더 매력적인 일을 달라고 요구해왔거든.

B 좋아. 그렇다면 그가 어떻게 해내는지 지켜보자고.

숙어 390 Make an exception 예외로 하다

A Have you seen Tina today?

B Now everyone is looking for her.

Unfortunately she called in sick.

A Again? I need to talk to her now. I had her make an appointment for my business trip to Japan.

B I'm sorry. You'd better wait for her to show up.

A She calls in sick like once a week.

Don't we have to make a decision about that?

B Mr. Burnett always **makes an exception** for her.

What can we do?

A 오늘 티나 봤어?

B 다들 티나를 찾는군.

오늘 아파서 결근한다고 전화 왔어.

A 또? 난 당장 그녀와 얘기해야 해. 근한테 내 일본 출장을 예약하라고 했단 말이야.

B 미안하지만 출근할 때까지 기다려야지, 뭐.

A 일주일에 한 번씩 결근이네.

뭔가 결정을 내려야 하지 않아?

B 버넷이 늘 그녀만 예외로 하는데 우리가 뭘 어쩌겠어?

숙어 391 Asking Price — 부르는 가격, 호가

A What's the **asking price** for the equipment?

B Eight million dollars for the whole shooting match.

A That's way out of line.

I'll bet we can get it for around six.

B But I suppose offers 15% below the **asking price** are unlikely to be accepted.

A 이 장비의 호가가 얼마지?

B 전부해서 800만 달러야.

A 터무니없군.

내 생각엔 600만 달러면 될 것 같은데.

B 하지만 호가에서 15%나 낮은 값으로는 받아들여질 것 같지 않아.

숙어 392 Throw in the Towel — 포기하다, 항복하다

A I heard N&N Corporation is in major trouble.

B That's true.

The company is currently losing their customers.

A I wonder what will happen to them.

B N&N is probably going to **throw in the towel** after losing all of its major customers.

A N&N 주식회사가 큰 곤경에 빠졌다고 들었어요.

B 맞아요.

그 회사는 현재 고객들을 잃고 있거든요.

A 어떻게 될지 궁금하네요.

B 아마도 N&N은 모든 주요 고객을 잃고 나서 문을 닫게 될 거예요.

숙어 393 Get the elbow — 거절당하다, 퇴짜 맞다

A What're you doing tonight?

B No plans yet.

A Can you give me a hand with these documents?

I can't go over it myself.

B Of course I can. But Mark is the right person to ask for help. He came up with most of these ideas.

A I've asked him already, but I **got the elbow**.

B You did? All right. I'll be with you.

A 오늘 밤에 뭐해?

B 별 계획 없어.

A 그럼, 이 서류들을 검토하는 것 좀 도와줄래?

혼자서는 좀 힘들어서.

B 도와줄 수는 있어. 그런데 마크가 더 잘 알텐데. 그가 대부분의 아이디어를 냈거든.

A 벌써 물어봤는데 거절당했어.

B 그랬어? 좋아. 내가 도와줄게.

숙어 394 Open the door | 기회를 만들다

A So the big day is coming. Is it tomorrow?

B If you're talking about the meeting with D&D, yes sir, it's tomorrow.

A Are you all set?

B I guess so.

I've been working on it for more than two weeks.

A What's the best result this company can possibly get?

B It's so obvious for both of us.

We reach an agreement to **open the door** to greatly increased sales.

A 거사가 다가오고 있지. 내일인가?

B D&D사와의 미팅을 말씀하시는 거라면, 맞습니다.

내일입니다.

A 준비는 다 됐나?

B 그렇다고 봅니다.

2주 이상 이 일에만 매달렸으니까요.

A 우리 회사가 얻을 수 있는 최고의 결과는 뭔가?

B 우리 회사나 상대방이나 분명합니다.

훨씬 향상된 판매수치를 위한 기회를 만들자는 것이지요.

숙어 395 keep one's head above water | 재정적 파탄을 겨우 면하다

A The recession threatens to put our whole division out of work.

B We're **keeping our heads above water.**

A Have y laid anyone off?

A 불경기 때문에 우리 부서 전체가 해고될 위기에 놓였습니다.

B 저희도 간신히 견디고 있는 정도입니다.

A 직원들을 해고하지는 않았나요?

숙어 396 Under the Table | 남몰래, 비공식적으로

A Have you turned in your tax report?

B No, I haven't Have you?

A My boss pays me **under the table**, so I don't have to pay income taxes.

B It is dangerous to get paid illegally.

A 세금 보고서 제출하셨어요?

B 아뇨, 아직 제출 안 했어요. 내셨어요?

A 우리 사장님은 임금을 비공식적으로 지급하셔서 저는 세금을 낼 필요가 없어요.

B 불법으로 봉급을 지급하는 건 위험한데요.

숙어 397 Praise someone to the skies — 치켜세우다

A How was the party last night?

B Don't even ask me. I don't want to think about it.

A What happened?

B It was just a normal house-warming party until Mr. President showed up. After he gave us a long lecture about business, all he did was to **praise Garry to the skies.**

A Oh, that's how it was messed up.

B Can you imagine how Garry's face was all night?
It was a good choice that you didn't come.

A 어젯밤 파티는 어땠어?

B 물어보지도 마. 생각하고 싶지 않으니까.

A 무슨 일 있었어?

B 회장님이 나타나기 전까진 그냥 평범한 집들이였지. 회장님은 업무에 관해 기다란 연설을 하신 다음, 온통 개리에 대한 칭찬만 하셨어.

A 분위기 망쳤겠군.

B 개리가 밤새 얼마나 의기양양했을지 상상이 가지?
너, 안 오길 정말 잘했어.

숙어 398 Fill someone in — ~에게 정보를 주다, 알려주다

A How did the conference go last night?

B I wasn't there. I was tied up with all the paper work almost until midnight.

A What? Oh, gosh.... I thought you could **fill me in.**

B Why didn't you go to the conference?
You're the one who had to be there.

A I had a terrible migraine and had no choice but to rush home.

B You have an excuse then.
Why don't you find someone else to fill you in?

A 어제 저녁 회의는 어떻게 됐어?

B 난 안 갔는데. 거의 자정가지 서류 작업에 매달려 있느라고.

A 뭐야? 이런…. 난 너한테 정보를 들을 수 있을 줄 알았는데.

B 너는 왜 안갔어? 너야말로 꼭 가야할 사람이잖아.

A 편두통이 매우 심해서 집에 갈 수밖에 없었어.

B 그랬구나. 어쨌든 회의에 대해선 다른 사람에게 물어보는 게 좋겠다.

숙어 399 Cut back — 절약하다, 줄이다

A Here is the new office policy.
Would you please distribute it?

B Sure, glad to help out.

A Thanks. This memo explains new guidelines for reducing office expenses.

B Well, the finance department is trying to **cut back** on expenses.

A 새로운 사내 방침입니다. 좀 배포해 주실래요?

B 물론입니다. 기꺼이 도와드리지요.

A 고마워요. 사무실 경비 절감에 대한 새로운 지침 내용입니다.

B 음…. 재무과에서 경비를 줄이려고 애쓰는 군요.

숙어 400 Return on investment (ROI) — 투자 수익

A She told me she studied the company's prospectus in great detail, and she was impressed.

B She told me she studied the company's prospectus in great detail, and she ws impressed.

A Market analysts forecast the value of the stock to triple in three months. If inflation remains low she stands to make a huge **return on her investment.**

A 제인은 그 회사의 주식 1000주를 샀습니다.

B 그녀는 그 회사의 주식발행 안내서를 아주 꼼꼼히 연구해 보고는 인상적이었다고 말하던데요.

A 시장 애널리스트들은 그 회사의 주가가 3개월 뒤에 세 배로 될 거라더군요. 만약 물가 상승률이 높지 않다면 그녀는 엄청난 투자 수익을 얻을 겁니다.

숙어 401 Dry Run — 연습, 리허설

A The material we've been working on is extremely important.

B We must make sure that we get it right.

A We do not have enough data to complete the presentation yet.

B Let's at least go through a **dry run** of it before we show it to the board of directors.

A 우리가 지금까지 작업해 온 자료는 매우 중요합니다.

B 제대로 입수했는지 확실히 해야 합니다.

A 프레젠테이션을 완성하기에는 아직 충분한 자료가 없습니다.

B 적어도 이사회에 보이기 전에 연습을 합시다.

숙어 402 The take — 매출

A Our sales have broken the record.

The take for today alone exceeds all of last week's.

B How much of this is profit?

A Somewhere around six or seven percent.

A 매출이 기록을 깼습니다.
오늘 매출만으로도 지난주 매출 총액을 넘어섰습니다.

B 그중에서 수익은 어느 정도인가요?

A 6~7%입니다.

숙어 403 Come to Think of it — 생각해 보니

A It took me 45 minutes to get here.

B Is that true?

I thought it would take 30 minutes maximum.

A At this time of the day there is a lot of traffic coming in to this area.

B **Come to think of it**, the recent construction on the freeway caused quite a few street closures.

A 여기까지 오는 데 45분 걸렸어요.

B 정말이세요? 전 길어야 30분이면 될 거라 생각했어요.

A 이 시간에는 이 지역으로 들어오는 차량이 많거든요.

B 생각해 보니, 최근에 고속도로 공사 때문에 많은 길이 차단됐네요.

숙어 404 Set straight — 오해를 풀어 주다

A Leo, can you speak French?

B Well... a little. Do yu need help in French?

A Yes. I've got an e-mail from our partner in Paris and I'm afraid he got me totally wrong in our last conversation.

B Then you've gotta **set him straight** right away. A tiny misunderstanding may cause a disaster in business.

A All right. I'm gonna write an e-mail and you make time to take a look at it, okay?

A 리오, 불어 할 줄 알아?

B 뭐…, 조금은. 불어 하는 데 도움이 필요해?

A 응. 파리에 있는 협력사에서 메일이 왔는데 지난번 대화를 완전히 오해한 것 같아.

B 그럼 당장 오해를 풀어 줘야지. 사업상의 사소한 오해도 큰 일이 될 수 있어.

A 맞아. 내가 지금 메일을 쓸테니 잠깐 시간 내서 좀 봐줘, 알았지?

숙어 405 To walk on eggs | 매우 조심스럽게 행동하다

A You seem quite joyful today. Something good must have happened to you, huh?

B Yeah, I'm allowed to take a day-off next Friday, which means I can go to my baby brother's graduation party.

A Oh, that's very nice. Was Mr. Callaway in that good mood to say yes?

B Yes. I felt like I was **walking on eggs** to ask for a day off, but he seemed unusually happy this morning.

A Glad to hear that. He's been really depressed recently.

A 오늘 기분 좋아 보이네. 좋은 일이 있는 모양이지?

B 응. 다음 주 금요일에 회사를 하루 쉬고 막 내 동생 졸업식에 갈 수 있게 됐거든.

A 야, 잘됐다. 캘러웨이씨가 허락한 걸 보니 이제 기분이 좀 괜찮은가?

B 응. 오늘 아침에 물어보러 갔을 땐 진짜 조심스러웠는데 의외로 기분 좋아보이던걸.

A 다행이다. 요즘 정말 저기압인 것 같더니.

숙어 406 To find one's feet | 새로운 상황에 적응해 효율적으로 일하다

A Do you think it's worth me doing an MBA?

B It depends how much you want to climb the career ladder?

A My new job's OK but there are lots of things I'm still not used to.

B That's normal. It always takes a few months before you **find your feet.**

A 제가 경영학 석사 공부를 할 가치가 있다고 생각합니까?

B 당신이 얼마나 업무적으로 성공하길 원하느냐에 달려 있겠지요.

A 새 일이 마음에는 들지만 여전히 익숙하지 않은 것이 많아서요.

B 당연하죠. 보통 몇 달은 지나야 새로운 상황에 적응하고 효율적으로 일할 수 있게 되지요.

숙어 407 goose egg | 빵점

A Did you win your game today?

B No, but we didn't lose either. We tied.

A What was the final score?

B We both got **goose eggs**. The score was zero-zero.

A 오늘 경기 이겼어?

B 아니, 그렇다고 진 것도 아니야. 무승부였거든.

A 최종 점수가 어떻게 됐는데?

B 두 팀 다 빵점이었어. 그러니깐 0대 0이었던 거지.

숙어 408 Over the hill — 한물 간

A Did you look for me? I was at the gym working out.

B You did go to the gym this morning?
What's going on?

A I read a really intriguing article on today's newspaper and I made up my mind to work out everyday.

B What was it about?

A A ninety-something-year-old man finished the marathon and proved that he wasn't **over the hill** yet. And I wanna be just like him when I get old.

B Oh, that's pretty impressive.

A 나 찾았다며? 체육관에서 운동하고 있었어.

B 아침부터 체육관에 가서 운동했다고? 무슨 일이래?

A 오늘 아침 신문에서 아주 고무적인 기사를 읽었는데 그것 때문에 매일 운동하기로 결심했어.

B 무슨 기사인데?

A 아흔이 넘은 할아버지가 마라톤을 완주해서 자신이 한물간 사람이 아니라는 걸 입증했대. 나도 나이 들면 그렇게 될 거야.

B 야, 그거 멋진데.

숙어 409 Keep a straight face. — 웃지 않으려고 애쓰다

A Did you see Mr. Chapel today?

B Nope. Why're you giggling?

A He got a new haircut and I had a hard time **keeping a straight face** when I saw him.

B Is it that funny?

A Funny is not a word for it. With a new haircut, he looks just like a lady.

B What? I've gotta check him out myself. Where's he?

A 오늘 샤펠씨 봤어?

B 아니. 왜 웃는데?

A 머리를 잘랐는데 그걸 보고 웃음이 나와서 참느라 얼마나 힘들었는지 몰라.

B 그렇게 웃겨?

A 웃긴다는 건 정확한 표현이 아니고 머리를 자르니까 꼭 여자같이 보여.

B 뭐야? 직접 가서 봐야겠다. 어디 있지?

숙어 410 have A do B — A로 하여금 B를 하게 하다

A Would you mind then telling me when I'd be able to speak to him?

B I'm sorry, sir, but I can't give you an exact time, but it won't be very long.

A I see.

B I'll **have him call** you back as soon as he comes in, sir, so if I can just have your....

A No need for that. I think it'd be better for me to call back.

A 그럼 그와 언제쯤이면 통화할 수 있는지 말해주겠어요?

B 죄송합니다만 손님, 정확한 시간은 잘 모르겠습니다만 그리 오래 걸리진 않을 겁니다.

A 알겠어요.

B 들어오시는 대로 연락드리라고 말씀드리겠으니, 제게….

A 그럴 필요 없습니다. 제가 다시 전화하는 게 날 것 같군요.

숙어 411 return an order — 반품하다

A J Crew. May I help you?

B Yes, please. I'd like to **return an order.**

A Yes, ma'am. Do you have the order number?

B Yes, I do.

A Could you give it to me, please?

A J Crew입니다. 무엇을 도와드릴까요?

B 네. 반품을 하고 싶은데요.

A 네, 손님. 주문번호를 알고 계십니까?

B 네.

A 제게 알려주시겠습니까?

숙어 412 explain oneself — 해명(변명)하다

A May I speak with your manager, please?

B May I ask what this is regarding, sir?

A I'm sorry but, I've no time or desire to **explain myself**. So if you don't mind, I'd rather speak to your manager directly.

B I'm sorry, sir, but the manager is currently unavailable.

A 매니저와 통화할 수 있을까요?

B 뭐 때문에 그러시는 거죠, 손님?

A 미안하지만, 전화 받는 분께까지 설명하고 싶진 않은데요. 그러니 괜찮다면, 매니저와 직접 얘기하고 싶은데요.

B 죄송합니다만 손님, 매니저께선 지금 부재중이십니다.

숙어 413 Out of the woods — 위험에서 벗어난

A Liz, I've been waiting for you.
You're coming from the hospital, aren't you?

B Yes. I've been with Ben since last night.

A So, how is Ben doing?

B The doctor said his condition has improved slightly but he's not **out of the woods** yet.

A Ben is the strongest person I've ever met, both physically and mentally. He will turn out all right.

B Yeah, I believe him. He will hang in there.

A 리즈, 기다리고 있었어.
병원에서 오는 길이지?

B 응. 어젯밤부터 벤 옆에 있었어.

A 그래, 좀 어때?

B 의사 말로는 약간 좋아지긴 했는데 아직도 위험한 상태래.

A 벤은 내가 만난 사람 중에 신체적으로나 정신적으로나 제일 강한 사람이야. 분명히 이겨낼 거야.

B 그래, 나도 믿어. 그는 꼭 견뎌낼 거야.

숙어 414 take a course — 어떤 방침을 취하다

A The government was bound to **take a course** on this issue.

B I know. The creditors were getting fed up with infeasible debt-reduction plans.

A But wouldn't they be on the losing end of the bargain if the restructuring goes through? Would they be able to retrieve their investment from the failing company?

B Better safe than sorry, right?

A 정부는 이 문제에 있어 반드시 어떤 조치를 취하게 돼 있었어요.

B 알아요. 채권자들은 실행 불가능한 채무감면계획들에 진저리가 났고요.

A 그렇지만 구조조정이 실행된다면 손실을 보는 건 채권자 쪽이 아닌가요? 파산 위기에 있는 기업에 투자한 자금을 회수할 수 있을까요?

B 후회하는 것보다는 안전한 것이 낫죠.

숙어 415 end in a draw — 동점으로 비기다

A Did you see the football game yesterday?

B You mean Korea versus Japan?

A Yeah.

B It was a close game. Korea was losing to Japan 2-1 in the first half. But Korea beat Japan 3-2 in the end. I was on the edge of my seat while watching that game.

A You sound excited.

B I was fortunate to be able to see the final game.

A I am so glad that the game didn't **end in a draw.**

A 어제 축구 경기 봤어?

B 한국 대 일본 경기 말이니?

A 응.

B 아슬아슬한 경기였어. 전반전에서는 한국이 일본에 2대1로 졌지만 마지막에는 한국이 일본을 3대2로 이겼어. 손에 땀을 쥐면서 경기를 봤다니까.

A 너 흥분한 것 같구나.

B 결승전을 볼 수 있어서 행운이었지.

A 게임이 동점으로 비기지 않아서 기쁘구나.

숙어 416 from the word go — 처음부터

A Something going on? Everyone seems so unusual.

B Didn't you hear the news?
Ken made a fake document and put a lot of money in his pocket.

A What? Oh, god....

B Did you sense he was hiding something?
You didn't like him **from the word go.**

A I just could tell when I looked into his eyes for the very first time.

B Is that so? From now on,
I'd definitely rely on you about everything.

A 무슨 일 있어? 다들 이상하네.

B 소식 못 들었어?
켄이 가짜 서류를 만들어서 엄청난 돈을 챙겼대.

A 뭐야? 세상에….

B 그가 뭔가 꾸민다는 걸 알았어? 넌 처음부터 그를 싫어했잖아.

A 그냥 처음 눈을 들여다봤을 때 느껴지던걸.

B 그래? 난 이제부터 무슨 일이든 네 의견을 전적으로 따르겠어.

숙어 417 step in — 간섭(개입)하다

A How's the restructuring going?

B Better than expected. They were trying to hold it off as long as they possibly could, but as soon as the government **stepped in**, the process was well on its way.

A Right. They were trying all sorts of legal maneuvers to buy time, but to no avail.

B Yes. In my opinion, government intervention was absolutely necessary since the so-called 'B&E Crisis' was causing a lot of anxiety in the financial market.

A 구조조정은 어떻게 되어가고 있습니까?

B 예상했던 것보다 잘 진행되고 있습니다. 가능한 한 시간을 오래 끌 줄 알았지만, 정부가 개입한 이후 순조롭게 진행되고 있습니다.

A 그래요. 시간을 벌려고 모든 법적인 조치를 취해봤지만 별 승산은 없었죠.

B 네. 제 의견으론 정부의 개입이 절대적으로 필요했다고 생각합니다. 소위 'B&E 사태'라는 것 때문에 금융계에 많은 불안한 요인을 조성하고 있었기 때문이죠.

숙어 418 To make waves — 파문을 일으키다

A What time did you get home last night?

B It was almost 3am when I finished taking a shower.

A I got home about 2am and slept only three hours. I don't feel good enough to function today.

B It's been a whole week. I don't think I can stand it any more.

A Me neither. I'm not trying **to make waves**, but I don't agree with Mr. Martin's policy.

B He doesn't seem to know that efficiency matters, not time, to do a good job.

A 어제 몇 시에 집에 도착했어?

B 샤워하고 나니까 거의 새벽 세 시더라.

A 나도 두 시쯤 집에 도착해 겨우 세 시간밖에 못 잤어. 오늘은 일할 수 있는 컨디션이 아니야.

B 이번 주 내내 그래. 난 더 이상 못 참겠어.

A 나도 마찬가지야. 문제를 일으키려는 건 아니지만 마틴씨의 정책에는 동의할 수가 없어.

B 일을 잘하려면 시간이 아닌 능률이 문제라는 걸 모르나 봐.

숙어 419 to hit the roof — 몹시 화내다

A Something wrong? Why're you so unhappy?

B I got a grade report on my final exam today.
It's just so awful.

A Uh-uh....
You really shouldn't have messed it up this time.

B I know. Dad is gonna kill me.
He will **hit the roof** after seeing this.

A Didn't you study pretty hard for this exam?

B Studying hard only a couple of days doesn't make any difference, you know.

A 뭐 문제 있어? 표정이 왜 그래?

B 오늘 기말고사 성적표를 받았는데 성적이 너무 안 좋아.

A 이런….
이번 시험은 진짜 잘 봤어야 하잖아.

B 그러게 말이야. 난 이제 아빠한테 죽었어.
이걸 보시면 불같이 화내실 거야.

A 이번 시험은 꽤 열심히 하지 않았어?

B 잠깐 공부한다고 성적이 잘 나오나 뭐.

숙어 420 not move a muscle — 털끝 하나 까딱하지 말고 그대로

A Stop, and put your hands over your head.

B But officer, I didn't do a thing.

A **Don't move a muscle**. I need to see if you're armed.

B Okay, I won't move. Just please don't shoot me.

A 멈추고 손을 머리 위에 올려.

B 경찰관님, 전 아무 짓도 안 했어요.

A 꼼짝 말란 말이야. 무기를 소지했는지 봐야 하니까.

B 네, 안 움직일게요. 제발 쏘지만 말아 주세요.

숙어 421 pig out — 게걸스럽게 많이 먹다

A Hey! You don't have to eat so fast.

B I'm not eating too fast.

A Yeah, you are. You are totally **pigging out**.

B I can't help it. This food is so good I just can't get enough of it.

A 야! 너 그렇게 빨리 안 먹어도 돼.

B 나 그렇게 빨리 먹는 거 아냐.

A 맞는데 뭘. 너 진짜 게걸스럽게 먹고 있어.

B 어쩔 수가 없어. 이 음식 진짜 맛있어서 먹어도 먹어도 계속 먹게 돼.

숙어 422 throw someone a curve ~의 뒤통수를 치다

A I have to go to the supermarket and buy some food.

B I thought that your wife was going to do that.

A That was the plan, but she **threw** me **a curve**. She can't go.

B She must have something else to do them.

A 수퍼마켓에 가서 음식을 좀 사와야겠어요.

B 당신 부인이 사올 줄 알았는데요.

A 그러기로 했는데 제 뒤통수를 치네요. 못 가겠대요.

B 뭐 다른 할 일이 있나보죠.

■ 직구(fastball)가 아닌 변화구를 던진다는 뜻으로, 일반적인 상황에서는 어떤 일이 예상치 못한 방향으로 진행될 때 쓰는 말입니다.

숙어 423 hit the sause 술을 실컷 마시다

A Has anyone seen Homer lately?

B I think he said he was going to the bar for a couple of hours.

A Is he **hitting the sauce** again?

B It sure sounded like it.
You know, he should really stop drinking so much.

A 최근에 호머 본 사람 있어?

B 두어 시간 술집에 가 있을 거라고 말한 거 같아.

A 또 술 마시고 있다고?

B 분명히 그렇게 말한 것 같아.
걔는 그렇게 과음하는 것 좀 그만 해야 되는데.

■ sauce는 속어로 '술'을 의미합니다.

숙어 424 cash cow 돈벌이가 되는 것

A How does you investment portfolio look?

B My holdings are up about 25% on the year.

A Wow! How did you get such a sizable return?

B I've got a couple of **cash cows** that are bringing in lots of money.

A 주식 투자한 건들은 어떻게 돼 가고 있어?

B 내가 가지고 있는 것들이 올해 25% 정도 올랐어.

A 와! 어떻게 그런 큰 이익을 낸 거야?

B 나한테 거금을 가져다주는 돈줄이 몇 개 있거든.

숙어 425 have ants in one's pants

안절부절 못하다

A Stop moving, and stand still for a minute!

B I can't help it! I'm too nervous.

A Calm down! You look like you **have ants in your pants.**

B I'm trying, but I just can't relax.

A 그만 왔다 갔다 하고 가만히 좀 있어!

B 나도 어쩔 수가 없어! 너무 긴장돼서 말이야.

A 진정해! 너 너무 안절부절못하는 것 같아.

B 나도 노력은 하고 있는데 진정이 안 돼.

숙어 426 let sleeping dogs lie

긁어 부스럼 만들지 않다

A What do you think I should do about this problem?

B You should just **let sleeping dogs lie.**

A But I'm already in a lot of trouble with my boss.

B And anything you say or do might make it worse.
Just try to ride out storm for a while.

A 넌 내가 이 문제를 어떻게 했으면 좋겠니?

B 괜히 긁어 부스럼 만들지 말고 가만히 있어.

A 하지만 이미 부장님하고의 사이에 문제가 많이 생겨버렸어.

B 네가 어떤 말이나 행동을 하면 상황이 더 나빠질지 몰라.
그냥 당분간 잘 참고 견뎌 봐.

숙어 427 in the bull pen

대기 중인

A Is Jay going to give you a ride to work?

B Yeah, he's going to pick me up around seven.

A But what if he can't make it?

B Don't worry. Harry is **in the bull pen** and will take me if jay can't make it.

A 제이가 출근길에 당신을 차에 태워줄 건가요?

B 네, 7시쯤에 태우러 올 거예요.

A 약속 시간에 못 오면 어쩌죠?

B 걱정하지 말아요. 해리가 대기하고 있으니까 제이가 못 오면 저를 태워갈 거예요.

숙어 428 down for the count — 완전히 뻗어서

A Somebody wake up Rick.

B No way. He's **down for the count** and won't be getting up until morning.

A Why is he so tired?

B He's been up late the last few nights trying to get his work all done.

A 누가 릭 좀 깨워봐.

B 절대 불가능해. 완전히 뻗어서 내일 아침까지는 못 일어날걸.

A 왜 그렇게 피곤한 거래?

B 일을 모두 끝내느라 지난 며칠 동안 밤을 샜거든.

숙어 429 turn a blind eye — 못 본 체하다

A Did you see Kevin cheating on the test?

B Yes, but I'm going to **turn a blind eye** to that.

A Don't you think we should tell the teacher?

B No. It's none of our business.

A 너 케빈이 시험에서 컨닝하는 거 봤니?

B 응. 그렇지만 난 못 본 척하려고.

A 선생님께 말씀드려야 할 것 같지 않아?

B 아니. 우리가 상관할 바가 아니야.

숙어 430 jump the gun — 성급하게 굴다

A John, you really **jumped the gun** back there.

B Do you think so?

A Yes. There was no need to speak up so soon.

B I guess I was just too eager to give all the answers.

A 존, 너 아까 너무 성급했어.

B 그렇게 생각해?

A 응. 그렇게 빨리 얘기를 해버릴 필요는 없었잖아.

B 모두 말해버리고 싶은 마음이 너무 컸나봐.

숙어 431 as free as a bird — 새처럼 자유로운

A You look really happy these days.

B That's because I'm **as free as a bird.**

A What are you talking about?

B Summer vacation started, so I don't have to do anything now.

A 너 요즘 정말 행복해 보여.

B 새처럼 자유롭기 때문이지.

A 무슨 얘기야?

B 여름 방학이 시작됐잖아. 이젠 아무것도 안 해도 돼.

숙어 432 spice things up — 분위기를 띄우다

A Hey, this is a party. Why is everyone so quiet?

B I don't know. I guess people just want to chat.

A Let's **spice things up** and listen to some good tunes.

B That's a good idea.

A 이봐, 지금 파티 중이잖아. 다들 왜 이렇게 조용해?

B 몰라. 그냥 다들 얘기나 하고 싶은가봐.

A 분위기 좀 띄우고 좋은 음악도 좀 듣고 그러자.

B 그거 좋은 생각이다.

숙어 433 cream someone — 묵사발을 만들다

A Wow! Did you see that hit?

B Yeah. John really **creamed** the other guy on that team.

A I don't even know if that guy is going to be able to get up again.

B Maybe not. That was a pretty hard shot.

A 와! 방금 치는 거 봤어?

B 그래. 존이 상대팀 선수를 완전히 넘어뜨렸는데.

A 저 선수가 다시 일어날 수나 있을지 모르겠네.

B 아마 못 일어날걸. 정말 세게 쳤거든.

숙어 434 spice of life — 인생의 색다른 맛

A What are you planning on doing this weekend?

B I think I'm going to try skydiving and see how that is.

A Wow! Are you crazy?

B Crazy? No. I just try to enjoy the **spice of life**.

A 이번 주말에 뭐 할 계획이야?

B 스카이다이빙을 한번 해보려고. 어떤 느낌인지 알아보게 말야.

A 야! 너 미쳤어?

B 미쳤냐고? 아니. 그냥 인생의 색다른 맛을 좀 즐겨보는 거지.